THE PAIN OF REFORMATION

THE PAIN OF REFORMATION

SPENSER, VULNERABILITY, AND THE ETHICS OF MASCULINITY

JOSEPH CAMPANA

Fordham University Press, New York 2012

Fordham University Press also publishes its books in a variety of electronic formats. Some content that appears in print may not be available in electronic books.

Library of Congress Cataloging-in-Publication Data
Campana, Joseph.
The pain of Reformation : Spenser, vulnerability, and the ethics of masculinity / Joseph Campana. — 1st ed.
p. cm.
Includes bibliographical references and index.
ISBN 978-0-8232-3910-8
1. Spenser, Edmund, 1552?–1599. Faerie queene. 2. Masculinity in literature. 3. Senses and sensation in literature. 4. Ethics in literature. 5. Reformation—England. I. Title.
PR2358.C35 2012
821'.3—dc23
2011037020

Printed in the United States of America
First paperback printing 2014
ISBN 978-0-8232-6168-0

Contents

Figures

Acknowledgments

Writing accumulates not merely words but also debt—happily so.

Since this is a study of a poem characterized by errancy, it was inevitable that its development would be characterized by straying through a variety of times, places, and institutions. My fascination with *The Faerie Queene* began in the classroom of the incomparable Sherron Knopp at Williams College. There I had the good fortune of learning from Karen Swann, Anita Sokolsky, Louise Glück, Clara Park, Kathryn Kent, Chris Waters, Regina Kunzel, David Eppel, and many others. This project incubated with mentoring from Jonathan Dollimore at the University of Sussex where I also had the pleasure of studying with Mandy Merck. Later, Gordon Teskey, now of Harvard University, proved an utterly singular example in his own scholarship and an unflagging supporter of mine. At Cornell, I had the privilege of working with him and with Winthrop Wetherbee, Mary Jacobus, Debra Fried, Reeve Parker, Scott McMillin, Barbara Correll, Alice Fulton, Roger Gilbert, and others. My colleagues at Kenyon College and Rice University have been unstintingly giving of their time and support. I thank both institutions for ample research funding and leave time. At Rice, the help of talented research assistants was vital; thanks to Anna Dodson, Nicholas Grant-Collins, Joanna O'Leary, Samitha Murthy, and Suzanne Rindell. Special thanks to Terry Munstieri for her extraordinary editing skills. The support of my Rice colleagues Helena Michie, Robert Patten, Caroline Levander, Rosemary Hennessy, Cary Wolfe, Alexander Regier, Edward Anderson, and Diane Wolfthal has been invaluable.

In the course of writing this book I have been humbled by the generosity of those initially unknown to me. Anonymity and distance characterize so many professional tasks but these are happily balanced by the collegiality of attentive readers, editors, and colleagues liberal with their counsel. Grateful thanks are owed to Bruce Smith, Patrick Cheney, Elizabeth Mazzola, Theresa Krier, Michael Schoenfeldt, Jennifer Summit, Richard Strier, Jan Frans van Dijkhuizen, Karl Enenkel, Wayne Rebhorn, Frank Whigham, Barbara Fuchs, Regina Schwartz, Linda Charnes, Katherine Eggert, Heather Dubrow, and Kevin Hart. For their friendship, collegiality, and patience, my thanks to Diane Cady, Zahid Chaudhury, Chi-Ming Yang, Scott Maisano, Katherine Romack, Michelle Duncan, and Janet McAdams.

Nolan Marciniec was my first guide in the dark forest of poetry. There's no repaying such generosity.

Chapter 1 appeared as "Reading Bleeding Trees: The Poetics of Other People's Pain in Edmund Spenser's Legend of Holiness," in *The Sense of Suffering: Constructions of Pain in Early Modern Europe*, ed. J. F. van Dijkhuizen and Karl Enenkel (Leiden: Brill, 2009), 347–76.

Chapter 3 appeared as "On Not Defending Poetry: Spenser, Suffering, and the Energy of Affect" in *PMLA* 120, no. 1 (January 2005): 33–48. My thanks to the International Spenser Society for the extraordinary community and programming they create and for recognizing this essay with the Isabel MacCaffrey Essay Prize.

Chapter 4 appeared as "Boy Toys and Liquid Joys: Pleasure and Power in the Bower of Bliss" in *Modern Philology* 106, no. 3 (February 2009): 465–96. My thanks go to the Modern Languages Association for the permission to reprint and to the GL/Q Caucus of the MLA for recognizing this essay with the Crompton-Noll Award.

We should all be grateful to Helen Tartar for the example she sets for humanities publishing. Thomas Lay, Eric Newman, and the staff of Fordham University Press should win awards for the quality and efficiency of their work.

Without the love and support of my family, launching myself into a life of thinking, reading, and writing would have been difficult at best. Without my partner, Theodore Bale, that life would have been impoverished beyond imagining.

Introduction

Perhaps nothing says more about a poet than praise lavished by that poet upon a predecessor. "Sage and serious" was how John Milton, in *Areopagitica*, characterized Edmund Spenser, perhaps his greatest and most complex precursor. This oft-cited assessment casts Spenser as a moral poet, exemplary in his description of "true temperance," and "a better teacher then *Scotus* or *Aquinas*."[1] Spenser's wisdom resides in the instruction he provides with respect to a matter central to Milton's own poetics: the knowledge of good and evil that endows the capacity to choose correctly between the two. Guyon's sojourn to the Cave of Mammon in the second book of *The Faerie Queene*, the Legend of Temperance, exemplifies the principle of continence: "that he might see and know, and yet abstain." Elsewhere, Milton expands on this: "He that can apprehend and consider vice with all her baits and seeming pleasures, and yet abstain, and yet distinguish, and yet prefer that which is truly better, he is the true warfaring Christian."[2]

The phrase "warfaring Christian" speaks to a persistent contradiction lodged at the heart of a religion responsible for extraordinary acts of violence and yet organized around a suffering divinity. What it meant to be a poet of virtue and a "warfaring" Christian was to prove especially complicated for all poets in post-Reformation England, even for Milton, whose thought and writing are characterized by an extreme and often violent clarity. Indeed, 1644 editions of *Areopagitica* emend "wayfaring" to "warfaring."[3] As editors point out, one finds biblical warrant for "wayfaring": "And an highway shall be there, and a way, and it shall be called the way of holiness; the unclean shall not pass over it; but it *shall be* for those: the wayfaring men, though fools shall not err *therein*"[4] (*Isaiah* 35:8, King James). And yet it seems, even before the emendation that has become common in editions of *Areopagitica*, that Milton clearly had "warfaring" in mind. Milton insists that virtue requires an armed encounter with evil: "I cannot praise a fugitive and cloistered virtue, unexercised, unbreathed, that never sallies out and sees her adversary, but slinks out of the race, where that immortal garland is to be run for, not without dust and heat."[5] For Thomas Luxon there seems to be little distinction between the two, as the pre-Reformation valorization of Christ's suffering, patience, and compassion finds itself displaced by a heroic ideal: "*Imitatio Christi* gives way to a new form of piety in which the faithful Hebrew prophet (Isaiah, Daniel, and especially David) is the model for Christian faithfulness—wayfaring and warfaring."[6] But "wayfaring" merely refers to following a way or taking a journey. Does following the way of holiness necessarily imply "warfaring" of the variety that motivated the Crusades and inspired whole genres of literature concerned with heroism and adventure?

In their edition of Milton's works, Jonathan Goldberg and Stephen Orgel find further warrant for the change from "wayfaring" to "warfaring" in *Ephesians* 6:11, which exhorts the true Christian to "put on the whole armor of God," and in the opening stanzas of the Legend of Holiness, which not only has *Ephesians* in mind but which introduces the young warrior Redcrosse as the exemplar of the way of Holiness and, as the poem later reveals, the future St. George, patron and defender of England.[7] There seems more than adequate support for this point of view in *The Faerie Queene*, which celebrates the heroic defense of virtue, glorifies England through a variety of allegorical embodiments of its sovereign, and announces in its proem that "Fierce warres and faithfull loues shall moralize my song" (1.proem.1).[8] When the Redcrosse Knight appears, he too embodies a certain contradiction between violence and vulnerability. He is "one for knightly giusts and fierce encounters fitt / And on his brest a bloodie Crosse he bore" (1.1.2). Is the bloody cross one more emblem in a martial imaginary and, therefore, consonant with the image of a knight fit for fierce encounter? The 1596 *Faerie Queene* revises "and" to "but." Perhaps the "bloodie Crosse" evoked too much pain, passion, and vulnerability to be an emblem of the triumphs of warfaring Christianity.

My subject here is not Milton's Spenser, a subject others have treated with complexity and nuance.[9] I would, however, suggest that

Milton's vision of Spenser as encapsulated in *Areopagitica* makes vivid a series of persistent assumptions about *The Faerie Queene*: that Spenser is a militant defender of Christian, indeed Protestant, virtue and the defense of that virtue required violence; that he is a moral poet, which might indicate a dedication to abstinence or at least a resistance to the lures of pleasure and sensation (even if Spenser's exemplary knights succumbed to pleasure or his hypnotic verse induced it); and that he is the proponent of an ideal of heroic masculinity that constellates gender, desire, and sexuality as the bedrock of a nationalistic and even imperialistic sensibility. Four centuries of richly textured readings of *The Faerie Queene* have caused readers rightly to question such values or even the values Spenser articulated in and about *The Faerie Queene*, either in his framing "Letter of the Authors" or in moments of direct commentary in the poem itself. What I propose is an account of why a particular and persistent set of assumptions about Spenser, which scholars have vigorously questioned but not displaced, are not so much incorrect as incomplete. Thus, if the claim can be made that *The Faerie Queene* was both "the greatest and, at the same time, the most representative product of the Protestant Reformation" and "a nationalistic epic," we must examine what effect Spenser's interest in an ethics and aesthetics of vulnerability might have on how we understand a wide range of phenomena, including the Protestant Reformation, the idea of a nationalistic epic, and the often unexamined varieties of masculinity on which such notions depend.[10]

To understand Spenser is to understand a host of contradictions both evoked and intensified by the fractious decades after the Reformation, as the violence of religious schism became a part of the fabric of life in England. *The Pain of Reformation* examines a triangulation of vulnerability, masculinity, and ethics common to many literary writers grappling with that peculiar admixture of triumph and trauma in the wake of massive religious and political changes. Literary writers register this phenomenon as a sense of vulnerability at the very time that the very terms for understanding and the ways of experiencing vulnerability—pleasure, pain, suffering, compassion, and other intense forms of affect and sensation—were themselves in flux.

Although my investigation began with Petrarchan plaints, bleeding trees, wounded bodies, and other explicit signatures of damaged masculinity in Spenser's singular poem, I came to apprehend *The Faerie*

Queene's capacity to index, under the rubric of vulnerability, a set of wide-ranging phenomena. To read Spenser's sustained conversation about vulnerability in the 1590 *Faerie Queene* is to explore poetry's role in recollecting urgencies and sensibilities scattered in the complex landscape of the post-Reformation; in exploring pleasure and pain and thereby understanding language's embeddedness in the sensorium of living flesh; in interrogating the fictions of masculinity in Renaissance England, fictions that undergird a range of ideologies, especially forms of nationalism; and in articulating an ethical imperative to investigate those limiting fantasies of invulnerability defined as forms of masculinity or the heroic. *The Faerie Queene* deploys an array of genres but makes a signature intervention in heroic poetry, one that, perhaps counterintuitively, explores vulnerability rather than violence. Rather than rejoicing in the necessary brutality of the Reformation or registering such violence as an obliterating trauma, Spenser makes vulnerability central to his idea of virtue, which he understands in a root sense as being related to manliness. Masculinity, or manliness, must then be reformed to accommodate vulnerability and an openness to the pain of others. Or one might say masculinity must be reformed to admit the possibility of vulnerability, and the reformation of masculinity to accommodate forms of vulnerability was for Spenser a deeply ethical project. The terms of this reformation work themselves out at first through quite obvious religious matters in the Legend of Holiness. But then Spenser's engagement with pain and vulnerability extends to aesthetics (in the Legend of Temperance) and sexuality (in the Legend of Chastity).

Spenser may indeed have sounded the trumpet of heroic virtue in the proem to *The Faerie Queene*. But in addition to invoking the muse of epic, he invokes Venus, the goddess of love, requesting she disarm the god of war, forcing him to set aside his "murderous spoyles and bloudy rage" (1.proem.3). Why begin a martial poem with a gesture of disarming? Homer sings of the wrath of Achilles, while Virgil conjures the talismanic "arms and the man" as his subject.[11] Spenser's more immediate predecessors, Ariosto and Tasso, appear to be diametrically opposed: the former devoted to wit; the latter, to melancholy. Both, however, invoke Christian heroism and the depravity of infidel invaders, either those Africans who invade France in *Orlando Furioso* or the denizens of Asia, Africa, and hell who threaten Christian efforts to recapture

Jerusalem in *Gerusalemme liberata*. The opening of *The Faerie Queene* adumbrates affinities with each of these epic projects, to be sure, but it resonates more powerfully with the project of Lucretius, whose *De rerum natura* begins by invoking Venus to soothe the violence of strife, Mars: "Cause meanwhile the savage works of war to sleep and be still over every sea and land. For you alone can delight mortals with quiet peace, since Mars mighty in battle rules the savage works of war, who often casts himself upon your lap wholly vanquished by the ever-living wound of love."[12] For Lucretius, the fractious "time of [his] country's troubles" motivates his invocation of Venus in the hope of peace.

England was not yet on the cusp of the Civil War to come, and such futures may not even have been imaginable for most at this moment in history. Still, the ongoing political and religious conflicts of Spenser's era reactivated a reservoir of conflict in response to what was often articulated as a great triumph but what was also a great trauma for England: the Reformation. Even as historians have offered increasingly complex accounts of the Reformation, the consequences of religious dissent altered fundamentally not only devotional practices and identities but also the way experiences of pleasure, pain, and vulnerability were construed and represented. Perhaps it is not surprising, then, that such tropes populate the landscape of heroic poetry in an age in which the fear of cultural and political vulnerability reached heights of intensity; the many signatures of vulnerability in heroic literature—bleeding trees, disarmed heroes, and exposed bodies of many varieties—were lent extraordinary resonance. Disarmed bodies must also be understood with respect to a larger iconography. Indeed, around and just after the decades in which *The Faerie Queene* was composed and published, Peter Paul Rubens painted portraits of Venus disarming Mars which drew on a stock of familiar images understood as an allegory of peace: love disarms war, bringing peace to a Europe racked by endless conflicts.

Spenser, naturally, would have responded to a more particular history of vulnerability. In spite of those fantasies of dominion later to become realized, England was, in the Renaissance, environed by a wilderness of sea with enemies in all directions. Every piece of good fortune—like the Spanish Armada being scattered, almost magically, by storm—was matched by myriad crises: uncertain succession (arguably ranging from the War of the Roses through the reign of Elizabeth and beyond), religious divisions that left enemies within and without, martyrdoms on both sides of the divide between Reformed and Roman faith, and attempted coups and royal murder plots were just the beginning. France, Scotland, and Ireland were all potential platforms for invasion (even Ireland was, in spite of the Tudor regime's brutalities, a colossal political failure that cost thousands of lives and financially crippled the nation). And Spenser lived just a generation or so after the one true universal church was (yet again) splintered, unleashing religious wars of shocking intensity that shaped the emerging nation-states of Europe. Moreover, the English ship of state was helmed by a virgin queen, the complexities of which have provided ample material for critical investigation into the way the sexed embodiment of the sovereign combined with an eroticized rhetoric of courtly service. What was often construed as passivity or timidity with respect to foreign policy drove heroically inclined courtiers like Sidney and Essex to states of distraction and provoked strategies of masculine overcompensation.

There were myriad responses to this sense of precarious life in Renaissance England. For some, a solution was the cultivation of virtue, which one can understand in its root sense. The defense against a pervasive sense of vulnerability that shook the foundations of a fledgling nation-state was so often the construction of an invulnerable, masculine, rational citizen, immune to immoderate pleasures, pains, and affects and emblematized by the figure of the knight whose body was safely encased in impenetrable armor. The failure of this fantasy provoked many responses—denial, defensiveness, anxiety, and shame. One need look no further than Philip Sidney to find the defensively sentimental and inadvertently self-parodying heroicization of masculinity in the *Arcadia*; than William Shakespeare to find an oscillation between a shamefully degraded heroic masculinity (in *Troilus and Cressida*, *Antony and Cleopatra*, and elsewhere) and a viciously naïve and brilliantly strategic, nationalistic masculinity (in the Henriad); or than Thomas Nashe to find masculinity ironized to the point of an incapacity that results in marketable but potentially fatal forms of buffoonery in *The Unfortunate Traveller*. But I will argue here that the most comprehensive meditation on vulnerability, masculinity, and ethics in the wake of the Reformation came from a poet who, in recent years, has been associated primarily with the brutalities of English rule in Ireland.

Who could argue with this position with respect to a poet who wrote *A Vewe of the Present State of Ireland* with the aim of thinking through the project of "reducinge that salvage nacion to better gouerment and Cyvilitye" by means of the most extreme and violent measures?[13] At the end of his life it was Spenser, the would-be civilizer, who was driven from the lands he occupied in Cork in the service of the Tudor regime. Richard Helgerson reminds us that early in his career Spenser cried out in a letter to Gabriel Harvey, "For, why a Gods name may not we, as else the Greekes, haue the kingdome of oure owne Language?"[14] Spenser participated, through literary debates about the nature of English verse, in the project of nation-building, a project racked by contradiction: "Prompted by the cultural breaks of Renaissance and Reformation," Helgerson argues, "sixteenth-century national self-articulation began with a sense of national barbarism, with a recognition of the self as the despised other, and then moved to repair that damaged self-image with the aid of forms taken from a past that was now understood as both different from the present and internally divided."[15] In his correspondence with Harvey, where Spenser deploys "the language of sovereign power eager to subdue rough words and have the kingdom of them, Harvey responds in terms made familiar by centuries of resistance to royal encroachment."[16] Even Georgia Ronan Crampton concludes, after a careful sifting of the works of Chaucer and Spenser in her study of the venerable *agere-et-pati* (to act and to suffer) topos, that "Spenser the Renaissance poet celebrates action; Chaucer, a medieval poet, sufferance."[17]

It has been easy to track those predictably violent formations of masculinity (defensive, anxious, retributive, failed, shattered, ashamed) that deny a sense of shared vulnerability at this moment in England's history. The very project of *The Faerie Queene* seems to fit this definition, making one ambition of the poem consonant with the creation of a nationalistic epic romance.

But Helgerson reminds us that it was Spenser's forebear, Torquato Tasso, who wrote in order to justify "the newly rationalized and absolute power of the state" and who produced a "strongly unified epic poem . . . in which unity of purpose and unity of rule are guarantors of neoclassical conformity." Tasso's project is, famously, rife with anxiety and paranoia about the success of this mission, yet as Helgerson succinctly states, "All this *The Faerie Queene* lacks."[18] Nations, like poetic projects, are more vulnerable than they would like to admit, making the longing for sovereign glory the stuff of fantasy. If the certainty of the triumphs of the English nation was in a constant state of doubt, might it not be the case that this crisis produced not only defensive gestures but also, more importantly, the capacity to reflect on vulnerability as the source of a new understanding of both masculinity and ethics, which might be united in the term *virtue*?

The interpretation of *The Faerie Queene* has always been tangled up in the problem of didacticism, so much so that *virtue* may seem too hackneyed a term to be of critical use. But in "A Letter of the Authors," Spenser articulates the intent to "fashion a gentleman or noble person."[19] As Maurice Evans argues in his study *Spenser's Anatomy of Heroism*, "Spenser's explicit concern is to fashion heroes, and he uses the heroic poem both as a means of anatomising the nature of heroism in his own sense of the term and of influencing the reader to embrace its values." Yet Evans locates in the didacticism of *The Faerie Queene* unexpected intricacies: "His moral theme is more subtle than is generally recognised, and his language has much of the paradox and complexity normally associated with the Metaphysical poets but usually denied to *The Faerie Queene*. A number of Spenser's lines, as we shall see, have a controlled ambiguity which lends itself to simultaneous and diametrically opposed interpretations."[20] For Spenser, paradox, complexity, and controlled ambiguity were the perfect tools for interrogating virtue and reflecting on the relationship between masculinity and ethics embedded in the idea of the heroic.

As Robin Headlam Wells points out, "For the Renaissance, the heroic ideal is essentially masculine. The qualities it evokes—courage, physical strength, prowess in battle, manly honour, defiance of fortune—may be summed up in a word whose Latin root means 'a man.' As English Renaissance writers understand the term, *virtus* signifies an ideal of manhood that derives partly from classical epic, partly from medieval chivalry, and partly from Italian *realpolitik*."[21] This heady brew of often contradictory associations with the cultivation of virtue certainly had political ramifications. Wells argues that "the conflicting political positions signaled by such coded phrases as 'courage-masculine' and 'manly virtue' caused deeper divisions in Elizabeth's and James's Privy Councils than any other topic of public debate in late-Elizabethan and early-Stuart England. Those conflicts very nearly resulted in the deposition of a reigning monarch and later provoked a bitter and embarrassingly public rift between her successor and the crown prince."[22]

Wells joins scholars like Diana Purkiss who expand the study of gender in early modernity by turning from representations of women and femininity to representations of men and masculinity. Indeed, Purkiss examines varieties of masculinity in and around the English Civil Wars "fissuring under the extreme pressure of the political events of the 1640s and 1650s."[23] Bruce Smith, who thinks of masculinity in his study of Shakespeare as "a matter of contingency, of circumstances, of performances,"[24] typifies approaches that rely heavily on medical texts, conduct books, and accounts of life changes from boyhood to manhood, among other sources. With respect to the works of Spenser, Lisa Cevlosky, one of the few to address masculinity, argues that "*The Faerie Queene* explores the masculine tensions that arise when men face the transition from bachelorhood to husbandhood."[25]

Other scholars have preferred not the sociology of manhood but rather a psychoanalytics of damaged masculinity. Thus Purkiss develops a historical account of masculinity in the English Civil War that rests on a series of psychoanalytic categories (castration and hysteria among others) that lead her to conclude that "masculinity is in any case always already broken."[26] Catherine Bates attends to early modern lyrics "populated by . . . figures who appear by choice to defy the period's model of a phallic masterly masculinity—these adopted positions of impotence, failure, and gendered discontent seeming willfully to pervert what might otherwise have been seen . . . as the patriarchal norm."[27] Lynn Enterline understands early modern masculinity to be shaped by narcissism and melancholia, producing myriad "images of self-reflection and images conveying a sense of loss that exceeds all compensation."[28] Many look back to Mark Breitenberg's *Anxious Masculinity in Early Modern England*, which characterizes masculinity as a perpetually anxious and fundamentally defensive formation.

The Pain of Reformation joins these studies of masculinity while differing from them in some respects. While I do not deny the importance of sociocultural definitions of manhood concretized by conduct books, medical treatises, and other sources, I understand masculinity throughout this study as an ethical state. In *The Use of Pleasure*, Michel Foucault describes an entire system of Greek thought with respect to the ethics of pleasure. As he puts it, "Foods, wines, and relations with women and boys constituted analogous ethical material; they brought forces into play that were natural but that always tended to be excessive; and they all raised the same question: how could one, how must one 'make use' of this dynamics of pleasures, desires, and acts? A question of right use."[29] For the Greeks of Foucault's account, the experience of pleasure was neither prohibited nor suppressed; it was, instead, deployed with "the 'virile' character of moderation" that enabled self-mastery, what Foucault describes as an "an ethics of men made for men," in which "an ethical subject consisted in setting up a structure of virility that related oneself to oneself."[30] Moderation of pleasure and a consequent self-mastery made ethical virility possible for Foucault's Greeks. But Spenser's era witnessed both a more severe ambivalence about pleasure and a systematic restriction of affect in the wake of the Reformation. As Max Weber's classic account *The Protestant Ethic and the "Spirit" of Capitalism* argues, early modernity witnesses a "combination of religious control of life and an extremely well developed business sense" coupled with a "negative attitude . . . toward all sensual and *emotional* elements in culture and subjective religiosity" and a "fundamental rejection of every kind of culture of the senses."[31] Ethical virility that eschewed the merely moralistic would have to result not from moderation but from an incitement and intensification of and openness to sensation and affect, pleasure and pain. Masculinity in *The Faerie Queene* is an opportunity for vulnerability, and it is vulnerability that makes ethical action possible.

Spenser's attention to vulnerability thus provides a transformative account of masculinity. The nature of masculinity, as described in mostly psychoanalytically inflected accounts, grounds a fundamental defensiveness in notions of anxiety, damage, or trauma. In a recent study, Patricia Cahill emphasizes "the complexities of a historical moment when martial performances might, at the very same time, suggest both the ordered rule of war and the unruliness of trauma."[32] Like most who refer to the body of work on notions of trauma, Cahill refers back to *Beyond the Pleasure Principle*, which describes trauma as the breach of "a protective shield against stimuli. . . . *Protection against* stimuli is an almost more important function for the living organism than *reception* of stimuli."[33] This masculine defensiveness surfaces also in references—by Enterline, Marshall, Purkiss, and others—to Jacques Lacan's mirror stage, in which the drama of the infant's encounter with the fictional coherence of a mirror image of the self results in "the succession of fantasies that extends from a fragmented body-image to a form of its totality . . . and lastly to the assumption of the armour of alienating identity, which will mark with its rigid structure the subject's entire mental development."[34] Scholars have attempted to find an antidote to the defensive and triumphant tenor of articulations of early modern masculinity commonly associated with martial prowess. As Wells reminds us, "For a brief period the collocation of 'martial' and 'masculine' took on a very specific and local meaning. In militant-Protestant circles it formed part of a pattern of praising martial values but characterizing them as masculine and depreciating eirenic values as feminine."[35]

Yet the impulse to disarm represented in *The Faerie Queene* and elsewhere suggests a middle ground between self-mastering masculinity and obliterated masculinity or, to borrow terms from Stephen Greenblatt and Cynthia Marshall, a middle ground between masterful "self-fashioning" and obliterated "self-shattering."[36] Contrary to Freud's premise that the need for "protection against stimuli" surpasses the need for "reception of stimuli," Spenser seems to have imagined a world in which instances of pain, pleasure, sensation, and affect might be experienced in a way that would be transformative rather than obliterating, that would suggest the importance of a concept of shared vulnerability, and that would reimagine a gendered split between masculine, martial values and feminine, eirenic values. Harry Berger Jr. has already suggested that the Legend of Holiness features a particular "ironic evaluation" of masculinity. "The quest of Christian identity," he argues, "is a quest of chivalric manhood: the problematic engaged by the former is that of narcissism, and by the latter, that of gynephobia and misogyny."[37] I would suggest here that Spenser's 1590 *Faerie Queene* advances more than merely an "ironic evaluation" of chivalric manhood. Furthermore, Berger's "quest of Christian identity" remains too general to pinpoint the particular struggle over masculinity and vulnerability in post-Reformation England.

As I have suggested, *The Pain of Reformation* attempts to explore the underside, or shadow, of violence, which is vulnerability. Contemporary criticism has enjoyed a certain vogue for the term. But why might this pertain to the writings of Edmund Spenser, who never, in fact, uses the terms *vulnerable* or *vulnerability* (a term not in use until the early 1800s), or any of the related forms of the word? Indeed, these terms were just entering into usage, their first instances appearing around the time of the publication of the 1590 *Faerie Queene*. Moreover, the earliest uses suggest an uncanny confusion between what we would now refer to as *vulnerable* and *invulnerable*. Forms of *vuln* and *vulned* refer, transitively, to the act of wounding or the power to wound, while late in Shakespeare's *Macbeth* (1605), Macbeth's mistaken sense of *in*vulnerability leads him to disdain Macduff's challenge, saying, "Let fall thy blade on vulnerable crests; / I bear a charmed life."[38] Macbeth subordinates the body's vulnerability to the idea of a "charmed life" in which harm is unimaginable.

Macbeth may have been naïve about his own vulnerability, but most early modern subjects were not. Yet even as early modern literature began to reflect both uncertainty about and a shift away from the ideal of warlike masculinity in the English aristocracy, the tropes and tendencies of heroic poetry remained useful for assessing a burgeoning awareness that forms of physical sensation and affective receptivity might be distinguished from forms of weakness or incapacity that threatened mortal harm. Indeed, later thinkers, notably Friedrich Nietzsche, might predispose us to consider an attention to vulnerability as merely another facet of a problematic and slyly aggressive valorization of weakness in the history of Christianity.[39] In spite of the relative novelty of the term in early modern England, *vulnerability* proves quite useful. As I have already suggested, *vulnerability* provides a critical alternative to *violence*. To be sure, gestures of disarmament connoted an opposition to war in early modern Europe. More importantly, this book attempts to describe the way states of vulnerability provide access to an experiential and imaginative aesthetics that resists the management, restriction, or expurgation of pain, pleasure, affect, and sensation. And while Nietzsche has proved both influential and useful in understanding the ideological deployment of Christian morality and the promulgation of forms of *ressentiment* that slyly deploy weakness in the service of fantasies of mastery, post-Reformation England provides an important historical index of the transformation or repurposing of pre-Reformation religious sensibilities to produce a notion of the self rooted in vulnerability, if not subjection, and a notion of sociality rooted in shared vulnerability.

The receding presence of affective piety and attention to the suffering Christ coupled with the rise of Protestant militancy provoked questions about both the centrality of physical and emotional pain and the importance of meditating and dwelling on the pain of others. In poetry these questions were posed with respect to the creation of an ideal: the masculine, rational, citizen whose citizenship was predicated upon defensive fantasies of invulnerability. And the possibility that a militant Christ and a defensible poetry were not ideals to be cherished made possible a reconsideration of the eroticization of subjection. Before I consider these subjects more fully in *The Faerie Queene*, I will explore some Renaissance contexts for the disarmed and vulnerable bodies to which Spenser's attention was so frequently drawn.

Lucretius identifies Venus as the mother of Aeneas and his line but also as a divine force capable of soothing the hostilities of Mars to bring peace to a troubled land. Note the difference between the role Venus plays in *De rerum natura* and the role she plays in that poem's successor in the epic tradition, Virgil's *Aeneid*. Mother of the scions of Troy, those refugees destined to found an empire to rival all others, Venus first appears as the aggrieved advocate of Aeneas and his men. In a poem that opens under the shadow of Juno's rage, Venus appears to be as vulnerable as her son. But this apparent vulnerability licenses a demand for power: "We, your offspring, to whom you grant the heights of heaven, have lost our ships—O shame unutterable!—and, to appease one angry foe, are betrayed and kept far from Italian shores. And this is piety honoured? Is this the way you restore us to empire?"[40] Even as she serves as a protective mother figure, Venus appears to her son disguised and alienated from him in the guise of a huntress reminiscent of the virgin goddess Diana. When finally she reveals herself to Aeneas just as she departs, he chides her for her unkindness: "Why, cruel like others, do you so often mock your son with vain phantoms? Why am I not allowed to clasp hand in hand and hear and utter words unfeigned?"[41] The dynamic that governs the quest of Aeneas is one of frustrated desire, its consequences violent. As Barbara J. Bono argues, "In the *Aeneid*, Venus eludes her son's grasp; her evanescence becomes a symbol for the pressure of mutability on mortals, which there leads to the strictest channeling and sublimation of desire into collective destiny."[42] But Virgil was a poet of empire, and his Venus, the nurturing mother of imperial destiny, retreats from a Lucretian Venus. For Lucretius, the fractious "time of [his] country's troubles" motivates the invocation of a nurturing peacemaker. Not just "the goddess of traditional religion and mythology, who was mother of Aeneas and the Roman people, who was loved by Mars," this Venus is "the Empedoclean principle of Love (as opposed to Mars = Strife), representing the creative forces in the world, and she is the personification of the Epicurean *summum bonum*, pleasure (*voluptas*)."[43] The tension between these visions of Venus was embodied in the imagery and furnishings of literary works identified with the epic or heroic tradition.

Heroic poetry casts its eye frequently upon the equipment of war, from gorgeously detailed arms, such as the shields of Achilles and Aeneas, to the noted depictions of warriors arming for battle, such as many scenes in *The Iliad* or the arming of the hero in *Sir Gawain and the Green Knight*. Conversely, for the heroic figure who refuses to arm or who finds himself disarmed, unarmed, or unprepared for battle would be reserved a potent mixture of vulnerability and opprobrium that clarifies in what ways the figures and tropes of heroic poetry construct a portrait of the ideal masculine citizen. Myriad characters lose their rational bearing, their erotic equilibrium, their moral purpose, and their masculine vigor as they lose or even cast aside their arms and armor. Achilles, selfishly and childishly refusing to arm against the Trojans in response to the perceived insults of Agamemnon, nurses his wrath and wounded pride in his tent as the battle rages on. Ariosto's Orlando, unhinged by evidence that his beloved Angelica loves another, tears off his armor and roams the woods like a mindless beast, senselessly killing those he encounters. Both Ariosto and Tasso treated the surrender of heroic arms and martial purpose in the face of erotic temptation; their characters Ruggiero and Rinaldo are lured into lascivious and effeminate abandon at the hands of Alcina and Armida. Of course, many of these episodes borrow from (and even allude to) the famous capture of the adulterous Venus and Mars under a net fashioned by the cuckolded Vulcan. Spenser's 1590 *Faerie Queene* is no different in featuring disarmed and vulnerable bodies as most of the titular knights find themselves in precarious states: the unarmed Redcrosse "pourd out in loosnesse on the grassy grownd" (1.7.7), Guyon unconscious after his sojourn to the cave of Mammon, the overly pleasured male bodies of the Bower of Bliss, or Britomart exposed in bed in the castle of Malecasta, to name just a few. On each of these occasions we find cause for alarm as these states of vulnerability connote shame, exhaustion, lapse of virtue, and mortal risk.

Yet there were other ways of understanding gestures of disarming that would value differently the experience of vulnerability. Although the legendary dalliance between Venus and Mars provides a potent emblem of shame, illicit sex, and emasculation (culminating in the lame Vulcan's voyeuristic capture of the copulating Venus and Mars under a net of his own fashioning), it also provides an allegory of peace, as the calming influence of love restrains the vicious impulses of war, resulting in the birth of harmony or concord. Edgar Wind's influential account of the "double life led by the average courtier, that of a warrior and of a lover," reads the battle between love and war as a larger cultural and philosophical paradox. To reconcile these forces, "the ancient 'mystery' upon which they seized"—Wind notes of poets, philosophers, and artists ranging from Plutarch to Pico della Mirandola and beyond—"was the unlawful union of Mars and Venus, from which issued a daughter named Harmony."[44] Wind continues: "The many and famous Renaissance idylls in which the victorious Venus, having subdued the fearful Mars by love, is seen playing with his armour, or allowing her cupids and infant satyrs to play with it, all celebrate this peaceable hope: that Love is more powerful than Strife."[45]

The potency of this allegory of peace should not be underestimated. For Pico della Mirandola the very structure of the cosmos was at stake in this pairing: "And since in the constitution of created things it is necessary that the union overcomes the strife (otherwise the thing would perish because its elements would fall apart)—for this reason it is said by the poets that Venus loves Mars. . . . Venus tames and mitigates Mars, because the tempering power restrains and overcomes the strife and hate which persists between the contrary elements."[46] Similarly, Marsilio Ficino argues that the very same principle applies to the astrological influences upon character development: "Mars surpasses the other planets in courage because he makes men braver. *Venus dominates him*. For when Mars is located in the corners of heaven, . . . he threatens evils to the person being born, but Venus often shackles, so to speak, the malignancy of Mars. . . . When Mars dominates at the birth of a man, he bestows greatness of soul and irascibility. If Venus comes near, she does not impede that virtue of magnanimity given by Mars, but she does restrain the vice of irascibility. Here she seems to make Mars more gentle and thus to *dominate* him. *But Mars never dominates Venus.*"[47]

A series of problems arises, however, that neither Wind nor these Italian Renaissance philosophers inquire into. First, might there not be deleterious consequences to conceiving of peace and concord through discourses of domination? Indeed, would we not need to conceive of forms of love and concord that were beyond subjection? What notion of concord could be guaranteed by a mythic structure that insisted on the subjection of masculinity, thus guaranteeing a potent mixture of shame and resentment? This scenario was foundational for England in an age famously ambivalent about the long rule of Queen Elizabeth I. Many have suggested this ambivalence lurks behind Shakespeare's poetic portrait of a domineering Venus wrestling her beloved Adonis into submission. Moreover, while these writers redeem the illicit, adulterous love between Mars and Venus, none seem to treat, as Rubens does, the consequence of disarmament, which would be the revelation of the male body rendered vulnerable to pleasure (as in the case of Mars) or pain (as in the case of Adonis). Yet epic and romance literature, from Homer to the Renaissance and beyond, takes up the trope of the discarding of arms primarily as an index of failure: the abdication of masculine fortitude in the face of erotic or emotional distraction. Achilles, Odysseus, Aeneas, Orlando, Rinaldo, and Tancred, among others, shamefully put off their arms or abandon their quests for love or for grief. How, then, to disentangle the vulnerability of the male body from the shame of emasculation? Moreover, might one distinguish between vulnerability and subjection?

The contradictions inherent in the ancient connection between the mythological and astrological figures of Venus and Mars can too easily be explained away, as Wind does, as a powerful instance of necessary contrariety, *discordia concors*. But these contradictions provided rich terrain for artists committed to the task of conceiving of a middle ground between martial violence and erotic subjection. In as much as the 1590 *Faerie Queene* is organized around the cultivation of moral value emblematized in heroic discourse, the primary virtue is not any of the poem's named virtues—Holiness, Temperance, Chastity, or even the sum total of all virtue, Magnificence, associated with the mythical Arthur. Nor is violence a primary virtue, however glorified it is in the seductive stanzas of this most sensuous of poems. Rather, the 1590

Faerie Queene proposes as its central virtue the capacity of the flesh to be receptive or vulnerable to sensation *and* to be a site of shared vulnerability that would constitute the ground of ethical behavior.

The work of Lucretius indicates that Spenser's quite singular attempt to explore vulnerability had, if not precedent, then at least a sympathetic predecessor. While it would not be accurate to say that Spenser had a successor, one could say that Spenser's near contemporary Peter Paul Rubens inherited and struggled with similar mythic constructs in an attempt to explore the possibility that war might be allayed by love. In 1630, having completed a mission to England to assist in the successful negotiations between Charles I and Philip IV of Spain, Rubens returned home to receive what Roy Strong has described as "the single most important artistic commission by the English Crown in the first half of the seventeenth century."[48] He was invited to complete a series of paintings for the ceiling of the Whitehall Banqueting House under the direction of Inigo Jones, paintings that celebrate the glory of the Stuarts in a positively heroic register. King James appears enthroned as a latter-day Solomon who revives the ancient empire of Great Britain, reigns over a golden age of prosperity, and finally ascends into the heavens, drawn upward by Justice herself. In the many panels morality persistently depends on martial endeavor, as classical figures such as Minerva and Hercules and allegorical personifications such as Justice and Temperance beat back vice and iniquity. Completed in the mid-1630s, these paintings culminated in the apotheosis of James I and, by extension, his son Charles I, who is allegorized as the glorious child (depicted in a painting referred to as either *The Judgment of Solomon: James I Re-creates the Empire of Great Britain* or *The Union of the Crowns* and in the sketch *The Apotheosis of James I* [see Figure 1]), magisterially indexed by an ascendant James. Rubens did not remain at the court of James, in spite of the king's invitations. Nonetheless, he participated in one of the greatest allegories of Stuart sovereignty and imperial aspiration, as imagined through exemplars of an invulnerable, heroic masculinity, reminding us that this was a nation that imagined its people were descended from Brutus, a scion of Troy, and its capital, London, was Troy reborn.

Note the contrast, however, between this celebration of heroic imperialism and the equally venerable subject Rubens turned to as he was finishing James's commission, a subject whose anticipation of

Figure 1. *The Apotheosis of James I and Other Studies: Multiple Sketch for the Banqueting House Ceiling*, Whitehall. (Tate / Digital Image © Tate, London 2009)

vulnerability and death contrasted sharply with the triumph of martial force in the Whitehall panels. In representing *Venus and Adonis* (1614 [see Figure 2] and 1635 [see Figure 3]), Rubens found inspiration in previous treatments of Venus's attempt to dissuade Adonis from what proves to be his final, fatal hunt. In both versions the tension in Adonis's body signals his resistance to her appeal. In the 1635 painting, Adonis has already planted his spear and nearly turned his muscular back to a seated Venus who reaches up to draw him back as Cupid tugs at his leg. Expressed here is a dynamic familiar to heroic narratives: the warrior, or hunter, resists the erotic supplications of the sensuous woman. Venus, vulnerable to her desires, fails to restrain Adonis, whose masculine indifference to her allure leads to his death. The death of Adonis is not depicted here, though Rubens treated this aspect of the narrative by approaching the spectacle of Adonis's death in the painting *Venus Lamenting Adonis* (1602) and in a series of unrelated

Figure 2. Peter Paul Rubens, *Venus and Adonis*, circa 1614. Oil on panel, 83 × 90.5 cm. (The State Hermitage Museum, St. Petersburg)

Figure 3. Peter Paul Rubens, *Venus and Adonis*, mid-or late 1630s. Oil on canvas, with added strips, 77¾ × 95⅝ in. (The Metropolitan Museum of Art / Art Resource, NY)

drawings (see Figure 4). In these works, Venus hovers over the prone body of the dead Adonis or holds his body in her arms. Adonis is consistently naked; the utterly disarmed hunter is now a portrait of vulnerable flesh tended by Venus and her minions with a care familiar from the portraits of a dead and broken Christ taken down from his cross to be attended by his mother or other devotees. No longer is Adonis the brash muscular hunter questing to prove himself against the beasts of the forest; he is, rather, a wounded body to be transfigured by a grieving goddess into a blood-red flower. A portrait of masculine prowess thus gives way to a portrait of wounded flesh as the vitality of the martial body gives way. Adonis's body possesses a measure of eloquent serenity reminiscent of Michaelangelo's *La Pietá*. Although the body remains unmarked by the goring, the brutality of death remains; in the painting, Adonis's eyes remain open, rolling up just enough to leave the corpse staring blankly at Venus.

Figure 4. Peter Paul Rubens, *Venus Lamenting over the Dead Adonis*. Watercolor on paper. (© Trustees of the British Museum)

Figure 5. Peter Paul Rubens and Jan Brueghel the Elder, *The Return from War: Mars Disarmed by Venus*, 1610–12. Oil on panel, 127.3 × 163.5 cm. (Acquired in honor of John Walsh, The J. Paul Getty Museum, Los Angeles)

The significance of Venus's frustrated love for the vulnerable Adonis becomes more pointed as it becomes entangled with the allegory of peace embedded in the iconography of Venus and Mars. The postures of Venus and Cupid in Rubens's treatment of the dead Adonis shadow those of his earlier collaboration with Jan Brueghel the Elder, *The Return of War: Mars Disarmed by Venus* (1610–12 [see Figure 5]), widely understood as a political allegory advocating peace in a conflict-ridden Europe. A similarly reclining Venus collapses, with all her sensuous heft, against the body of Mars as a host of putti work to relieve him of his arms and armor. Around these figures we see scattered the cast-off (or not yet taken-up) armaments of Vulcan's forge, where Venus has lured Mars for their dalliance. Again it seems that the feminine, erotic principle restrains, distracts, or interrupts martial endeavor. In a roughly contemporary work on the same subject, Rubens's *Venus Disarming Mars* (1615–20 [see Figure 6]), it is Mars who collapses into the seated body

Figure 6. Peter Paul Rubens, *Mars and Venus*, 1618–1620. Oil on canvas. (The State Hermitage Museum, St. Petersburg)

of Venus, his eyes almost rolling up into his head as she and her army of putti, one of whom takes the reins of his dismounted steed, begin the work of uncasing his martial body, which sinks into sensual abandon as a pair of doves meet or mate in a tree above. These interlocking mythic complexes suggest a series of contradictions to which myriad Renaissance artists and writers would return. The sensual abandon of Mars constitutes a form of submission inimical to heroic virtue, but the masculine indifference of Adonis proves fatal. To submit to love is to be vulnerable, and yet vulnerability, for the heroic figure, constitutes a shameful lapse of manhood. But to fail to submit to love is to court annihilation for Adonis or for all civilization. Rubens also depicted the consequences of the failure of Mars to surrender his ferocity in the face of the gentleness of Venus. In *The Horrors of War* (ca. 1638), Mars, in a gesture not unlike Adonis's, turns his back on Venus, unleashing destruction upon all.

Spenser and Rubens, the secretary and the diplomat, were both artists and political functionaries who shared in the task of fashioning works that deployed heroic and mythological motifs to allegorize and justify the sovereign fantasies of a nation eager to emphasize its own glorious past and its ever-expanding senses of possibility under the sign and influence of an imperious Mars. At the same time, both artists also drew from an inheritance that, with reference to a similar cast of heroic and mythological motifs, emphasized the pacification of martial impulses and the cessation of violence through the life-giving influences of the loving, nourishing Venus. Lisa Rosenthal has argued that Rubens was centrally concerned with "the creation of compelling allegories promoting the desirability of peace and depicting the horrors of war."[49] In the process, Rubens, like Spenser, comes to "problematize heroic masculinity as an effective model for statehood" and inquire into the possibility of a masculinity that can coexist with the aims of civilization and peace.[50] Yet in his painting, also for Charles I, the *Allegory of the Blessings of Peace* (1629), Rubens's rapacious Mars is not seduced into surrender but must be beaten back by an armed Minerva; elsewhere in Rubens's paintings it is Hercules (sometimes allegorizing heroic virtue) who stands between violence and figures of vulnerability. In such canvases dedicated to the militant defense of peace, neither Venus nor Adonis is anywhere to be found. Certainly Rubens, like most, could only conceive of Adonis as the brash and eager hunter, rippling with martial intent, or as a body consumed by mortal, not erotic, lassitude. If this late Rubens teaches us anything, it is that true peace is not to be found in even the obliterating and sometimes calm aftermath of violence so great that it preempts response. Nor is the armed defense of perceived weakness an encounter with those forms of vulnerability in which all living things participate. For that one must move from Rubens back to Spenser.

As I have suggested, the primary virtue of the 1590 *Faerie Queene* is vulnerability. Spenser recalibrates the age-old dynamic between love and war in heroic poetry, making vulnerability—an openness to sensation and affect that implies an ethical openness to others—the poem's governing ideal. Spenser dwells on the many implications of the dalliance between Venus and Mars and traces a mythographic transit from Venus's pairing with Mars to her pairing with Adonis to suggest that the pacification of martial violence through submission must be superseded by a wholesale refashioning of masculinity through the sensate flesh of a body vulnerable to pleasures and pains located outside of regimes of either martial or erotic subjection. A critical impression of the historical Edmund Spenser—who is often viewed as an apologist for colonial violence and with whom is often associated the militant Protestantism and hatred of Catholicism characteristic of the New English settlers of Ireland—may have obscured aspects of this most complex, multilayered, and variegated of poems. What is at stake in the 1590 *Faerie Queene* is the question of whether poetry can or should contribute to the project of creating an invulnerable, heroic, rational, masculine citizen (resistant to compromising incitements of pain, pleasure, bodily sensation, and affect) on whom a nation might be founded. And if not, what should be the work of poetry if not to posit the fundamental vulnerability of the flesh as a new ground for ethics?

To focus on vulnerability was to negotiate the complexities of poetry's place in the wake of the Reformation. Like so many of his era, Spenser grappled with the question of how to reconcile the politics of religious affiliation with the complex transformations that accompanied them. How does one understand literature's relationship to the losses that followed from the Reformation consequent to figures of Christian militancy that displace the influence of affective piety and devotion to the figure of the suffering Christ? Moreover, this was an age in which the many literary treatises of justification and apology drew on a potentially restrictive set of tropes to articulate the purpose and function of poetry. How can poetry be disentangled from a fundamental defensiveness that depends on moral heroism for its validity? Religious and poetic discourses provide two contexts for Spenser's exploration of vulnerability while erotic discourse supplies the last. If love was to serve as a pacifying influence over war, how might the gendered violence and the forms of subjection endemic to erotic subjectivities—represented in epic romance, Petrarchan lyric, and allegory, those fundamental genres of *The Faerie Queene*—inhibit the project of disarming the violence of heroic masculinity? How must masculinity be reconceived to accommodate erotic vulnerability and the project of peace?

Of course, myriad gestures mark the 1590 *Faerie Queene* as a typically heroic poem, written in a tradition stretching from Homer and Virgil to Spenser's England by way of medieval Continental romance and Italian Renaissance epic. One might imagine that Spenser's goal was to maximize the thrust of heroic poetry, making it an organ resounding with the triumph of Elizabeth's Protestant state. But like those slippery, hypnotic alexandrines, the stanzas of this first incarnation of *The Faerie Queene* displace, and by displacing refocus, the task of heroic poetry, deploying its tropes and landscapes for a new purpose, one that may seem, for readers accustomed to the weight of centuries of interpretation, like a glimmer or a whisper in a dark forest. Perhaps there was no way to anticipate the opening gambit of the 1590 *Faerie Queene*—announcing as it does a full-scale reformation of the contours of heroic poetry, which provided governing metaphors for crucial ideologies in early modern England—and of the central virtues, both the moral qualities and the masculine efficacy, explored by each legend. Mary Beth Rose has argued that "during the early modern period the claims of both active and passive heroism are intensely scrutinized" and, more pointedly, that "the gendering of heroism from the late sixteenth to the late seventeenth centuries in England does not reveal an accelerating idealization of that which is male, public, and active, but rather the opposite." Rose sees the emergence of a new brand of heroism, one that contributed to the idealization of the private, domestic realm of women: "Rather than acts of killing and conquest, the patient suffering of error, misfortune, disaster, and malevolence is idealized in a newly and self-consciously constructed heroism of endurance that privileges the private life and pointedly rejects war." Rather than "privileging privacy and passive suffering" and contributing to "the larger cultural effort to distinguish and distinctly gender private and public spheres," Spenser imagines anew the problematic figure of masculine heroism, the notion that vulnerability connotes passivity, and the gendering of vulnerability into discrete spheres.[51]

The proem, with great fanfare, announces both Spenser's Virgilian advancement to greater levels of poetic achievement and the articulation of his poetic purpose: moral, heroic poetry. The full panoply of knights and ladies, shepherds and muses, trumpets and reeds, praise and blazon, and war and love confirms these gestures:

Lo I the man, whose Muse whylome did maske,
As time her taught, in lowly Shephards weeds,
Am now enforst a far vnfitter taske,
For trumpets sterne to chaunge mine Oaten reeds:
And sing of Knights and Ladies gentle deeds,
Whose praises hauing slept in silence long,
Me, all too meane, the sacred Muse areeds
To blazon broade emongst her learned throng:
Fierce warres and faithfull loues shall moralize my song.
(1.proem.1)

Modeled as it is on lines prefacing Renaissance editions of Virgil's *Aeneid*, Spenser announces his intention to cast off the "lowly Shephards weeds," represented by his *Shepheardes Calendar*, and take up the "trumpets sterne" and "sing of Knights and Ladies gentle deeds." The famous alexandrine of that first stanza ("Fierce warres and faithfull loues shall moralize my song") seems to confirm the turn from pastoral pleasures (and woes) to heroic deeds, which is represented in Richard Stanyhurst's translation of *The Aeneid*, where the Virgilian poet turns from his "rural sonnet" to "manhood" and "martial horror."[52] Stanyhurst's phrase "martial horror" translates the appended phrase "horrentia Martis," and the reference to Mars proves critical for Spenser as he transforms the intent of moral, heroic poetry by shifting the object of his invocation. If at first Spenser addresses "the sacred Muse," that "holy Virgin chiefe of nine"—who might be either Calliope, the muse of epic, or Clio, the muse of history (1.proem.2)—he turns instead to the powers of love:

And thou most dreaded impe of highest *Ioue*,
Faire *Venus* sonne, that with thy cruell dart
At that good knight so cunningly didst roue,
That glorious fire it kindled in his hart,
Lay now thy deadly Heben bow apart,
And with thy mother mylde come to mine ayde:
Come both, and with you bring triumphant *Mart*,
In loues and gentle iollities arraid,
After his murdrous spoyles and bloudie rage allayd.
(1.proem.3)

The Mars Spenser invokes in the proem is one whose "murdrous spoyles and bloudie rage" have been "allayed" by Cupid, who the narrator asks to set his "deadly Heben bow apart." The two would then enter, with Venus, into a loving triad with "gentle iollities arraid."

Spenser's imagined scenario, in which Cupid and Mars, *eros* and *heros*, are alike disarmed, sets the tenor of the action to follow, as does the proem's compassion for Arthur, "that most noble Briton prince" who "so long / Sought through the world and suffered so much ill" (1.proem.2) questing for the elusive Gloriana. Quest, the fundamental engine of romance, structures the 1590 *Faerie Queene*. David Lee Miller describes Arthur's longing for Gloriana as the quest for an "anticipated-but-deferred wholeness of the ideal body," which resonates with humanity's "quest for the body's wholeness and informs every realm of social and cultural experience."[53] Of the central quest in the *Faerie Queene*, A. Bartlett Giamatti argues that "the impulse to go from the wild edges to what one hopes is the ordered clearing at the center—of the world, of the self—is the great movement of *The Faerie Queene*. And the desire to know and to possess in the flesh of the mind the ideal vision is Spenser's great theme."[54] As both positions suggest, quest depends on the fantasy of possession, a fantasy that is no less potent when faced with the constitutively frustrated nature of the quest. Spenser quests not for "the body's wholeness" or for some ideal vision but rather for varieties of experience that can only be encountered when the masculinity enshrined by heroic poetry, which stands in for other ideological uses of force, can be disarmed and reconstituted through radical experiences of pain and pleasure. Spenser, at the close of this proem, refers to his "afflicted stile" (1.proem.4) as a mode of representation lowly before the grandeur of Elizabeth; one might borrow that phrase to describe the style Spenser adopts to convey what concerns him most in the *Faerie Queene*, a kind of vulnerability that must be suffered, or undergone, for the poem to realize its purpose. These objectives are not realized in the centripetal trajectory toward either the central clearing of Gloriana's hierarchical court or the culminating battle between Gloriana and the Paynim king, both of which figure in the imaginative (and unrealized) scheme for the poem described in "A Letter of the Authors"; rather, Spenser engages in the task of conveying the experience of what it is to be a vulnerable body—a moving, speaking, feeling, thinking thing that suffers change, time, and pain in an obscure forest of other people and things.

Notions of vulnerability have been central to how some critics have understood the nature of literary texts in the Renaissance. Scholars such as Thomas M. Greene and Jane Tylus have understood Renaissance vulnerability, not, as Spenser did, as an opportunity to reinvent masculinity and reconceive of a whole culture of subjection, but rather as the consequence of the pathos of humanism.[55] Heroic or martial poetries of love and war, poetries often referred to as epic, romance, or epic romance, create a world in which vulnerability is not only inconvenient but counter to the urgencies of these associated genres with their scenes of combat, adventure, and endeavor. Epic has long been thought of as the genre of the glorification and aestheticization of violence, conquest, and domination featuring the "purposive empire-building of the hero."[56] At the same time, as Leo Braudy points out, the heroic genres pose affective problems for how masculinity is understood. "The medieval warriors in *The Song of Roland*," he writes, "can simultaneously slice an opponent entirely in half with one blow and weep copiously over a dying comrade in a manner that more tight-lipped definitions of masculinity reject."[57]

Colin Burrow attempts to describe the root of the affective paradoxes of heroic poetry, arguing that whereas Homeric epic was intimately "concerned with the nature of sympathy and its relation to complex social rituals such as guest-friendship and supplication," the Virgilian model of epic so influential for Renaissance Europe "shows a repeated tendency to *oppose* something like pity to something like imperial duty."[58] Yet in spite of Virgil's influence in the Renaissance, Burrow argues that "sixteenth-century writers in the vernacular approach Virgil through a web of Christian values, and through a significant manifestation of those values: the widespread European tendency for *pietas* to shift and soften in meaning toward our word 'pity.' This semantic change, and the changes in mentality to which it testifies, effectively invents romance as a genre. Pitiful heroes do not go in straight lines toward their duty. They delay, they pursue attractive and pitiable ladies endlessly, they desire. Their narratives do not follow straight lines: they exfoliate, digress, and endlessly ramify." Hence, for Burrow, the paradox of epic emerges: "'Epic' here implies not just an effort on the part of heroes to enact some imperial or dynastic purpose; it also implies an effort on the part of the author to comprehend and embrace alien forms of feeling."[59] Yet, as I argue in Chapter 1, "Reading Bleeding Trees," this surprising heroic impulse for pity would encounter imperatives of Reformed theology that resisted both vulnerability and pity.

If for Burrow the dynamics of heroic poetry respond to the paradoxical coincidence of that alien feeling, sympathy, and violence, David Quint characterizes romance and epic as genres that express opposing relationships to the assertion of violent mastery in the form of imperial fantasy: “To the victors belongs epic, with its linear teleology; to the losers belongs romance, with its random or circular wandering. Put another way, the victors experience history as a coherent, end-directed story told by their own power; the losers experience a contingency that they are powerless to shape to their own ends.”[60] The defeated, Quint suggests, not only experience but celebrate what he calls their powerlessness. They “valorize the very contingency and open-endedness that the victors’ epic disparages: the defeated hope for a different future to the story that their victors may think they have ended once and for all.”[61] Romance, Quint stresses, “bears a subversive relationship to the epic plot line from which it diverges, for it indicates the possibility of other perspectives, however incoherent they may ultimately be, upon the epic victors’ single-minded story of history.”[62] The subversive potential Quint identifies with antimonarchical politics Patricia Parker and Jonathan Goldberg associate with romance’s Derridean *différance*, the continuous deferral of meaning and assertion of difference characteristic of language. Indeed, Parker refers to romance as “a form which simultaneously quests for and postpones a particular end, objective, or object.”[63] The deferrals and diversions of romance come to be marked as feminine, perverse, and decidedly non-Western. As Quint remarks, “Epic’s losers, the enemies of empire whom epic ideology assimilates with the East, woman, nature, irrationality, and chaos, consequently also embody a potential, indeed inevitable, collapse of narrative.”[64]

Violence and vulnerability structure how both Burrow and Quint see the landscape of heroic poetry. What renders romance abject or failed from the perspective of epic teleology is precisely what makes it creatively suited to the task of exposing and exploring vulnerability in Spenser’s poem. As accounts ranging from Quint and Burrow to Geraldine Heng emphasize, heroic poetry has proved uniquely capable of not merely witnessing violence but registering forms of bodily, affective, and cultural vulnerability. Heng has argued that “the evolution of romance, . . . through the Middle Ages and beyond, attests to the successful tenacity of the genre in harnessing the characteristic resources of a literary empire of fantasy, so that in the hands of able manipulators romance may offer a ready and—equally important—a *safe* language of cultural discussion, and cultural transformation, in the service of crisis and urgent contingency."[65] In her study of romance, Heng reveals the extent to which the otherwise unspeakable possibility that Christians of the First Crusade committed cannibalism surfaced safely in romance. Heng argues, "Romance does not repress or evade the historical—as has sometimes been claimed—but *surfaces* the historical, which it transforms and safely memorializes in an advantageous form, as fantasy."[66] This variety of romance responds, ultimately, to "the desire of culture to give voice to, and speak, its traumas in a safe medium."[67] Such traumas include "shock, pollution, and self-denaturing that accompany the violation of horrific taboos—and cultural fantasy was instantiated in order that the indiscussable, what is unthinkable and unsayable by other means, might surface into discussion."[68] Moreover, Heng argues, medieval romance turns trauma into triumph, making the magical aura of the genre an enabling locus for medieval Europe's imperial longings. "The impetus of romance," she argues, "is toward recovery—not repression or denial—but surfacing and acknowledgment through stages of transmogrification, and the graduated mutating of exigency into opportunity."[69] Heng shares with Jameson and Quint an understanding of an impulse within romance to transform confusion, transition, trauma, and loss into the certain and triumphant assertion of ideology. But might the chaotic world of romance contingency, indirection, and irreality provide an ideal medium, not merely for representing violence inflicted on bodies to elaborate fantasies of conquest but, rather, for conveying fundamental bodily and social vulnerabilities?

When Spenser made vulnerability central to his endeavor in heroic poetry, he, too, was responding to a trauma experienced both socially and corporeally, and this trauma provides the first of three contexts for my study. That trauma one might refer to as the Reformation. The unspeakable was not, for Spenser, the Reformation itself or a religious identity as Reformed or Protestant, which Spenser certainly was comfortable avowing, but rather the losses that accompanied cultural transformation. Nor was the trauma of the Reformation restricted to the substantial body count resulting from the strife between Catholic and Protestant factions within England or the skirmishes among the nations of a strife-ridden early modern Europe. The triumphant rhetoric of Reformation was accompanied by losses felt imaginatively in the body, even by staunch Protestants. It will no doubt be clear that my own sense of Spenser's relationship to his religious identity has been shaped by what some refer to as revisionist accounts of the Reformation, accounts that emphasize the violent and even unbidden nature of religious change in and following the reign of Henry VIII.

Eamon Duffy has influentially argued that "the Reformation as actually experienced by ordinary people was not an uncomplicated imaginative liberation, the restoration of true Christianity after a period of degeneration and corruption, but, for good or ill, a great cultural hiatus, which had dug a ditch, deep and dividing, between the English people and their past."[70] More than two decades ago, Christopher Haigh argued that the account of religious and political transformation in A. G. Dickens's authoritative *The English Reformation* was really a version of John Foxe's propagandistic *Acts and Monuments*, both of which "traced the rise of reforming Protestantism at the expense of deficient Catholicism, and both used the trials of heretics as evidence for the spread of Protestant beliefs."[71] Moreover, he suggests that "the fact that there *was* a Reformation does not mean that it was wanted: it does not imply that there was a deep-seated popular demand for religious change."[72] J. J. Scarisbrick is even more blunt in arguing that, "on the whole, English men and women did not want the Reformation and most of them were slow to accept it when it came."[73]

This once dissenting view of the Reformation now fosters its own form of dissent, as in Norman Jones's *The English Reformation*,[74] which David Aers and Nigel Smith cite in a special issue of the *Journal of Medieval and Early Modern Studies* entitled "English Reformations" (a title Haigh deployed decades earlier to address the multiple, overlapping, and "haphazard" efforts at religious reform which "had limited success").[75] Aers and Smith argue that "the current historiographical situation for writing about the early sixteenth-century English Reformation has been shaped by the triumph of what is often called 'revisionism'";[76] they resist the extreme polarities that characterize Reformation historiography: "It is our view that we cannot adopt or revert to a 'good Middle Ages, bad Renaissance' any more than we can sustain its opposite."[77] They argue, instead, for a greater sense of "continuity and successive transformation" that would resist periodization. "The reformers of the later Middle Ages and the early modern period," they argue, "were a very subtle group of thinkers, and there is a vast array of viewpoints, arguments, and interpretations to be considered together."[78]

To honor Aers and Smith's call for attention to the great subtlety and complexity of literary responses to the English Reformations is to reconsider Spenser's relationship to religious reform. If, with these revisionist historians, then, we set aside the view of Protestant Reformation as a triumph and an index of progress and conceive of the Reformation (or reformations) as "a deep and traumatic cultural hiatus,"[79] how does romance represent and respond to such trauma? Moreover, how might one avoid the problem of the discourse of trauma, which suggests varieties of experience that are obliterated, inaccessible, or, in Cathy Caruth's powerful formulation, unclaimed? I would suggest that Spenser's 1590 *Faerie Queene* does mark the waning of an intimate, affective, embodied worldview rooted in the suffering body of Christ, a body rent by the iconoclastic fervor of early modern England. But it was in this wounded body of Christ, a body whose pain solicited witness and compassion and whose materiality yoked together words and things, that Spenser found resources for articulating the importance of vulnerability as the qualities associated with Christ's body were absorbed into the tropes of heroic and allegorical poetry.

Spenser was, as he has been traditionally understood to be, the impresario of Protestant epic, satirizing and demonizing Catholic and pagan monstrosities. In this sense Spenser was politically, culturally, and biographically a Reformation subject and author of a Reformation epic. Thus, it has been easy to describe Spenser, as Linda Gregerson has, not only as an author engaged in the arduous task of reclaiming epic for Reformation iconoclasm ("to imagine a new Rome, a new Troy cleansed of the intervening abuses of Roman Catholicism"), but also as an author dedicated to creating "a virtual manifesto for imperialist monarchy."[80] As Robin Headlam Wells points out, "For a brief period the collocation of 'martial' and 'masculine' took on a very specific and local meaning. In militant-Protestant circles it formed part of a pattern of praising martial values but characterizing them as masculine and depreciating eirenic values as feminine."[81] For Richard McCabe, the gendered implications of this "imperialist monarchy" both "registers the failure of the fairy queen, a failure implicitly attributable to the monarch's lack of 'masculine' resolve," and results in representations of "anti-heroic emasculation," demonstrating that "to sing of arms and the woman proved far more difficult than to sing of arms and the man."[82] But Spenser's poem also archives the pain inflicted by the Reformation, a sense of lost possibility that accompanied jubilant and often violent change. Romance was a way of recording and transforming the trauma of those losses and, more importantly, conveying an affiliation with lingering aspects of pre-Reformation Christianity that, if not unspeakable in the hybrid religious landscape of post-Reformation England, were at times discomfiting. The poem that begins by articulating, in epic terms, the Protestant resolve of the English nation becomes quickly a poem that attempts to account for the trauma of the Reformation and that dedicates itself to disarming a militant, Protestant masculinity indifferent to or wary of the corporeal, affective, and ethical consequences of the waves of Reformation sweeping across Europe. To miss this facet of the poem is to base totalizing assumptions about the religious and imperialistic leanings of Spenser's poem on tenuous and unexplored assumptions about masculinity in *The Faerie Queene*.

The Legend of Holiness grounds its exploration of vulnerability in the wake of the Reformation with respect to an evolving post-Reformation Christology. As Spenser's "A Letter of the Authors" makes clear, the quest of the Legend of Holiness takes its inspiration, in part, from Paul's Epistle to the Ephesians. Paul urges, "Put off concerning the former conversation the old man, which is corrupt according to the deceitful lusts; And be renewed in the spirit of your mind; And that ye put on the new man, which after God is created in righteousness and true holiness."[83] On the one hand, one commits to true holiness by putting on "the new man," casting off the lusts of the flesh, and, on the other hand, as Paul recommends later, standing "strong in the Lord, and in the power of his might" and putting "on the whole armour of God."[84] The militancy and morality of these statements sound familiar, especially as applied to what has often seemed to be the least complicated of the books of *The Faerie Queene*, the Legend of Holiness. Yet we should also remember that Paul's exhortation to "put on the new man" and "the whole armour of God" is also an exhortation to cultivate patience and compassion: "Let all bitterness, and wrath, and anger, and clamour, and evil speaking, be put away from you, with all malice: / And be ye kind one to another, tenderhearted, forgiving one another, even as God for Christ's sake hath forgiven you."[85] This tension between Protestant militancy and Christ-like mildness will prove constitutive for the Legend of Holiness; more globally, the attempt to refashion a "new man" or masculinity capable of vulnerability will be the task of the 1590 *Faerie Queene*.

As visual and literary representations of the suffering Christ declined in tandem with an increasing discomfort with the vulnerability of Christ, Spenser sought a way of returning to representation the ethical value of conveying and responding to the pain of others. Chapter 1, "Reading Bleeding Trees: The Poetics of Other People's Pain in the Legend of Holiness," examines the hybrid and embattled nature of affective piety as lingering devotion to the suffering of Christ collides with a growing disdain for the role of pain and compassion in Christian worship. Pain and compassion come to be conceived of as idolatrous because they activate or energize a material body that should, instead, demonstrate submission and obedience in the face of divinely sanctioned violence, as the writings of Jean Calvin and William Tyndale dictate. Spenser exposes the excision of suffering from Protestant devotion in the Redcrosse Knight's adventures; this excision enables a dangerous concatenation of beauty, violence, and sentimentality, which Una, the exemplar of Protestant truth, embodies in her travels through the Legend of Holiness. As Una embodies the dangerous alliance between beauty, innocence, and violence, the progress of the Redcrosse Knight dramatizes the forcible replacement of a discourse of integrative suffering with a discourse of pain as a form of punishment for or a heroic fortitude against the pull of physical experience. As Redcrosse becomes first the object and then the subject of this iconoclastic violence, the burden of both suffering and sympathy devolves upon the bodies of idolaters whose moral status is at odds with their participation in an ethics rooted in pain and compassion. Spenser also notes the extent to which iconoclastic assaults on pain and compassion imply an assault on the capacity to imagine the pain of others. Thus, Spenser's instance of the marvelous epic trope of the bleeding tree provides what Spenser will later find in Adonis, an alternative to the lost figure of the suffering Christ, one that returns to representation a staple of pre-Reformation devotional practice: the impulse to imagine the pain of others and respond ethically to that pain.

In the tropes of heroic poetry Spenser found a way of relocating the ethical impulses associated with pre-Reformation Christology. In allegory Spenser found an obscure wood in which to secret the materiality of Christ's body in an age that witnessed the rise of a textualized Christ, persistent assaults on idolatry of all varieties, and competing notions of the Eucharist and other sacraments, many of which downplay or eliminate the real presence of Christ.

In Chapter 2, "Spenser's Dark Materials: Representation in the Shadow of Christ," I argue that Spenser's concern for the potentially idolatrous nature of poetic representation conceals a deeper fascination with the receding physicality of Christ that would become the basis for a materialist poetics that was ultimately sacramental, if not Catholic. Indeed, one must understand sacrament to be an occasion for making contact with the body of Christ and not merely an occasion for solidifying a religious identity in the midst of the violence of post-Reformation England. As representations of the bodily nature of Christ wane in Reformation England, so, too, does the mediating materiality of Christ's body. As such, Spenser's "satire" of Catholicism reveals an attempt to find in idolatry a productive discourse for imagining mediation, that is, for construing the relationship between words and things. This desire for mediation in the wake of an absent Eucharistic or incarnational poetics appears in a shadow world of materiality in the Legend of Holiness: dark forests, monstrous bodies, women's bodies, dreams, Hesiodic cosmogonies, and harrowing underworlds.

Poetry, then, was to absorb the functions of pre-Reformation devotion by providing alternate locations for the vulnerable materiality of the body of Christ. Yet poetry had its own complex history with respect to the ideal of heroic invulnerability, which was one of the many inheritances Spenser's age grappled with in the struggle to define the purpose and defend the validity of literature. While Renaissance authors fed on a steady diet of Horace, urging poetry that was sweet but useful (*dulce et utile*) and whose task was to delight and to educate (*delectare et educare*), Plato's earlier infamous banishment of poets from his ideal city in *The Republic* first provoked the compensatory construction of the moral heroism of the masculine, rational citizen; this was to be the purpose of poetry, rendering it acceptable for the sake of its cultivation of virtue. Indeed, before Plato resorts to banishing poets late in *The Republic*, he first attempts to limit their practice to its least offensive embodiment to protect the upbringing of the guardians of the ideal city. In so doing, he begins to construct the invulnerable citizen by excluding that which provokes excess pain and pleasure or extreme states of affect. As Socrates argues, "If you accept the honeyed Muse, in song or poetry, pleasure and pain will be twin kings in your city in place of established custom and the thing which has always been generally accepted as best—reason."[86]

Fear that pain and pleasure would have sovereign power over the rational, masculine subject motivated a burgeoning early modern literary critical apparatus to seek the moderation of extreme states of affect, which incited both social and physical vulnerability. The Legend of Temperance explores the consequences of this anaesthetic impulse for early modern moral and poetic discourses. In Chapter 3, "On Not Defending Poetry: Spenser, Suffering, and the Energy of Affect," I explore Spenser's alternative to early modern defenses of poetry, such as Philip Sidney's influential *A Defence of Poetry*, which respond to longstanding anxieties about the validity of poetry by asserting the primacy of its moral function. Sidney's heroic rhetoric locates poetry's "power" in its capacity to create iconic portraits ("speaking pictures")[87] of unchanging moral truths. Spenser departs markedly from Sidney's static moral vision of the function of poetry, one invested in the heroic assertion of the clarity of truth. Whereas Sidney privileges *enargeia*, or vividness, *The Faerie Queene* works consistently to disarm the heroic masculinity that violently produces *enargeia* as a form of iconic, moral clarity. Spenser's Legend of Temperance finds *energeia*, or vitality, in moments of suffering and in corresponding moments of sympathy. Through suffering Spenser highlights the dense networks of affect and obligation that defy moral and visual clarity. As the legend's opening spectacle of the suffering Amavia and Guyon's later sojourn in the cave of Mammon indicates, Spenser's true task in the Legend of Temperance is to mine experience for the painful intensity that lends poetry its energy, efficacy, and appeal and that draws subjects together into dense networks of affect and obligation. For Spenser poetry resonates with the affective energies of corporeal experience from which language derives its capacity to move.

The attempt to neutralize extreme states of affect extends from the body in pain to the body in pleasure. In Chapter 4, "Boy Toys and Liquid Joys: Pleasure and Power in the Bower of Bliss," I argue that once one understands the energizing effect of painful affect in The Legend of Temperance, one can then understand the valuable role of a perverse liquidity associated with sexual and poetic pleasure. As the persistent, rhyming evocation of feminine joys, wanton toys, and lascivious boys indicates, the second book of *The Faerie Queene* emphasizes, rather than merely condemns, this liquidity. Far from condemning the Bower of Bliss (or merely reveling in forbidden pleasures), Spenser conducts an experiment in redefining the relationship between pleasure and the generation and distribution of the physical energies of the body. Indeed, a series of uxorious men, autoerotic women, and homoerotic pairings reveals that the disarming of violent masculine force releases an extraordinary energy into the landscapes and seascapes of the Legend of Temperance. Spenser's flagrant displays of liquidity indicate an interest in the extent to which even morally problematic flows of pleasure allow readers to reimagine the contours of the bodies and the narratives on which agency depends. The Bower of Bliss represents a realm in which gender can be analyzed not as an assemblage of bodily parts or cultural roles but as a vulnerability to physical energy. This clarified relationship to power reveals heroic masculinity to be a form of alienated labor that may be repaired as femininity and masculinity are rendered vulnerable to and reshaped by radical experiences of pleasure.

As I have argued, one cannot ignore the proem to the 1590 *Faerie Queene*, which announces its goal of epic disarmament as the force of love, Venus, neutralizes the force of war, Mars. At the same time, Spenser tells readers in "A Letter of the Authors" that his main purpose is to "fashion a gentleman or noble person." The reconciliation of these two impulses, the construction of an ideal portrait of masculinity and the disarming of the martial man, requires the reconstitution of heroic masculinity as a new vulnerable masculinity. Moreover, it forces us to ask what varieties of love create the "new man" of the Epistle to the Ephesians and finish the reformation of masculinity initiated by the 1590 *Faerie Queene*. It is perhaps not surprising to find the answer to these questions, and the culmination of Spenser's poetic project, in The Legend of Chastity, a book that explores desire and its consequences in an attempt to rearticulate the erotic scenarios of Petrarchan lyric, heroic poetry, and allegory, all of which locate varieties of gendered violence at the heart of amatory discourse. Moreover, as these genres become those through which the intelligibility of the self becomes possible, that self emerges either as subject to external shaping forces, such as the will of an elusive sovereign, or through a fantasy of self-fashioning. Thus, the

Legend of Chastity must explore the erotic modalities of that disarmed masculinity that generate an embodied and vulnerable subject.

In Chapter 5, "Vulnerable Subjects: Amoret's Agony, Britomart's Battle for Chastity," I argue that the action of the Legend of Chastity, which culminates in the rescue of Amoret from the enchanter and torturer Busyrane, responds to a crisis of masculinity dramatized through the erotic scenarios central to the conventions of romance narrative and Petrarchan lyric, all of which proved vital to the social imaginary of gender in the era of Queen Elizabeth. Whereas romance positions women as the objects of violent, masculine desires, Petrarchan sonnets elevate the beloved woman to an imaginary position of violent supremacy and power, leaving the man to suffer abjectly the woman's wrath and disdain. The interlocking nature of these discourses produces a seemingly inescapable dialectic of violence and victimization that devolves painfully on the bodies of women. In the context of the Legend of Chastity, many identify Spenser as the torturer Busyrane and have identified Busyrane with a variety of vicious sadomasochism characteristic of early modern eroticism. Yet dismissive references to "mere sadomasochism" in the castle of Busyrane index the larger problem of conceiving of subjectivity outside of subjection. That is to say, a simplistic paradigm of heteroerotic power as either submission or domination has made it hard to see the extent to which Spenser marshals Petrarchan lyric and heroic poetry to find a way out of the gendered violence of sexual subjectivity through a form of vulnerable subjectivity. When one remembers that, for Michel Foucault, sadomasochism and friendship provide ways out of restrictive implantations of sexuality, one comes closer to an understanding of Spenserian chastity. Spenser's solution to the crisis of masculinity in the 1590 *Faerie Queene* comes as sympathetic identification that occurs through a masochistic theatricality implicit in the Petrarchan lyric. Spenser positions the male poet as the tortured Amoret, who can only be rescued by the female knight Britomart, who comes to represent the ideal of a chaste and vulnerable masculinity. The union of Amoret and Britomart represents the articulation of sympathetic, erotic friendship (imagined here between women) as the social complement to the virtue of shared vulnerability. The project of reforming masculinity drives Spenser to create cross-gendered, vulnerable subjects in Amoret and Britomart, subjects for whom friendship provides an alternative to other forms of social life rooted in gendered violence.

In Chapter 6, "Damaged Gods: Adonis and the Pain of Allegory," I assess the problem of structural violence in the gendered relationships endemic to allegorical representation in the Legend of Chastity. To do so, I return to the mythopoetic scenarios with which I began this study. By foregrounding damaged iterations of crucial cultural myths, such as the encounter between Diana and Actaeon, Spenser advances his project of disarming heroic masculinity and thereby reformulating the sexual contracts that govern not only the intimate logic of gender identity but also the structural relationships between matter and form that govern embodiment, as the workings of allegory make evident. The surprising encounter between Diana and Venus represents a fundamental revision of the relationship between *eros* and *heros* and of the relationship between militant virginity and erotic desire. When the heavenly Venus descends to the mortal realm in search of Cupid and surprises the bathing Diana, these goddesses of seemingly diametrically opposed purpose encounter one another in states of vulnerability. This revision of the myth of Actaeon severs the identification between *eros* and violence secured by Diana's vicious retribution. This scene relocates the erotic encounter, as Diana and Venus become vulnerable in one another's presence and open to matter in two important senses; in addition to being materialized as bodies that are sites of both pain and compassion, Venus and Diana develop a new relationship to matter as both become parental figures that mark Belphoebe and Amore, the progeny of Chrysogonee, with their own character. No longer is matter the mere receptacle in which masculine form reproduces itself; rather, matter emerges as the aftermath of an erotic scene between two female divinities drawn into a vulnerable materiality through experiences of suffering and sympathy, which culminate in the idealized figure of Adonis, who becomes a figure of masculine, suffering matter through whom the passivity of feminine materiality comes to be refashioned, just as allegory comes to be rooted in the pain of organic matter as it suffers change and lives in time. Adonis not only provides yet another poetic location for the suffering body of Christ but also, as in the paintings of Rubens, supplants Mars in the primal scene of the 1590 *Faerie Queene*'s proem.

The task of Spenser's poetry was to process the consequences of the Reformation and to reform masculinity by making a virtue of vulnerability, and it is in this respect that Spenser's project may be of interest considering recent critical reflection on violence and contemporary politics. I approach this subject in my conclusion while also considering the fate of Spenser's project when the extension of the 1590 *Faerie Queene* in its later editions changed the tenor of Spenser's reflection on vulnerability, ethics, and masculinity as the 1596 *Faerie Queene* struggles to understand the seductive lure of violence through the operations of shame. Spenser's poem may be too complex to sustain simple moral principles, but as it fashions gentle persons, it aims to create subjects capable of reflecting ethically on experiences of violence and vulnerability at the moments in which such experience seems most resistant to the possibility of common feeling.

Milton understood perhaps better than anyone the weighty implications of choice. But such burdens are also a form of liberty. *The Pain of Reformation* is, like all studies, built around a range of choices, some clear, others still inchoate. I close here by reflecting on some of those choices.

Why make Virgilan epic, one reader asked, not Ovidian poetics, a centerpiece of a study of vulnerability? After all, Ovid's impact on Spenser and the poets of his era was substantial, as many scholars have argued.[88] Moreover, *The Metamorphoses* provides a ready language for the materiality of the body as it experiences the often literally transformative effects of passion, be it in the form of suffering, grief, or a host of other affects that motivate Ovidian metamorphosis. Indeed, William Keach demonstrates the wide-ranging affective valences of the Renaissance Ovidian epyllion, valences ranging from irony to pathos that Spenser made great use of.[89] The Virgilian emphasis intensified as the focus of this book coalesced around the analysis and reformation of heroic forms of masculinity, and as, simultaneously, the invocation of the allegory of the disarmed Mars seemed increasingly central to the project of the poem.

One might ask why the principal focus of this study is the 1590 *Faerie Queene*, which consists of the legends of Holiness, Temperance, and Chastity, and not the 1596 *Faerie Queene*, which excised stanzas from the 1590 *Faerie Queene* to help accommodate a narrative expansion to include the legends of Friendship, Justice, and Courtesy; the 1609 *Faerie Queene*, which for the first time included Two Cantos of Mutabilitie and constituted what many have come to think of as the "whole" poem; or, more broadly, all of Spenser's poetry and prose. It is both convenient and commonsensical to refer to *The Faerie Queene* as the sum total of these various installments, but both the publication history and the complexity of Spenser's verse constantly force us to ask exactly what a poem is. I would suggest that it might be equally correct to refer to each of these versions—1590, 1596, 1609, or simply *The Faerie Queene*—as different if not discrete poems. Moreover, the 1590 edition, I would suggest, coheres as an intervention organized around the exposure of forms of vulnerability, the reformation of masculinity to accommodate vulnerability, and the production of an aesthetics suitable to these tasks. The luxury afforded by attending to the 1590 *Faerie Queene* as a coherent focal point in fact broadens the scope of this inquiry and makes it possible to generalize more broadly about the way literary authors engage with the complex religious and political landscape of Spenser's era.

If this is a study of pain, what about other cultural discourses? Neo-Stoicism, for instance, concerns itself with pain, invulnerability, and virtue. The influential writings of Justus Lipsius were certainly in vogue in Spenser's moment, and one wonders about the relationship between Lipsius's *De Constantia* and the "two cantos of Mutabilitie," also referred to as the Legend of Constancie. At the moment, however, Spenser's relationship to Stoicism has drawn little interest, and the bulk of publishing on Renaissance neo-Stoicism and English literature concerns itself with Renaissance drama or with Milton's generation.[90] But most importantly for this study, the Stoic (and neo-Stoic) goal of virtue achieved through an indifference to pain and vulnerability was yet another manifestation of the ideal of masculine invulnerability Spenser sought to interrogate and reform. Moreover, although the dispassionate nature of Stoicism seemed, to many, to provide resources for conflict resolution or at least a retreat from political violence, Renaissance neo-Stoicism also fomented strife. As Andrew Shifflett argues, "If the idea that Stoicism could countenance and even encourage strife, violence, and war seems strange to us, it did not seem at all strange to its sixteenth- and seventeenth-century critics."[91]

Along these lines, some might wonder at the relative lack in this study of attention to medical, anatomical, and humoral discourses in Spenser's poem. Certainly there has been a healthy expansion of work on those subjects and on the early modern passions.[92] Spenser was conversant with such subjects as some of his allegorical set pieces make clear, especially the Castle of Alma in the Legend of Temperance. But in the evolution of the project, *The Pain of Reformation* became more about an aesthetics of vulnerability than about a cultural poetics of pain. It seems to me the latter approach would be more attentive to how Spenser's depictions of pain compare with cultural discourses of early modern medicine and physiology—including anatomy, the humors, and the passions—and might work in concern with varieties of historical phenomenology practiced by Bruce Smith, Gail Kern Paster, Michael Schoenfeldt, and now many others.[93] While pain remains surprisingly underemphasized in such approaches, my interest lies more in what I would call the aesthetics of vulnerability. Although the term *aesthetics* dates from the Enlightenment, my interest is not to apply to Renaissance artworks later historical sensibilities. Rather, it seems helpful to remember that the etymology of the word traces back to embodied sensation. My interest, then, has been in how poetry evokes and transmits affect, sensation, and understanding by virtue of its specifically poetic qualities. The point is not to isolate poetry, or literary modes of intensity, from other forms of discourse. Recent scholarship makes clear there is no danger of that. My desire has been to understand the particular resources poetry has for addressing the sense and sensation of vulnerability, which to my mind has ultimately ethical ramifications for what happens in the experience, or exposure, of one's own vulnerability; in encountering the vulnerability of another; or in a state of shared vulnerability.

The liberty Milton advocates in *Areopagitica* depends on the capacity to know both good and evil and to choose appropriately. This capacity is a rational one, and one consequence of Adam and Eve's transgression in the garden is that the capacity to make rational choices itself degrades. For *Paradise Lost*, all consequences flow from the choices Adam and Eve make, from the release of Sin and Death into the world to the English Civil War. Another hope arises in *Paradise Lost*. After his lapse, Adam learns his lesson from the course of history narrated by Michael. He states that lesson succinctly near the poem's end: "to obey is best."[94] For Milton, radical liberty inheres in obedience, in the human choice to be devoted and subservient to God.

For Spenser, vulnerability was a radical choice and ultimately an ethical choice. This becomes clear, in the course of the 1590 *Faerie*

Queene, as the deleterious consequences of fantasies of invulnerability become all too vivid. It might even be fair to say that for Spenser a radical liberty inheres in vulnerability because *The Faerie Queene* imagines anew the notion of submission often associated with vulnerability. For most, the word liberty conjures the freedom of individuals, but Spenser came to discover the world as a web of shared vulnerability in which individuals could not help but find themselves embedded in and open to experiences and structures far larger than themselves. If we allow ourselves the luxury of lingering in the dense thickets of this most singular of poems, we might just discover *The Faerie Queene* to be a work of great compassion.

PART I

The Legend of Holiness

CHAPTER 1

Reading Bleeding Trees: The Poetics of Other People's Pain

Near the opening of the Legend of Holiness, that legend's exemplary figure, the Redcrosse Knight, plucks a branch from a tree in a dark wood to fashion a garland for his ill-chosen beloved, Fidessa, who is, in fact, Duessa, the seductive Catholic whore of Babylon and the physical manifestation of sinful carnality in *The Faerie Queene*. As so often is the case in Spenser's poetry, complexity wells up to contaminate obvious surface significance, as errant romance complicates the stricter tendencies of allegory. In Redcrosse's encounter with Fradubio, that complexity wells up as blood: "He pluckt a bough; out of whose rifte there came / Smal drops of gory bloud, that trickled downe the same" (1.2.30). Then the tree bleeds and speaks:

> Therewith a piteous yelling voice was heard,
> Crying, O spare with guilty hands to teare
> My tender sides in this rough rynd embard,
> But fly, ah fly far hence away, for feare
> Least to you hap, that happened to me heare,
> And to this wretched Lady, my deare loue,
> O too deare loue, loue bought with death too deare.
> Astond he stood, and vp his heare did houe,
> And with that suddein horror could no member moue.
>
> (1.2.31)

Ready-made interpretations for even the most marvelous events spring up easily in the Legend of Holiness, the most commonly read book of *The Faerie Queene*, one all too often read as an emblematic version of allegory written in support of rather obvious Protestant moral impulses.

The tree, readers learn, was once Fradubio ("brother doubt" or "amidst doubt"), and his capitulation to Duessa's seduction results in his transformation to a rationally lower, vegetative form of life.[1] Fradubio seems, then, to stand not only as one of the many moral signposts in *The Faerie Queene* but as one pointing directly to Redcrosse, who has been seduced by Duessa and led astray from the path of righteous Protestant truth and violence.[2]

Signposts such as these (Ovidian mythic and Virgilian epic tropes, etymologically instructive names, and monstrous female bodies) seem to instruct readers as to what they should do at this moment in the allegory: note Redcrosse's error and ongoing fall into sin; beware the treachery of appearances; vilify Duessa, Catholics, and so forth. However, Redcrosse's encounter with Fradubio, by invoking the trope of the bleeding tree, activates that trope's capacity to consider both the nature of pain and the ramifications of violence. But the essential mystery of the bleeding tree is not just the infliction of violence but the experience of suffering matter, for one must remember that the Greek for *wood*, *hyle*, is also the word for *matter*. If a tree cries out in pain in a dark forest, is there anyone to hear it? In what way are representations of pain real? How do we hear and receive other people's pain? How is pain communicated and does its communicability make us spectators, participants, or members of a community? This last question is of particular import since so often the tree knows its assailant as brother or brother-in-arms, parent, or friend. Suffering is intimate, elemental, and enigmatic; one might say that trying to understand other people's pain, even one's own, is like standing in an obscure wood in which an uncanny voice echoes, demanding some response. Does imagination encourage or obstruct a capacity to experience and respond to our own pain or the pain of others?

As Redcrosse makes this seemingly idle gesture, he already signals his unwitting participation in intertwining histories of pain embedded in *The Faerie Queene*. Spenser invokes a literary history of bleeding trees in order to think through the relationships governing pain and the imagination, on the one hand, and beauty and violence, on the other, in the wake of the Reformation. These literary marvels enable Spenser to consider the ethics of witnessing, experiencing, appropriating, or responding to pain and to consider the extent to which it is *suffering* (not violence) in which both a sense of lived embodiment and the possibility of subjectivity might be rooted. Spenser translates the bleeding tree from an epic inheritance to a poetic compensation for the diminishing importance of the figure of the suffering Christ in the early modern Protestant imaginary, a figure that embodies the importance of the lived experience of pain and provides the ground of an ethics rooted in compassion. The Legend of Holiness dramatizes as romance adventure the consequences of Reformation religious ideology: (a) the disappearance of the suffering Christ, which produces an emphasis on Christian morality as expressed through heroic masculinity; (b) the conversion of suffering to obedient reception, rendering the body an allegorical signifier of virtue and thus alienating the body from its lived experience, which renders actual suffering inconsequential; (c) a consequent inability to apprehend the suffering of others and to respond compassionately, which derives from the derogation of both pain and the imagination; and (d) the relegation of suffering and compassion to forms of idolatry, which produces a cult of sentimental beauty that incites violence and relegates suffering and sympathy to "evil characters" vulnerable to iconoclastic attack.

The separate adventures of Redcrosse and Una suggest competing economies of idolatrous suffering (and sympathy), on the one hand, and iconoclastic violence (and beauty), on the other. As Redcrosse sinks into idolatrous attachment, we witness not merely a moral lapse but the critique of a heroic masculinity constituted as a form of iconoclastic violence. Redcrosse and a series of "evil" characters thus return to representation textures of suffering and sympathy that provide an ethical ground for subjects. As we follow Una, we witness her conversion into a figure of sentimental beauty whose appeal and triumph are underwritten by a displaced violence directed at demonized figures of feminine materiality, such as Duessa.[3] While this legend witnesses the correction of Redcrosse by Protestant ideology and the defeat of the problems of pain and sympathy (in the form of Duessa, Orgoglio, and the dragon), it also witnesses in such correction the loss of the texture of lived experience from which emerges an ethics rooted in common experiences of pain and in compassionate responses to the pain of others, pain one can only understand as one peels back the layers of obfuscation that render suffering at best inconsequential and at worst idolatrous.

Pain poses particular problems in the wake of the Reformation. As Michael Schoenfeldt has argued, "the significant cultural productions of early modern Europe were deeply invested in the cultivation and the articulation of pain."[4] Yet one consequence of the Reformation was a deep divide on the nature of pain, as Jan Frans von Dijkhuizen argues of this "watershed moment in what we might call 'the history of pain.'"[5] "One central idea that was upheld and attacked in equal measure by religious writers," he argues, "was that suffering pain, and experiencing it in all its physical intensity, is theologically and spiritually meaningful and efficacious, and is therefore something to be actively sought."[6] Moreover, he continues, "the Protestant Reformation, in its preoccupation with the theological role of the human body, and of the physical world in general, did much to forge what was in some respects a radical revision of Catholic conceptions of bodily anguish, while the Catholic Reformation was in part an attempt to reassert some of the Catholic attitudes toward pain that reformers were at pains to discredit." The result, in England, was a kind of "religious hybridity" on the subject of pain in the wake of the Reformation.

To a great extent, that wake extends to and conditions influential contemporary thinkers on the subject. Like other Christian apologists, C. S. Lewis, in *The Problem of Pain*, relies on sin and evil to justify the often-violent ways of God to men. Pain provides a corrective force that neutralizes sin by inciting benign violence. As Lewis argues, in a phrase worthy of Milton, pain "plants the flag of truth within a rebel fortress."[7] Although Lewis argues that pain is central to being created, it is, at best, "sterile" or "disinfected" evil.[8] Lewis's *The Problem of Pain* inscribes itself in a long tradition of ambivalence about suffering, which results in a language of pure negativity. Pain is privative, sterile, aversive, evil: its only validity comes when it signifies something other than itself, such as obedience, humility, mortification, or love. The conversion of pain to a signifier without a signified, a *verbum* independent of any *res*, occludes the experience of human suffering as it naturalizes both violence and the patient acceptance of violence. Suffering points away from the lived experience of the body, and sympathy, what one might call suffering's social dimension, can have no role when pain is understood as righteous violence applied to the fallen.

For Lewis the fundamentally negative character of pain emerges from the fallen nature of humanity. For Elaine Scarry pain is similarly an experience of privation. Her influential *The Body in Pain* presents a decidedly secular account of pain that traces its negative character to the fundamental structures of the brain. Pain destroys the capacity for language and consciousness by rendering an individual purely physical with no room for the communicative gestures of civilization, without which one reverts to a "pre-language of cries and groans" and loses the capacity to project "the facts of sentience into speech."[9] The suffering body, unable to exert will on external objects, becomes an object as a consequence of the "corporeal engulfment," that is, being reduced to "sheer material factualness" in pain.[10] Pain traps the subject in self-involvement, alienating those who suffer from others. "Pain's triumph" is the "temptation to invoke analogies to remote cosmologies" in order to apprehend the pain of others; pain "achieves its aversiveness . . . by bringing about, even within the radius of several feet, this absolute split between one's sense of one's own reality and the reality of other persons."[11] Here, too, suffering prevents signification and renders sympathy a false analogy.

While a reliance on theology in Lewis's *The Problem of Pain* must, at first glance, seem alien to a recourse to cognitive science in Scarry's *The Body in Pain*, these influential views of the nature of pain must also be considered as a consequence not only of the tension between suffering and violence in the history of Christianity but also of the massive sea changes of the Reformation, in which declining representations of the suffering Christ participate in a larger prohibition of representational acts endemic to an iconoclastic spirit reaching back to the Byzantine iconoclastic controversies and, further still, to the early church fathers. Nowhere was the tension between violence and suffering more heightened than in the early modernity of Spenser's England, marked as it was by escalating religious violence, proliferating doctrinal and sectarian differences, and a fundamental ambivalence about theological opinions and ritual practices centered on the incarnate Christ. Noting the lack of Calvinist passion narratives, Deborah Shuger claims, "The figure of the crucified Jesus slips to the margins of English Protestantism, which favored dogmatic theology and devotional introspection over retelling the story of Christ's suffering and death—the pervasive focus of late medieval and Tridentine Catholicism."[12] The move away from "affective piety" produces, then, "curious and problematic texts, particularly in their ambivalent fascination with revenge, torture, and the dialectics of male violence and victimization."[13] Ernst B. Gilman identifies this ambivalence about images of the suffering Christ and other devotional images associated with pre-Reformation affective piety, along with the broader disdain for images resulting from the profound iconoclasm of the era: "Few people are likely to have envisioned an 'image'—certainly in its most narrowly proscribed form as a representation of the Trinity, of Christ or his cross, of the Virgin or the saints—without at the same time, perhaps for a fleeting instant charged with horror or glee, envisioning that image destroyed."[14]

This potent blend of brutality and victimization, horror and zeal, results in a conception of pain from the perspective of infliction, requiring suffering to be no more than the passive, obedient reception of violence. Thomas Luxon observes, "*Imitatio Christi* gives way to a new form of piety in which the faithful Hebrew prophet (Isaiah, Daniel, and especially David) is the model for Christian faithfulness—wayfaring and warfaring."[15] This transition was accomplished visually by the typical iconoclastic gesture to remove or replace figures of Christ's Passion in churches. As Patrick Collinson has noted, "So efficiently did the Elizabethans eradicate the life-sized figures of Christ on the cross . . . which had commanded the devotion of the worshippers in every parish church, that today only one set of pre-Reformation images survives, in a small church in Wales."[16] Thus "the royal arms" came to be "substituted for the holy rood."[17] As such, the virtues associated with the suffering body recede before the power associated with righteous, royal militancy.

The problem of pain in the Legend of Holiness is not solely a problem of theology but also one of genre. The varieties of Christian epic romance to which Spenser was indebted not only included *meraviglie* (such as bleeding trees) that had to be justified but also emphasized spectacular violence, featuring either invading infidels who had to be beaten back by virtuous Christian knights, as in Ludovico Ariosto's *Orlando Furioso*, or infidels who occupy the holy city of Jerusalem, as in Torquato Tasso's *Gerusalemme liberata*. The sanctity of homeland and holy land alike depended upon the successful exercise of righteous violence, which prevented the victimization of Christianity, leaving, it would seem, little room for suffering, charity, or compassion. Moreover, when the poem is read as a Protestant epic defending itself from Catholic as well as Saracen or pagan incursions, another obstacle to our understanding of the role of pain in this poem emerges from the very reading of Spenser's *Faerie Queene* in its purportedly Protestant nature.

Such readings emerge early in the history of the poem's reception, as in John Dixon's annotations of a 1590 edition. As Graham Hough relates in his introduction to these annotations, Dixon remains "interested in Book I almost entirely as an allegory of the English Reformation." He is, furthermore, "indifferent to the courtly and romantic aspects of *The Faerie Queene*; like Milton in the next generation he is inclined to see Spenser as 'a better teacher than Scotus or Aquinas'; and it is the Protestant divinity, the ascetic morality and the national history that concern him. He looks very like a Puritan parson of moderately scholarly tastes."[18]

For the most part, Spenser's identity as not merely Protestant but as a proponent of a fiercely Protestant poetics has seemed dominant if not uncontested. John N. King argues that Spenser began his career articulating "Reformation themes" in his early poetry and later "self-consciously adopted the mantle of the Protestant visionary poet."[19] For all that "literary historians have," according to Jeffrey Knapp, "given new life to the subject of religion in Spenser's works" by "resisting the old urge to enlist Spenser in one sectarian camp or another," many of these "eclectic" approaches, even Richard Mallette's refusal to locate *any* doctrinal or religious identity, through action or inaction reify Spenser's identity as a Protestant poet.[20] As King puts it, "despite the indeterminate open-endedness of Spenserian allegory, consensus exists concerning the reformist Protestantism of Spenser's romantic epic."[21]

Kenneth Gross, however, has noted the ways in which the violence of religious iconoclasm in Spenser's treatment of religious virtue comes to pose at least as great a danger as idolatry, leading one to "fear the unstable power mobilized in acts of iconoclasm as much as it does idolatry."[22] Sean Kane also has argued that the true problem for Spenserian holiness is not the behavior or practices of other religions but the virulence of Protestant, reformist religiosity, which fantasizes the threat of pagans, Saracens, and Catholics to feed its own violent fervor. Kane suggests that Spenser was wary of the "dependence for definition on the negation of a rival [that] made Protestantism its own worst enemy."[23] Noting disparaging marginalia in an early edition of the *Faerie Queene*, Stephen Orgel argues, "Vices and virtues, villains and heroes often do look the same in the poem, and this is certainly part of its moral structure; but our Puritan reader also provides a good index to the degree to which Roman Catholicism remained an indispensable and genuinely troubling element in Protestant poetics, as in the Elizabethan religious imagination generally."[24]

More useful, it seems, than attempting to extract from Spenser's poetics a clear sense of religious identity or doctrine, is the project of locating *The Faerie Queene* in a landscape described by Regina Schwartz and Deborah Shuger, one in which literary compensations replace lost sacramental forms or religious emphases in the wake of the Reformation. Shuger describes Renaissance poetry as the only medium capable of absorbing the energy and function of confession.[25] Schwartz investigates the literary return of the Eucharist in Milton and Herbert as an index of "a persistent nostalgia for material presence" that articulates a "hunger" for prohibited modes of sacramentality.[26] Spenser's hunger was not for a specific sacrament but for the corporeal and affective resources adumbrated by the suffering, bleeding body of Christ. For, indeed, the problem of pain in the Renaissance was also the problem created by Protestant disavowals of the suffering body: "the Protestant attempt to downplay the importance of Christ's physical suffering may have been an effective means of chipping away at a central pillar of early modern Catholicism, yet it also created a problem. The identification with the passion had been a way of enlisting the body as a spiritual tool—of attaching meaning to bodily sensation and integrating it into an overarching theology. In disparaging this, reformers ran the risk of robbing the faithful of a crucial aspect of religious experience."[27] Spenser's challenge at the opening of *The Faerie Queene* was to articulate pain as an integral part of holiness, succumbing neither to the temptations of violence endemic to epic-romance nor to narratives of militant Christian defense nor to the reduction of suffering to a passive, aversive, or negative state. To do so, Spenser dramatizes the ramifications of the neutralization of the suffering of Christ as a consequence of Reformation iconoclasm while championing pain as an index of the texture of lived experience and the ground of a sociality rooted in sympathy.

A certain tension between suffering and violence appears early in the Legend of Holiness, as Spenser introduces his hero, the Redcrosse Knight, "pricking on the plaine." Among other figures that establish the active, even carnal, nature of Redcrosse is the horse that we see not only "pricking" on the plain but also "chid[ing] his foming bitt" and "disdayning to the curbe to yield" (1.1.1). For John Calvin, the unruly horse describes the relationship between human passion and divine will: "When [God] seeth that we be dull vpon the spurre, and that we be ouerslowe and restie: he muste needes pricke vs so much the more roughly: according as we commonly say, A rough horse must have a rough ryder."[28] Calvin justifies human suffering as the necessary if painful goading of erring humanity; God as "rough ryder" must break a disobedient steed. It is perhaps no surprise that Calvin makes this remark in the midst of a massive exegesis of *The Book of Job*. There, suffering is the furnace in which the purity of the soul is tested, as in the case of gold; it is nothing in itself other than the display of obedience or disobedience. Regarding Job, the important thing for Calvin is God's function as "our buckler and shielde, our wall and trench, our rampyre and bulwarke, our towre and fortresse."[29] Calvin's conception leaves room not for the experience of pain but only for militant defense against depravity. Although Calvin wrote 159 sermons on *The Book of Job* and though Job may have suffered silently and stoically at first, his later ravings provoke condemnation: "For Job raungeth out of his boundes and useth such excessive and outrageous talke, that in manie poyntes he seemeth a desperate person. And specially he so chafeth, as it seemth that we would even resist God."[30] That even Job is a poor example suggests Calvin's hostility to representing bodies experiencing pain, bodies that should instead demonstrate obedience.[31]

If the suffering Job was eminently fallible and if the suffering Christ was increasingly unavailable in representation, how might the experience of suffering be conveyed in a poem concerned with holiness? This is precisely the question Spenser raises with the figure of the fallible Redcrosse, who is not merely a triumphant Christian hero caught in a Calvinist dialectic of masculine violence and victimization but rather a subject learning to experience pain. Redcrosse may be the martial man, a "iolly knight . . . one for knightly giusts and fierce encounters fitt," but he is also a bearer of pain. His armor, "wherein old dints of deepe woundes did remaine, / The cruell markes of many' a bloody fielde" (1.1.1), itself marks more than a contrast between experience and naïveté. Redcrosse must grow into the armor he wears, learning to endure and experience pain—his own and other people's. That is, he must not become hardened to it, as the Latin verb *indurare* might suggest; rather, he must bear up in the experience of pain in time. Redcrosse is, after all, named for the symbol he bears:

And on his brest a bloodie Crosse he bore,
The deare remembrance of his dying Lord,
For whose sweete sake that glorious badge he wore,
And dead as liuing euer him ador'd.
(1.1.2)

Redcrosse pays homage to Christ as a crusading knight who defeats the opponents of holiness while wearing the traditional armaments of the patron of the Order of the Garter, Saint George. He is the hero of Christian epic: a martial saint. But his shield is not merely an abstract sign of holiness. Rather, it reintroduces the suffering and salvific body of Christ in a way that was problematic for Orgel's Puritan annotator of *The Faerie Queene*, who tersely remarks in the margins of this passage, "This is not the way to adore him."[32]

The encounter with Fradubio represents another attempt to reintroduce the texture of suffering to a landscape denuded of corporeal and affective experience by heroic, iconoclastic violence. Redcrosse has at this point shifted his allegiance from the pure Una to the duplicitous Duessa, with whom he makes a "fair seemely pleasaunce." In a clear echo of Una and Redcrosse's initial adventure in the wandering wood, the two seek respite from the sun, thus shifting from epic action to romance pleasure, from pricking on the plain to cooling in the shade. Here, Redcrosse endeavors to fashion an object of beauty, making for Duessa a garland. To fashion beauty, however, is to commit violence; as Redcrosse plucks branches from a tree, "drops of gory bloud" pour forth from the "rifte" of the wound (1.2.30). Redcrosse's attempt to adorn his lady with a beautiful ornament of his own fashioning turns out to be the forceful fashioning of another person's body and constitutes a form of violence with shocking consequences. Redcrosse's response to the "piteous yelling voice" makes this clear: "Astond he stood, and vp his heare did houe, / And with that suddein horror could no member moue." Redcrosse's horror closely resembles another scene of heroic masculinity's dis-identification with suffering: that of Aeneas faced with the voice of his slain companion and compatriot, Polydorus, whose blood pours from a myrtle tree Aeneas rends in order to consecrate an altar for the sake of a new Trojan settlement named after him. Redcrosse's initial paralysis embodies the shock of masculinity faced with a materiality that is neither docile nor silent; he faces, instead, the threat of the voice of another person's pain, which summons the hearer into a state of compassionate witness and prevents the gesture of heroic, nation-building self-assertion.

Redcrosse's paralysis derives from a particularly masculine lack of receptivity to pain; he experiences the pain of others as an obstacle or an assault. Just prior to this incident, Redcrosse wins the hand of Duessa from the Saracen knight in a battle that exposes the consequences of heroic violence. Redcrosse, "prickte with pride / and hope," does not notice, as the narrator does, the consequence of his pricking, which (even prior to the battle) devolves on another body. In this case, his horse "spurred fast" begins to bleed: "adowne his coursers side / The red bloud trickling staind the way, as he did ride" (1.2.14). Like the dwarf who bears Una's material "needments," the horse, here, bears the suffering flesh on which the aggressive and sexual impulses of Redcrosse's "pricking" depend. Though this moment foregrounds the suffering bodies on which masculinity depends and against which it exercises itself, the battle itself reveals the way a dedication to violence renders masculine subjects incapable of conceiving of suffering and the veritable outsourcing of pain (as labor) to the bodies of others. Redcrosse and Sans Foy fall on each with extraordinary vigor; they are

> daunted with theyr forces hideous,
> Their steeds doe stagger, and amazed stand,
> And eke themselues too rudely rigorous,
> Astonied with the stroke of their owne hand.
> (1.2.15)

Like "two rams," they pound one another, producing repeated concussive shocks and a resulting bewilderment (1.2.16). These men, "Astonied both, stand sencelesse as a blocke." Paralyzed, "vnmoued as a rocke," the two hold "idely, / The broken reliques of their former cruelty" (1.2.16); violence incites idolatry as epic masculinity leaves "reliques" of cruelty in its wake.

Despite the obliterating nature of violence, markers of suffering—such as the blood of Redcrosse's horse and the blood and voice of Fradubio—stain the landscape of the Legend of Holiness. Fradubio insists upon his experience of pain, and in contrast to the shock of masculine violence, which produces stony insensibility, he assures Redcrosse of an intense if vegetative sensibility: "For though a tree I seme, yet cold and heat me paines" (1.2.33). Redcrosse gets over his initial surprise once the "dreadfull passion / was ouerpast, and manhood well awake" (1.2.32), suggesting at first that masculinity is incompatible with the experience of either pain or compassion. He attempts to contain the potentially overwhelming experience of that suffering, trading the experience of pain for the experience of comfort by encouraging Fradubio to express himself in a cathartic narrative: "He oft finds med'cine, who his griefe imparts; / But double griefs afflict concealing harts" (1.2.34). Redcrosse uses a familiar language of suffering as that which can be purged from the body, cured as a disease, or conceived of in the logic of economy. To imagine a calculus in which pain is a quantity to be doubled or canceled would be to denude pain of the qualitative, experiential intensity that grounds Fradubio's capacity for both sensation and sentience.

Built into the narrative of Fradubio's fall—and the failure of masculinity—are the seductions of beautiful appearance, which produce violence and occlude suffering. Duessa, with her "forged beauty" (1.2.36), entices Fradubio to battle another knight and win her hand. By virtue of her "hellish science," Duessa then casts a "foggy mist" over Fraelissa's beauty, which is not just dimmed but replaced with a "foule vgly forme" (1.2.38). Fradubio's response is not just to shun but to destroy the seemingly grotesque Fraelissa. Without Duessa's restraint he "would haue kild her" (1.2.39). Yet Fradubio discovers Duessa to be what Fraelissa seemed: a foul, deformed hag:

> Her neather partes misshapen, monstruous,
> Were hidd in water, that I could not see,
> But they did seeme more foule and hideous,
> Then womans shape man would beleeue to bee.
> (1.2.41)

One might read the scene as a manifestation of Duessa's sinful carnality or of Spenser's misogyny or of both. But an odd interplay of seeing and seeming ambiguates the scene. The spectacularly gruesome genitalia of the hag Duessa were "hidd" so that Fradubio "could not see," yet they also "seeme" to him plain in all their horror. Does Fradubio see Duessa as she is in a moment of revelation? Or does he see the manifestation of a woman's body as grotesque depravity? That this scene is constructed retrospectively suggests that Fradubio's "vision" is a projection that compensates for the vulnerability that compromises heroic masculinity by shifting the burden of suffering to a figure of demonized, feminine materiality.

While it is easy to dismiss Duessa as morally culpable or as the projection of a misogynistic culture, she functions to draw attention to a series of problems for heroic Protestant masculinity, one of which is the valuation of the flesh. Some scholars have attempted to locate a more positive view of corporeality in *The Faerie Queene*. In the 2004 Hugh McLean Memorial lecture, "Revaluing the Body in *The Faerie Queene I*," Janet Adelman argued quite elegantly for a vision of the Legend of Holiness that makes room for both the rather negative "story of a man's [Redcrosse's] fall into the generative world and the sexual body" and "another story . . . one in which excessive guilt and horror at the body (rather than bodily sin) are exactly what Red Cross [*sic*] needs to be cleansed of."[33] Adelman argues that the Legend of Holiness revalues this scene of female grotesquerie to teach Redcrosse "that the material body is the vehicle through which God's love is experienced and directed outward into the world."[34]

Yet what are we to make of the displacement of Fradubio's love, Fraelissa, who slips in and out of a narrative concerning the conflict between violent masculine subjectivities and the feminine materiality in which such subjectivities are rooted? We see in that displacement the emergence of sentimentality, which responds to beauty instead of pain. Just before Redcrosse encounters Fradubio, he allies himself to Duessa, having won her in combat and having experienced great pity for her (fabricated) tale of dispossession and exile:

> He in great passion al this while did dwell,
> More busying his quicke eies, her face to view,
> Then his dull eares, to heare what shee did tell,
> And said, "Faire lady, hart of flint would rew
> The vndeserued woes and sorrowes, which ye shew.
> (1.2.26)

To be sure, this is another instance of Duessa's duplicity, as she manipulates the compassion of a knight eager to rescue suffering damsels. Yet the real shock comes from the masculine psychology produced by the mingling of beauty and the *appearance* of suffering. Duessa is more attractive not only for having been "won" in battle but for seeming to have suffered; her visual appearance alone consumes his attention, while his "ears are dull" to her dubious tale. Masculinity of Redcrosse's variety seeks out feminine beauty either to win as a trophy through the exercise of force or to defend from the highly arousing violence of others. The suggestion of sympathy with masculine suffering, however, paralyzes Redcrosse. Fradubio's voice produces stony, insensate paralysis, as Redcrosse's hair literally bristles in defensive horror.

Redcrosse's failure to learn from Fradubio has to do less with moral turpitude than with an inability to genuinely and compassionately respond to the suffering of others, a problem especially keen for male, heroic subjects for whom identification with abject masculinity is all too real a possibility. Feminine objects of desire are easily rendered sentimental objects of pity, making suffering valid only when subsumed under the expression of the beautiful. Despite Redcrosse's failure to free Fradubio and Fraelissa, the episode closes with contrition:

> When all this speech the liuing tree had spent,
> The bleeding bough did thrust into the ground,
> That from the blood he might be innocent,
> And with fresh clay did close the wooden wound:
> (1.2.44)

However naïve, Redcrosse's gesture is one of reparation and repair, as violated organic matter returns to a nurturing earth. The previously implacable, silent tree gains a voice, a history, and, perhaps, a projected future. One might say that Redcrosse fashions, in this act of reparation, a living idol, as if bodies reduced by violence to stock matter may be returned to organic fecundity.

Redcrosse is, of course, distracted from real suffering and the possibility of reparation by a closing display of false suffering from Duessa. It is no surprise that Spenser might associate duplicitous suffering with Duessa. The real surprise comes as Duessa becomes a figure of real suffering and genuine compassion in the Legend of Holiness while the virtuous Una comes to exemplify sentimentality in which the alliance of compassion and beauty distracts from real suffering. Immediately following Duessa's false suffering, Una appears as an object of sympathy in the first eruption in *The Faerie Queene* of a tremulous narrative "I":

> Nought is there vnder heau'ns wide hollownesse,
> That moues more deare compassion of mind,
> Then beautie brought t'vnworthie wretchednesse

Through enuies snares or fortunes freakes vnkind:
I, whether lately through her brightnes blynd,
Or through alleageance and fast fealty,
Which I do owe vnto all womankynd,
Feele my hart perst with so great agony,
When such I see, that all for pitty I could die.

(1.3.1)

The obtrusive narrator affirms the dangerous link between compassion and beauty already present in the legend. Then, in a gesture that exceeds any moralizing rhetoric, the narrator identifies himself as an "I" through an experience of painful sympathy with the suffering of Una. This suffering identification presents simultaneously the first narrative intervention in the body of the poem *and* a hazard to the narrator's existence. The very writing of *The Faerie Queene* seems to be threatened by this sympathy, the narrator nearly "steepe[s]" its "lines with teares" (1.3.2). Such sentiments find extreme articulation in the Legend of Friendship; there, the narrator's "softened heart" makes him "wish" his narrative "neuer had bene writ" (4.1.1).

Of course, there may be something more than a little disingenuous about a work whose narrator plunges women into distress over and over again only to bemoan their constant peril. One might wonder, then, if this is not, rather, some variety of veiled sadism, in which a taste for the distress of vulnerable, beautiful women finds shelter in a histrionic display of sympathy. Yet the events of the canto depart nervously from this moment of heart-piercing compassion. The suffering Una is also the beautiful Una, whose beauty enables mastery. Having lost the protection of her knight-errant through Duessa's machinations, Una encounters a lion who desires "to haue attonce deuourd her tender corse." As these rhymes confirm, that desire is transformed by beauty, as Una "his bloody rage aswaged with remorse" (1.3.5). Beauty "maister[s] the most strong" just as "simple truth" can "subdue auenging wrong" (1.3.6).

Where beauty is involved, we come to learn, compassion becomes a degraded form of sentimentality that masks violence. Una's relationship to the lion succinctly demonstrates the displacement of violence from beauty. Una may continue on—vulnerable, humble, beautiful and true in her seemingly innocent wanderings—*because* the lion provides not only protection but also enviable offensive capabilities of which she remains blissfully unaware. Indeed, as Una and the lion come to the home of the Catholic idolaters Abessa, Corecca, and Kirkrapine, the narrative emphasizes her weariness and need of shelter, as if to justify the lion's violence. Upon hearing nothing from the cottage of the idolaters, the lion rips open the home to allow Una entrance, thus terrifying the occupants, who huddle in the corner "nigh dead with feare, and faint astonishment" (1.3.13). Having terrified her hosts, Una belatedly requests lodging for the night and then lies down to lament the loss of the Redcrosse Knight.[35] This is the consistent pattern of events; Una's suffering and weariness come to the fore in a narrative in which expressions of beautiful suffering are juxtaposed with outbursts of violence. The next idolater astonished by Una's lion is Kirkrapine (church rapine): the lion "Vnder his Lordly foot him proudly hath suppress" (1.3.19). We return to the same discourse used to describe the proud beast that submitted himself to the weak Una, though the violence of lordly pride operates in her service as she weeps in a corner for her lost lord, oblivious to the ongoing slaughter:

> His bleeding hart is in the vengers hand,
> Who streight him rent in thousand peeces small,
> And quite dismembred hath: the thirsty land
> Dronke vp his life; his corse left on the strand.
> (1.3.20)

The target of iconoclastic violence is not merely greed or the luscious trappings of Catholic worship. Rather, violence is directed against a familiar signifier of devotional adoration: the bleeding heart. Suffering, too, becomes the target of violence. Una sleeps through this dismemberment, waking the next morning to continue her search. Beauty proceeds ignorant of pain as violence, beauty's restless and disavowed unconscious, exerts gruesome force.

Beauty, posing as truth, becomes in Spenser's analysis the idolatry enabling and inciting iconoclastic violence, as is clear in the scene of Una's rescue at the hands of "A rude, mishapen, monstrous rablement" of fauns and satyrs (1.6.8). Compassion for the beautifully suffering Una drives the action. As the troop comes upon the maiden, they are captivated by her appearance:

> All stand amazed at so vncouth sight,
> And gin to pittie her vnhappie state,

All stand astonied at her beautie bright,
In their rude eyes vnworthy of so wofull plight.
(1.6.9)

The repetition of "amazed" intensifies our sense that Una's beauty—later referred to as "beauty sovereign" (1.1.48)—is at the heart of the problem here, as opposed to the extent to which these rude savages display the errors of primitive idolatry. Idolatrous beauty encourages sentimentality, in which one's sympathy ("compassion of her tender youth" [1.6.12]) becomes a source of pleasure. To be utterly absorbed in one's pity for others is, to be sure, a species of idolatry, one that encourages the representation of gorgeous and overwhelming spectacles of suffering of the variety Una experiences. As postures of suffering beauty incite idolatry, iconoclastic violence becomes all the more necessary. Beauty and violence are, for Spenser, sides of the same coin.

That retribution might be the secret heart of suffering Friedrich Nietzsche argues in *On the Genealogy of Morals*, where he claims that Judeo-Christian values come to be rooted in a slave mentality characterized by an inversion of values that valorizes weakness and suffering. The consequence is the "submerged hatred, the vengefulness of the impotent" that produces a dangerous form of *ressentiment* lodged within an apparently meek exterior.[36] More recently Wendy Brown has parlayed Nietzsche's notion of *ressentiment* into the idea of a "wounded attachment" whereby an identity or an entire community comes to be defined by the memory of past suffering, which lodges an intense *ressentiment* at the heart of those identities and communities, serving only to perpetuate violence and animosity.[37] While Brown refers to identity politics in the contemporary world of a liberal politics of toleration and multiculturalism, one might argue that the virulent zeal of iconoclasm conceals itself within the wounded attachment to Protestant obedience. Una demonstrates this inasmuch as she represents an early modern ethos depicted in William Tyndale's *The Obedience of a Christian Man* (1528), which advises believers to "despise not the chastising of the Lord, neither faint when thou art rebuked by him. For whom the Lord loveth him he chasteneth: yes and he scourgeth every son whom he receiveth. . . . If ye be not under correction (whereof all are partakers) then are ye bastards and not sons."[38] For Tyndale, as for Calvin, suffering is the sign of obedience to the will of God. One questions

God no more than one questions the physician who causes pain to cure the patient, an analogy that reveals his attitude to the body: "The surgeon lanceth and cutteth out the dead flesh, searcheth the wounds, thrusteth in tents, seareth, burneth, seweth, stitcheth and layeth corsies to draw out the corruption, and last of all layeth to healing plasters and maketh whole."[39] While Tyndale aims at the health of the body, the violence of the methods reveals that though the body should not be "killed" it should "be tame."[40] The only healthy body is a punished body. For all that the works of Nietzsche and Brown may, in their skepticism about suffering, make the project of attending to its experiential dimensions more difficult, they are themselves a product of intense suspicion about suffering consequent to the iconoclastic zeal of Tyndale and others.

Indeed, the dialectic of violence central to Tyndale has serious ramifications for a poetic project such as Spenser's. A consequence of the valorization of stern, divine, masculine violence is that, despite exhortations to suffer patiently without seeking revenge or relief, a veritable armory of retributive fantasies lurks behind the placid surface of obedient Christianity. Though Christians should follow "the peaceable doctrine of Christ" and "obey and suffer," they can hope that God will "take vengeance of his enemies and shooteth arrows with heads dipped in deadly poison at them and poureth his plagues from heaven down upon them and sendeth the murrain and pestilence among them, and sinketh the cities of them and maketh the earth swallow, and compasseth them in their wiles and taketh them in their own traps and snares, and casteth them into the pits which they digged for other men, and sendeth them a dazing in the head and utterly destroyeth them with their own subtle counsel."[41] The logical end of Tyndale and Una's vision of Protestant truth is that it must utterly denude the body of its capacity for suffering or sympathy, both of which constitute idolatry. Tyndale's ultimate target is, not surprisingly, followers of the Catholic faith, whose disobedience manifests itself, interestingly enough, as addiction to both pain and the imagination. Not only are Catholics all too wedded to penance "after the example of Baal's priests which (3 Kings 18) cut themselves to please their God." Like Calvin, Tyndale stresses the extent to which idolaters rely on "the maliciousness of their own imaginations or inventions" and the visions of the crazed who "do things which they of Bedlam may see that . . . are but madness."[42] Imagination comes to be intimately associated with the suffering body, and as the imagination becomes the locus of idolatrous error, it becomes the primary route to the suffering body and to compassion for the pain of others. Even Luther, who was more friendly to art and the intense affects evoked by religious devotion and who was not inclined to banish images of the suffering Christ, found the involuntary nature of being seized by the image of Christ's pain chilling. As Valentin Groebner recalls "Luther's well-known description of his youthful fear of images of Christ, which had made him, according to his own words, 'lower his eyes and wish to look at the Devil instead.'"[43]

Against a Spenserian poetics dedicated to conveying the enigmatic, lived experience of the flesh, whose texture is pain, and the enigmatic workings of sympathy, which is the basis of social life in *The Faerie Queene*, we see juxtaposed the transformation of the Redcrosse Knight into the ideal allegorical body of Protestant theology. Already, as Arthur rescues the Redcrosse Knight and hauls his body up from the dungeon of Orgoglio, Redcrosse is constituted as the abject, alien, suffering body of pre-Reformation theology. Hearing the woes of Redcrosse through an iron door, Arthur, like Polydorus and Redcrosse before him, experiences disorientation:

> Which when that Champion heard, with percing point
> Of pitty deare his hart was thrilled sore,
> And trembling horrour ran through euery ioynt,
> For ruth of gentle knight so fowle forlore.
> (1.8.39)

The danger of compassion inheres in a threat to the inviolable masculinity of subjectivity, a masculinity threatened by the conflation of sufferer and witness. Heroic masculinity responds, as Arthur does, with defensive violence: "He rent that yron dore, / With furious force, and indignation fell" (1.8.39). While Arthur spares neither "long paines" nor "labors manifold" to draw Redcrosse from the dark pit of his prison, he remains unable to contemplate the spectacle of suffering masculinity and abstracts the scene, reading suffering in a crudely allegorical way:

> This daies ensample hath this lesson deare
> Deepe written in my heart with yron pen,
> That blisse may not abide in state of mortall men.
> (1.8.44)

Despite that carnal figure of words and lessons written "in [the] heart with yron pen," Arthur avoids the distasteful suffering of the Redcrosse Knight hauled up from the dungeon just as so much post-Reformation theology lowers its gaze before the figure of the suffering Christ. The body is replaced with the moral lesson it teaches, allowing Arthur to avoid an encounter with the pain of another.

The peril of identifying with suffering flesh, as in the narrative commentary on Una's suffering, is not, of course, limited to the narrator or to heroic knights. Even Una, who engineers the rescue of the Redcrosse Knight, must be purged of pain. Despite her resolve to wander patiently in search of him, an overpowering and physical grief overpowers her. Coming upon Redcrosse's abandoned arms and hearing some report of her lord from the dwarf, Una collapses, her very body seeming to flicker in and out of appearance: "Yet might her pitteous hart be seene to pant and quake" (1.7.20). Indeed, later the dwarf must bring Una back from a deathlike swoon and make the "flitted life" return to "her natiue prison" (1.7.21). When she meets Arthur, she speaks in "bleeding words" and must be convinced by him to exorcise her dark and troublesome passion, bringing her to the rule of right reason. In an oddly pat exchange, we see again pain rendered manageable by articulation, as Arthur encourages Una to narrate her grief despite her inclination not to:

> But griefe (quoth she) does greater grow displaid,
> If then it find not helpe, and breeds despaire.
> Despaire breeds not (quoth he) where faith is staid.
> No faith so fast (quoth she) but flesh does paire.
> Flesh may empaire (quoth he) but reason can repaire.
> (1.7.41)

Conceived as a prison, Una's troublesome body, not only in spite of but in opposition to her pain, must be ruled by reason, which is what Arthur offers in the form of this advice. The excessive, repetitive speech tags in this dialogue ("quoth he," "quoth she") are particularly of note. As William Flesch points out, the lack of typographic conventions for the quotation of reported speech lends extra function and interest to speech tags.[44] Here they serve to emphasize the stifling regularity and marked predictability of the nuggets of wisdom that follow. Spenser stresses in this little dialogue the way in which Una and Arthur bring the bleeding words of pain into a safer economy, one that depends on semantic, prosodic, and formal structures to discipline Una's wayward and unreliable body. Likewise the rhyming repetition—"paire," "empaire," and "repaire"—acts to render pain reasonable. For Una, the body is a prison that suffering renders feeble and unreliable. But just at the moment Una finally gains a body through suffering Redcrosse's loss, Arthur draws her back to the ineffable realms of truth, reason, and light. He seeks out the dark wound of Una's suffering, convinces her to "disclose the breach," and brings it to light in order to exorcise it, all the while acting the part of Tyndale's physician.

The surgical precision with which Arthur excises Una's grief offers considerable contrast to the canto's singular moment of visceral compassion, which comes as Duessa throws aside her rich garments to mourn Orgoglio:

> Such percing griefe her stubborne hart did wound,
> That she could not endure that dolefull stound,
> But leauing all behind her, fled away.
>
> (1.8.25)

It is not danger or capture Duessa flees but a "stound," which is the doleful reverberation of Orgoglio's passing. If earlier Duessa feigned suffering to ensnare the Redcrosse Knight and distract him from the tale of Fradubio and Fraelissa, here she casts aside objects of beauty and power, losing the opportunity to escape as grief pierces her stubborn, recalcitrant heart. Remember the efforts of Duessa to save her previous consort, Sans Foy, nearly slain by Redcrosse. Duessa distracts Redcrosse and conceals Sans Foy's body to prevent "his thirsty blade / To bathe in blood of faithlesse enimy" (1.5.15). As Redcrosse's wounds are tended and "*Duessa* wept full bitterly" (1.5.17), the narrator interrupts to comment on the lure of false grief:

> As when a wearie traueiler that strayes
> By muddy shore of broad seuen-mouthed *Nile*,
> Vnweeting of the perillous wandering wayes,
> Doth meete a cruell craftie Crocodile,
> Which in false griefe hyding his harmefull guile,
> Doth weepe full sore, and sheddeth tender teares:

> The foolish man, that pitties all this while
> His mournefull plight, is swallowed vp vnwares,
> Forgetfull of his owne, that mindes anothers cares.
> (1.5.18)

The stanza's opening suggests a moralizing comparison that oddly misses its mark. What does the simile refer to? Who is the crocodile? Duessa's grief is not, in fact, false, even if she often is. Furthermore, Duessa is, at this moment, powerless to harm anyone. She is, rather, overly concerned with the harm that has befallen Sans Foy. Redcrosse is not even privy to her grief—no less victim to it. Indeed, it is far too late for the Knight of Holiness, who has already been taken in and who cannot, for the moment, think of anything but killing infidels. It seems unlikely that this warning would be addressed to the reader, as Spenser goes on to narrate Duessa's great labor to bring Sans Foy back to life. Tortured by grief, she descends into the underworld, into the ancient realm of "grisly Night." Duessa elicits sympathy from the dread Night:

> Her feeling speaches some compassion mou'd
> In hart, and chaunge in that great mothers face:
> Yet pitty in her hart was neuer prou'd
> Till then: for euermore she hated, neuer lou'd.
> (1.5.24)

Despite the warning to beware crocodiles and their false tears, the narrative gives us no reason to doubt Duessa's pain. Her grieving display performs the miraculous feat of drawing feelings of compassion from the previously inaccessible heart of Night. Pain wells up from a dark cosmogony attended by Duessa, whose compassion brings life to a mortally wounded body. In one of the many ironies of *The Faerie Queene*, Duessa briefly becomes the locus of genuine sympathy in the Legend of Holiness, as if her material duplicity were the only place for suffering and compassion to lodge given the denuded, excoriated body of Protestant theology.

Like her compassion for Sans Foy, Duessa's oddly touching grief for Orgoglio is also dismissed upon her defeat. Duessa is, on Una's insistence, stripped to reveal "her misshaped parts." Fradubio's misogynistic fantasy is at last fulfilled in the revelation of the nether parts of "a loathly, wrinckled hag, ill fauoured, old" (1.8.46). She is, as has been much noted, a monstrous mix of bestial pieces. Her disgusting appearance, minutely anatomized, reveals the monstrosity of flesh and alludes to earlier instances of gross carnality: breasts "lyke bladders lacking wind," from which "filthy matter" wells, and "skin as rough, as maple rind" (1.8.47).[45] Duessa bears the burden of female matter, a burden made more palpable in the experience of pain. Whereas Arthur could dig into Una's pain and, with emphatic reason, scourge any taint of suffering physicality, Duessa combines features from the monster Error (in her grossly productive genitalia), the wood of Error (in her rough skin), and Orgoglio (in his bladderlike body). Duessa embodies the taint of sinful matter and thus is subject to violence; she can be stripped, demonized and cast out. That is her function in the Legend of Holiness. After crude flesh has been banished, the heroes may enjoy the spoils of Orgoglio's castle: "Where store they fownd of al, that dainty was and rare" (1.8.50). Marking the transition from the moment of Redcrosse's greatest physical need, the sustenance offered to him comes as a banquet replete with choice foods, thus enforcing the distinction between the gross substances associated with Duessa and the ethereal beauties associated with Una.

Arthur's moralizing commentary, along with the stripping of Duessa, marks the beginning of the reclamation of the Redcrosse Knight and his transformation into the allegorical body of Protestant theology. In the House of Holiness, his "dainty corse" is arrayed in ashes and sackcloth. He fasts and prays constantly. His wounds swell up and "the superfluous flesh" is treated to hot pincers, the "iron whip" of Penance, the sharp "prick" of Remorse, the stinging salt water of Repentance, all of which are allegorical operations that aim at rendering the dark matter of the body transparent and obedient. In the dungeon of Orgoglio and the House of Holiness alike, we find those "curious and problematic texts" described by Shuger in which the collision of Protestant Passion narrative and martyr discourse display "their ambivalent fascination with revenge, torture, and the dialectics of male violence and victimization."[46] These acts of purification strikingly intermingle a Catholic rhetoric of penance with the discourse of torture common to accounts of martyrdom so effectively deployed by English Protestants. Moreover, they anticipate a phenomenon Walter Benjamin associates with baroque aesthetics, when "martyrdom prepares the body for emblematic purposes."[47] As Julia Reinhard Lupton emphasizes, "Baroque martyrology . . . did not use emblems to represent torture so much as it used the disarticulating apparatus of torture to carve up the body into material for emblems."[48] The violence inflicted in the House of Holiness, that veritable factory of bodily obedience, runs counter to devotional practices of suffering rooted in the *imitatio Christi* that predates the Reformation. In his study of voluntary flagellation, Niklaus Largier discusses practices of self-mortification stretching from early Christianity through the Counter-Reformation in which pain served not just to mortify the flesh but to enliven it, awakening thoughts, feelings, and the imagination, making "real pain and suffering into the foundation of an imaginary unity with Christ."[49]

In place of "the connection of pain with the absolute affirmation of life embodied by Christ as God-man," the House of Holiness delivers the emblematic body of Protestant theology. At the end of his scourging, Redcrosse encounters Contemplation, who represents the result of such discipline:

> There they doe finde that godly aged Sire,
> With snowy lockes adowne his shoulders shed,
> As hoary frost with spangles doth attire
> The mossy braunches of an Oke halfe ded.
> Each bone might through his body well be red,
> And euery sinew seene through his long fast:
> For nought he car'd his carcas long vnfed;
> His mind was full of spirituall repast,
> And pyn'd his flesh, to keepe his body low and chast.
> (1.10.48)

The bones and connecting sinews read clearly—as if the body were a holy X-ray. Contemplation presents the ideal body of the burgeoning science of anatomy, a discipline that, however important to the history of medicine, demonstrates the consequence of ideologies that rendering the body a source of evidence or knowledge communicated visually: ocular proof requires dissection. Contemplation is no more than the carcass of a half-dead tree, a starved and obedient Fradubio. Suffering sentience, replaced by discipline, leaves behind the palest form of allegory.

The representatives of truth, goodness, and beauty must purge themselves of pain and its representative physicality, creating Reformed bodies. The burden of pain must therefore be outsourced, lodging in the bodies of the enemies of Protestant truth. At the close of the Legend of Holiness, the dragon is at once the goading engine of heroic violence and the recipient of the burden of suffering. The dragon, struck once,

> cryde, as raging seas are wont to rore,
> When wintry storme his wrathful wreck does threat,
> The rolling billowes beat the ragged shore,
> As they the earth would shoulder from her seat,
> And greedy gulfe does gape, as he would eat
> His neighbour element in his reuenge:
>
> (I.II.21)

Pain becomes a deafening and unintelligible noise as its catastrophe threatens to engulf its surroundings in "a gushing riuer of blacke gory blood" (I.II.22). Yet even the dragon's fire causes temporary harm to a Redcrosse increasingly impassive, impervious, and miraculously restored in the face of pain. As Redcrosse sheds his searing armor as if it were a troublesome layer of flesh, the narrative shifts from his experience of pain to the memory of heroic labor:

> Not that great Champion of the antique world,
> Whom famous Poetes verse so much doth vaunt,
> And hath for twelue huge labours high extold,
> So many furies and sharpe fits did haunt,
> When him the poysoned garment did enchaunt
> With *Centaures* blood, and bloody verses charmd,
> As did this knight twelue thousand dolours daunt,
> Whom fyrie steele now burnt, that erst him armd,
> That erst him goodly armd, now most of all him harmd.
>
> (I.II.27)

Little trace remains of the shock of sympathy that briefly passes between Redcrosse and Arthur in the dungeon of Orgoglio. Instead, the comparison between Redcrosse and Hercules highlights competition: a quantification of the violence ("twelue thousand dolours" instead of twelve labors) withstood by the warriors. The pain of Hercules' temporally extensive labors is compressed here into the annihilating instantaneity of fiery violence. The medieval and early modern association of Christ with Hercules further indicates an occlusion of Christian suffering by heroic violence. The suspended, suffering Redcrosse in Orgoglio's dungeon has no place here, where the martial comes to the fore in the exercise of righteous violence.

The defeat of the dragon is the defeat of the idolatry constituted by suffering and sympathy. These experiences are replaced by the virtuous violence of a martial Christianity, for which the fall into sinful, suffering flesh constitutes the wounding incursion of the past on the present that justifies righteous combat. The wounded past is redeemed by present violence. Yet if the *telos* of the Legend of Holiness was never in question, the aftermath of the fight, featuring, as it does, the bodies of the victor and the vanquished, raises questions about the idolatry of violence. While the court celebrates Redcrosse's victory, a crowd—"the raskall many ran, / Heaped together in rude rablement"—surrounds the victor and all admire him with "gaping wonderment" (1.12.9). It seems even citizens of Una's righteous kingdom constitute a naïve and unsophisticated rabble prone to idealizing and idolizing a Christian conqueror. Their "gaping wonderment" smacks of the same stupefaction produced by the violent beauty of Una unveiled.

If Redcrosse himself spurs a potentially idolatrous following, the body of the dragon, marked by violence, inspires fascination. When we hear the crowd is dismayed with "ydle fear" we must take the word "idle" seriously. In one sense, the dragon is dead and the people's fear unwarranted. The aftermath of the battle's spectacular violence fascinates these spectators, even though the object of fascination is an immobile corpse:

> Some feard, and fledd; some feard and well it faynd;
> One that would wiser seeme, than all the rest,
> Warnd him not to touch, for yet perhaps remaynd
> Some lingring life within his hollow brest,
> Or in his wombe might lurke some hidden nest
> Of many Dragonettes, his fruitfull seede;
> Another saide, that in his eyes did rest
> Yet sparckling fyre, and badd thereof take heed;
>
> Another said, he saw him moue his eyes indeed:
> One mother, whenas her foolehardy chyld
> Did come too neare, and with his talants play
> Halfe dead through feare, her litle babe reuyld,
> And to her gossibs gan in counsell say;

How can I tell, but that his talants may
Yet scratch my sonne, or rend his tender hand.
So diuersely themselues in vaine they fray;
Whiles some more bold, to measure him nigh stand,
To proue how many acres he did spred of land.
(1.12.10–11)

The Legend of Holiness begins by asking what it is to experience suffering. It closes by asking how we witness and respond to violence. Thomas A. Prendergast suggests that the "idolatrous seductions of violence" are a central concern for *Beowulf*, noting that, like much heroic poetry, the poem "unfolds as an idolatrous memorialization of the pleasures of violence, a pleasure compulsively repeated in the very language of the text."[50] A core concern for *Beowulf* is the potentially unstoppable cycle of retribution aided by compulsive iterations or memories of violence. Indeed, as René Girard argues, "Vengeance . . . is an interminable, infinitely repetitive process."[51] Spenser's rabble believes that at any moment the beast could spring back to life and spawn new dangers, as if a host of offspring lay in wait to pour forth from its body. Even the admittedly hysterical mother of Spenser's passage recognizes a real, if not a literal, threat. The community that assembles here at the close of the legend comes together in victory, and their unity is marked by a fascination with spectacular violence and its gory aftermath. The very attempt to "measure" the dragon, to quantify its body, runs counter to the way bodies are experienced (how they suffer and live) or imagined (this is, after all a dragon). In the same way, anatomy creates knowledge through the disarticulation of bodies; to see their physical truth, they must be cut apart. Contemplation, then, is not merely a spiritual state to attain but a worldview requiring the sacrifice of imagination and lived experience for the rigor of moral discipline.

In the Old English devotional poem *The Dream of the Rood*, the rood in question is that tree hewn into the cross on which Christ was crucified. Like Fradubio, it bleeds and speaks, which frightens the narrator of the poem. The rapturous glory provoked by the tree, bedecked with treasure and witnessed by hosts of angels, is inseparable from the suffering that marks it, rendering stock, hewn matter a living, speaking tree. While the poem imagines Christ as a hero in the terms of Anglo-Saxon warrior culture, such militancy is never isolated from suffering. Fradubio reminds Redcrosse of the centrality of an active, engaged experience of pain, one so thoroughly alienated in the wake of the Reformation that suffering appears as if in a dream or in the remnants of mythic and literary inheritance, where it is the task of the imagination to return to the body its sense of lived experience through pain, emblematized in the flow of blood from a speaking tree. No trees bleed or speak in the landscape of Contemplation, and all the dragons have been slain, for the fervor of Reformation iconoclasm wills the reduction of complexity of thought, feeling, and imagination to a state of passive, obedient witness in the face of extreme violence. Such violence is hypnotic, whether in the form of the beautiful or the grotesque, in the delicacy of Una's progress or in the convulsions of the dragon's death and its morbid aftermath. If there is not merely a critique of violence in the Legend of Holiness, which there surely is, then there is also, in the experience of lived embodiment so centrally embedded in Spenser's poetics, a form of resistance. The familiar features of *The Faerie Queene*, those very features that seem to render Spenser difficult, obscure, nostalgic, or conservative, are the stylistic correlatives of an alternative Spenserian modernity—the nearly hypnotic rhymes of the Spenserian stanza, the shudderingly visceral style, the willfully antiquated language, the patterns of repetition, variation, and dilation. One might construe such features as a response to the willful excision of history "at the heart of the Edwardine reform," including "the necessity of destroying, of cutting, hammering, and scraping, or melting into a deserved oblivion the monuments of popery, so that the doctrines they embodied might be forgotten."[52] Spenser may have written as part of "a generation . . . which had known nothing else, which believed the Pope to be Antichrist, the Mass a mummery, which did not look back to the Catholic past as their own, but another country, another world."[53] At the same time, that other country, that other world lingered in traces of pre-Reformation corporeal habits and ethical sensibilities that comprise the substance and experience of Spenserian holiness. Faced with the alienating violence of iconoclasm, Spenser locates in fairyland and in the fabric of poetry a world in which what it means to suffer, to sympathize, or to socialize—even the capacity to experience ourselves, each other, and the world around us—might be excavated from the fantastic archaeology of national and religious history in order to be imagined anew.

CHAPTER 2

Spenser's Dark Materials: Representation in the Shadow of Christ

Idolatry haunts the history of poetry. In his treatise on the genealogies of the pagan gods, Boccaccio traces the art of this "fervid and exquisite invention," poetry, to one of three primal scenes: the deification and worship of nature, the rituals and sacrifices of the Hebrews, or the Babylonian devotions enacted under the rule of Nimrod, who is described as "the founder of idolatry."[1] While pagan animism deifies the wonders of the natural world, Babylonian idolatry mistakes the useful or the enjoyable for the divine, as in the case of fire. Animism and idolatry fail to grasp the scope of the relationship between the Creator and the created world. Thus it was left to the ancient Hebrews to discover, or to have revealed to them, the true means of communicating with the Creator, in part through sacrifice. For Boccaccio, Moses, in his communion with the Holy Ghost and reception of the scriptures, becomes the model poet. The poet, then, is the conduit between a spiritual message and a fallen world all too inclined to misread it. By this point in the treatise, Boccaccio has set aside primitive pagan animism and has dismissed depraved Babylonian idolatry, saying "of the beast Nimrod I take no account."[2]

Lurking in the shadows of history, however, is a desire to take into account poetry's fundamental materiality. And while many have approached this materiality as what inheres in textuality itself or in the media of transmission, one still wonders what it is that makes poetry neither merely imagination nor medium nor text. This question becomes especially keen in an early modernity in which the aftermath of the Reformation meant not only the waning presence of the suffering Christ but, moreover, the waning presence of Christ, Word made flesh, to mediate between the spiritual sources of poetry and its physical manifestations.

Michel Foucault's influential *The Order of Things* famously posits an early modern crisis of representation in which classical systems of knowledge and order, rooted in regimes of resemblance, come to be ruptured at and as the emergence of modernity, a time in which the "profound kinship of language and the world was dissolved" as signs come to refer only to other signs.[3] Not only are "things and words . . . to be separated from one another" but also language and literature lose an "enigmatic, monotonous, stubborn, primitive being" as well as a "peculiar existence and ancient solidity of language as a thing inscribed in the fabric of the world." While there is value in understanding language, especially poetic language, as endowed with "enigmatic, stubborn, primitive being," Foucault's account is not particularly attentive to the ways in which early modern crises of order were embedded in religious conflict. Post-reformation debates about the nature of the Eucharist—was it endowed with physical, divine presence or was it no more than an abstract sign or reminder?—provide a central instance of a truly massive representational crisis rooted in the now troubling flesh of Christ.

As Regina Schwartz has argued, "When Reformers gave up the doctrine of transubstantiation (even as they held on to revised forms of the Eucharist), they lost a doctrine that infuses all materiality, spirituality, and signification with the presence of God."[4]

Furthermore, Michael O'Connell describes how early modern Europe witnessed, as a result, a shift away "from visual, sensible, 'incarnational'" modes of meaning to "logocentric" modes of meaning as "'Christ as text'" comes to "replace the sacramental Christ, the visualized Christ." As a consequence "in much of Europe, attitudes would shift so dramatically that what had before been created by highly developed artistic expression would, a few years later, be destroyed as a religious abomination."[5] To explore the means by which poetry attains its "ancient solidity as a thing inscribed in the fabric of the world" is to risk the "abomination" of primitive or depraved idolatry, yet in idolatry we find the sensuous particularity that lends poetry its efficacy.

It is no accident, then, that Spenser begins *The Faerie Queene* with the Legend of Holiness. Holiness, with its vested interests in idolatry and iconoclasm, articulates appropriate relationships to matter, to the complex substances of bodies and things, and to the world through which those bodies and things pass. Spenser's concerns as a writer are much like those of his naïve paragon of holiness, the Redcrosse Knight, who is, in fact, the youthful St. George—martyr, dragon slayer, and patron saint of England. Jacob de Voragine's *Legenda Aurea*, translated by William Caxton in 1483, offers etymologies for *George*, deriving the name from words for earth, holy wrestler, pilgrim, and councilor, associating the qualities of each with the saint. The primary association, one Spenser echoes, is that of the earth: "George is said of geos, which is as much to say as earth, and orge that is tilling. So George is to say as tilling the earth, that is his flesh."[6] Derived from Greek (*ge*, "earth," and *ergon*, "work") the knight who will be St. George works in and as earth. For Spenser, as for Caxton, George signifies both earth and flesh.[7] Late in the Legend of Holiness, Contemplation narrates Redcrosse's history, revealing the fact of his earthly, as opposed to fairy, origins. Redcrosse is a changeling stolen by a fairy:

> Thence she thee brought into this Faery lond,
> And in an heaped furrow did thee hyde,
> Where thee a Ploughman all vnweeting fond,
> As he his toylesome teme that way did guyde,
> And brought thee vp in a ploughmans state to byde,
> Wherof *Georgos* he thee gaue to name.
> (1.10.66)

Here, etymology is genealogy as Redcrosse rises up as a worker of and in matter. The fairy who steals him from the earth plants him in a "heaped furrow" where he is found by a cultivator of the land, as if he were a seed or an anticipation of Adonis growing from his fecund garden in the Legend of Chastity. St. George's earthiness is taken by Voragine to signify either humility or the vulnerability of flesh to temptation. Here, however, Redcrosse as proto–St. George serves as the element that grounds the world of romance: Spenser plants quotidian earth in the midst of his "Faerie lond."

Redcrosse, like many readers of *The Faerie Queene*, may ultimately take the side of Contemplation, who emphatically pronounces, "So darke are earthly thinges compard to things diuine" (1.10.67). But to read *The Faerie Queene*, Spenser's "darke conceit," is also to sense the extent to which dark, earthly things are not the abject physicality above which holiness must rise but, rather, its constitutive element. Boccaccio, like other early modern mythographers, places at the origin of pagan gods a figure Spenser would also invoke in *The Faerie Queene*, Demogorgon, whose name was explained either "as *daimon-gorgos* ('terrible daemon or terror to daemons') or *daimon-georgos* ('god of the earth')."[8] This double etymology encourages us to wonder how to understand and experience physicality when matter is deemed monstrous. As Jean-François Lyotard suggests, "Matter thus denied, foreclosed, remains present in this violently modern thinking: it is the enigmatic confusion of the past, the confusion of the badly built city, of childhood, ignorant and blind."[9] Lurking behind terrible demons and evil specters of the Legend of Holiness is a fundamental materiality in which Spenser locates a vitality that animates subjective, sensuous experience and the poetry that colors and conveys that experience. Nowhere is this fundamental materiality more present than in the monsters and idolaters on which Spenser lavishes his attention, along with the ancient, chthonic presences in the wood of Error, the realm of Morpheus, and the House of Pride. By knowing intimately the matter of these monsters, we come to understand Spenser's interrogation of poetry's fundamentally sensuous properties. Spenser conveyed the horror of the iconoclastic assault on sensuous experience by invoking the machine, which turns living substance into deadened matter, inert and obedient like the suffering bodies examined in the previous chapter. In Spenser's romance landscapes and in the antiquated character of his language, we learn that poetry draws its power from idols and icons of old now banished to the shadows to which the body of Christ was also banished.

When, in the "Letter of the Authors," Spenser described *The Faerie Queene* as a "darke conceit" he referred to a conventional definition correlating allegory with obscurity.[10] The rhetorical treatise *On Style*, once commonly attributed to Demetrius, distinguishes allegory from the commonness of plain speaking and associates it with the obscurity of religious mysteries, specifically the Elusinian Mysteries, which "are revealed in an allegorical form in order to inspire such shuddering and awe as are associated with darkness and night. Allegory also is not unlike darkness and night."[11] The sublimity of shuddering and awe, though palpably present at moments in *The Faerie Queene*, may not have been the goal of this allegory, but mystery seems an appropriate way of construing the oddity of the religious landscapes of Spenser's poetry. In the Legend of Holiness, the patent obscurities of allegory have encouraged polarizing moral readings of the poem or allegorical reading strategies that attempt to extract religious identity or doctrines. Carol Kaske has, in fact, developed this into a tactic for reading the poem through religious images presented *in bono* and *in malo*.[12] Yet as Anne Lake Prescott admits in a survey of recent scholarship on Spenser and religion: "Identifying Edmund Spenser's beliefs so as to illuminate his poetry further has proved no easy task."[13]

Perhaps the problem, indeed, is the notion that a poem, like the figure of Contemplation in the Legend of Holiness, whose nearness to the light of truth quite nearly illuminates the bones of a body whose flesh is starved into submission, could be held up to the light and the outlines of its doctrines "illuminated" within the shell of a poem's tropes, ornaments, events, or moral sentiments. For it was in the shadows of allegory that Spenser secreted two aspects of pre-Reformation religious sensibility. In Chapter 1 I discussed the extent to which the epic trope of the bleeding tree offered a location for the suffering, vulnerable Christ derogated or ignored by much Reformed theology, thus offering Spenser an opportunity to reflect on a world in which representations of beauty and violence allied with Protestant truth inhibit the capacity to apprehend or remedy the pain of others, the contemplation of which was a traditional focus of pre-Reformation religious practice. Here, I will suggest that allegory became one location for the contentious materiality of the body of Christ in an age in which both the idea of the real presence of Christ and, by extension, the nature and efficacy of sacraments were hotly contested.

O'Connell has described such contestations "as primarily a clash between religious systems, one based on an incarnational structure of religious understanding and the other resting on the logocentric assumptions of Renaissance humanism empowered by print culture. In the case of England the contest meant the official replacement, though by no means total or unambiguous in the culture at large, of one system by the other. There, as in much of Northern Europe, Reformation iconoclasm brought to an end a semiotic and symbolic field for apprehending and imagining the sacred."[14] The consequence, O'Connell suggests, "was an increasingly sophisticated use of verbal modes of knowing and expressing, the fruit of which in England would be a religious culture based on the vernacular Bible and on preaching, a culture that finds aesthetic expression, for example, in the poetry of Donne, Herbert, Vaughan, Marvell, and Milton. What was lost was a visual aesthetic that had materialized religious concepts in traditions of painting, sculpture in stone and alabaster, wood carving, stained glass, and theatrical performance." Although Spenser has never been thought of as a religious poet in the same way as Donne, Herbert, Vaughan, or Milton, poets who seem to have eclipsed Spenser in considerations of the nature of religious poetics in this era, nonetheless we find in the monsters and machines of the Legend of Holiness an attempt to understand poetry as more than merely textual or merely visual. Ernst Gilman too traces tensions in early modern representation caused by post-Reformation iconoclasm, arguing that poetry's relationship to its sister art, painting, produces a particularly complex relationship to visuality. "The creative power of sixteenth- and seventeenth-century literature," he argues, "is released at crucial moments when the visual resources of the poet are challenged by a conception of language disinfected, in its blind and often violent purity, of any appeal to the eye."[15] While later I consider more closely poetry's relationship to visuality, here I concentrate on the capacity of poetry to evoke a sensual experience of materiality, a capacity that becomes the location of the problematic physicality of a post-Reformation sacramentality, as if it too were made of those elements of stone, alabaster, wood, and stained glass lost as post-Reformation England destroyed religious art in some of the most severe iconoclastic purges in the history of Christianity.

But this aspect of Spenser's religious poetics has been obscured by an insistence on identity as a primary lens for interpreting, or "illuminating," his poem. John N. King, perhaps the most trenchant defender of Spenser's Protestant poetics, claims that "even though soft Catholic tropes permeate Spenser's imagination, the poem allegorizes hard opposition to the ritual, worship and sacerdotalism of the Church of Rome."[16] *The Faerie Queene*, in this sense, is the source of "soft Catholic tropes" or, as he puts it elsewhere "soft poetic images" as if poetry were the mere shell that must be shucked to find the hard truth of doctrine. But the general trend in Spenser studies has been to admit to a more flexible religious rubric. Prescott suggests that "for a firm Protestant, Spenser seems strangely friendly toward some Catholic practices and texts."[17] Harold Weatherby admits an even greater complexity of identity faced with the same complexity of reading Spenser's religious poetics: "What conclusions, then, should one draw? Not that Spenser was a 'Church papist' or crypto-Catholic, but neither that he was always and consistently Protestant in his every address to religious matters. Most critics assume that Spenser's incontestable dislike for the Papacy and the Roman Church precludes the possibility of his embracing other aspects of Catholicism and that we must explain away seemingly Catholic beliefs and attitudes."[18] C. P. Brand similarly argues that "Notwithstanding the poet's evident anti-Romanism, his characterizations of the sacraments in the last three cantos of Book one betray more than a natural resemblance with their Catholic models and hints at a number of conventional similarities and temperamental affiliations with the sacramental understanding of pre-Reformation of Catholicism."[19] Brand also suggests that, "writing out of this fluid historical moment, Spenser gives us not only his hopes for a revivified nation and a Reformed Church, but also perhaps his nostalgia for elements of 'the old religion' and his longing for the beauty, coherence, and efficacy of sacramental presence."[20]

If sacramentality, rather than identity, provides a more helpful way of understanding in what way Spenser is a religious poet, how are we to understand sacramentality in *The Faerie Queene*? Is it merely the representation of particular sacraments, as much of the criticism suggests, or does sacramental presence refer to a broader range of experience? Prescott, rather, insists that the question of Spenserian sacrament allows the reader to raise questions about the nature of bodies, signs, and space in the wake of the Reformation.[21] Kenneth Borris suggests that "the whole action of *The Faerie Queene* could be termed, in a sense, 'sacramental.' . . . And the sacraments centrally express union or joining in the body of Christ, just as the term 'sacrament' implies membership in a united group on account of its etymological relation to the Latin *sacramentum*, the Roman soldier's oath of military allegiance and integration."[22] As such he sees, throughout *The Faerie Queene*, Arthur as a type of Christ while "the patron knights partly constitute a trope for membership in Christ." Borris exposes here a potential conflict between membership in the body of Christ as an identity with respect to Christian institutions and membership in the body of Christ as a form of union with the materiality of Christ's body. The former requires, it seems, the heroic gesture of a soldier's oath, which also implies the heroic investment in a religious identification armed against hostile foes; clearly, this produces the identity skirmishes in Spenser and other post-Reformation texts. But if union with Christ means union with the flesh of Christ left vulnerable to Reformation iconoclasm, this would also mean a union with a materiality easily deemed idolatrous. As Lee Palmer Wandel has argued of the Eucharist, "The anguish of the sixteenth century centered around these two words [my body]. What did it mean for Christ to have a body? What kind of body? How was Christ present among the community of Christians? Could he be known physically to his followers or did they simply have a disembodied memory of him?"[23] Out of this anguish Spenser sought to disarm the politics of Reformed identity to craft a sacramental poetics rooted in and drawing efficacy from a potentially idolatrous relationship to the vulnerable materiality of Christ's body.[24]

Written by hostile iconoclasts, accounts of idolatry remain suspicious about the materiality at the heart of the idol, rendering such idols mutely opaque or fantastically unreal. Kenneth Gross identifies in *The Faerie Queene* the danger of the idol as "the threat of the empty, blank and yet infectious image."[25] Elsewhere it is not the insubstantial shadow but rather "the empty, blind, petrified sign, the dead or never living idol that is no-thing."[26] This understanding of the idol as both vain shadow and lifeless or "never living" matter is nothing if not the result of the violent rhetoric of iconoclasm. W. J. T Mitchell describes the nature of iconoclastic revolutions whereby "the repudiated image is stigmatized by notions such as artifice, illusion, vulgarity, irrationality; and the new image (which is often declared not to be an image at all) is honored by the titles of nature, reason, and enlightenment."[27] Referring to the "fundamental illusion" or "radically false conception" constituted by "negation," "the void," and "the nought," Henri Bergson points out the source of such strategic invocations.[28] He argues, "'Disorder' and 'nothingness' in reality designate . . . a presence—the presence of a thing or an order which does not interest us, which blunts our effort or our attention; it is our disappointment being expressed when we call this presence absence."[29] Daniel Tiffany suggests that in modernity materiality "emerges as the 'other' of language, a thing inimical to reflection or representation, which we overlook even when we mean to confront it. . . . When we do suffer to entertain the stuff, or to think about which bodies 'matter,' we tend either to trivialize 'substance,' as if it were a toy, or to endure it, as if it were a climate."[30]

In the iconoclastic attack on idols, matter becomes a haunting absence: mutely physical but perilously illusory. As the lingering presences of pre-Christian thinking are driven away, the numinous world gives way to a world of created matter, shaped by an all-powerful fashioner. Idolatry, as Augustine insists, is the confusion that results from "worshipping . . . the created order or part of it as if it were God."[31] The physical, substantial world, according to Augustine, exists not to be enjoyed for its own sake but to be used to come closer to God. Even the physical trappings of worship can become dangerous distractions. Boccaccio's pagan pantheists seem wholly occupied with ritual objects; indeed they "fashioned of gold the drinking cups, candelabra and whatever other vessels they used."[32] Yet, Augustine reminds us, "we ourselves who enjoy and use other things are things."[33] Matter creates potentially threatening chains of communicability. The vicious iconoclasm of the early church fathers recognizes this danger. Tertullian believed that not only should idolaters receive the most severe of punishments but so too should the craftsmen who fashioned the objects that served as idols even when ignorant of the uses to which those objects were put.[34]

A similarly dangerous communicability inheres in the materiality of language. Augustine was especially concerned for Christians who might be "incapable of raising the mind's eye above the physical creation so as to absorb the eternal light."[35] Despite Augustine's vigorous iconoclasm, his desire to "destroy the material basis of all superstition," he runs into a series of quandaries about the palpability of language, ritual, and idolatry.[36] As Clifford Ando argues, in Augustine's writing, "things, and words about things, possess the same metaphysical status."[37] Naturally, early Christian philosophy and literature were founded on classical traditions and texts. Augustine, like other commentators, advocated using these pagan texts, like the ancient Israelites who, under the direction of God, chose wisely among "the ancient treasures of Egypt" with its combination of "idols and heavy burdens" and more valuable "vessels and ornaments of silver and gold."[38] While this would mean extracting the truths of morality and monotheism from the "false and superstitious fantasies" of pre-Christian writing, the process would still be like the integration of pagan *spolia* into the architecture of Christian buildings. There would still be material reminders of a past negated (as disorder or vanity) or demystified (as outlandish fiction) or assimilated to moral, allegorical narratives.[39] If this was the founding role of hermeneutics, poetry holds out the possibility of communicating the memory of a materiality never fully excised by iconoclasm. The possibility of such poetic creation haunts the history of idolatry.

In a defining text of the Reformation, *Institutes Institutiones Christianae Religionis*, Calvin associates idolatry with making and generation. Opposing the claim that idolatry derives from the veneration of slain heroes and ancestors, Calvin claims "Mens idolum genuit: manus peperit" (The mind generates forms: the hand brings them forth).[40] The mind and the hand here form a circuit. Although *genuit* (*gingo*, *gingere*) and *peperit* (*pario*, *parere*) imply both organic generation and physical making, recent translations of Calvin stress the lifeless nature of idols, rendering them in the language of mechanical production. Henry Beveridge's translation names the mind "a perpetual forge of idols."[41] Sean Kane, relying on a similar translation that names the mind as a "factory" of idols, describes the faculty of the fantasy, which coins idolatrous shapes in the mind that are then fashioned into objects.[42] While "forge" and "factory" may convey some sense of the artifactuality of Calvin's idolatry, these translations supply Calvin with mechanistic metaphors in their effort to transform the threatening physicality of idolatry into psychology. But idols are neither merely specters of the imagination nor improperly revered lumps of mute stuff. For Calvin, the idol was a hybrid of sensuous experience and imagination, one that could not—as it was deployed against the sacramental and devotional culture of early modern Europe—help but bear the trace of an idea that Christ's real presence could endow ordinary physicality with vital, sacred plenitude.

Reformation iconoclasm was to find even in Christ's flesh the danger of such idolatry. The Reformation Christ was, then, not only no longer a suffering God; he had become less physical, less of the world than of words. As Thomas Luxon points out, "The early reformers had removed the 'body' of Christ from the altar and relocated it in the scriptures, redefining Christ's 'true' body as a discursive body—the Word."[43] Of course, as O'Connell indicates, reformers only enhanced a development already underway in Renaissance Europe: "For Erasmus—and for humanism more generally—'Christ as text' replaces the painted, sculpted Christ. For succeeding reformers, Christ's real presence as text would also eclipse his real presence in the visible, tactile Eucharist."[44] Erasmus extols the virtue of scriptures above and beyond representations of the

Christ, for "the latter represents only the form of the body—if indeed it represents anything of Him—but these writings bring you the living image of His holy mind and the speaking, healing, dying, rising Christ himself, and thus they render Him so fully present that you would see less if you gazed upon Him with your very eyes." More important than the body is scripture, which does not so much represent Christ as "let us continually occupy ourselves with it, let us fondly kiss it, at length let us die in its embrace, let us be transformed in it, since indeed studies are transmuted into morals."[45]

Erasmus turns away from the mere body, which could never "fully present" Christ—indeed, what was viewed as an idolatry of the body—to a hermeneutics nearly idolatrous in its fervor, one that guarantees salvation at least in part through the morally beneficial study of scripture. More emphatically, "Calvin's Christology," Luxon argues, "emphasizes the distinction between rather than the combination of the divine and human. The divine is never human. . . . The two remain as distinct as sign and signified."[46] As Mary Aston has noted, "The fanatics who thought (as Luther put it) that 'nothing spiritual can be present where there is anything material and physical' were constantly faced with this disillusioning limitation of the human condition. If it is human to err we are all subject to the error of being incarnate."[47] The price of the Reformation valorization of the Word as scripture was the denigration of the materiality of bodies, things, and the resonance of words with their affective and physical heft.

If, in the history of Christianity, the idol rarely had defenders, the icon did, for all that Reformation iconoclasts hardly distinguished between the two. Indeed, the advocates of icons were the victors in the Byzantine iconoclastic controversies. As Marie-José Mondzain makes clear, the stakes for such debates were as high as they were in the Reformation: "We are dealing with a crisis in which the relationship between each and every symbol and the real, the imaginary, the fictitious, the deceitful, and the true were all at stake."[48] Whereas iconoclasts and iconophiles produced an intense cultural and political dialogue in the Byzantine Empire, Reformation iconoclasm witnessed astonishing violence. Aston argues, "Reformation iconoclasm destroyed more objects in more places than any previous iconoclasm [for] Protestant iconoclasts believed that widespread destruction was necessary for the renewal of an entire religious system."[49] In their defense of the icon, Byzantine iconophiles mounted not only a trenchant defense of the fleshly nature of both Christ and Christians, they also offered an alternative to the textualization of Christ, conceiving of icons as no mere symbols. As St. John of Damascus argues, "I do not worship matter; I worship the Creator of matter who became matter for my sake, who willed to take His abode in matter; who worked out my salvation through matter. Never will I cease honoring the matter which wrought my salvation! I honor it, but not as God. How could God be born out of lifeless things?"[50] Moreover, St. Theodore the Studite offers a striking analogy to explain how icons of Christ were neither Christ nor mere representations. If, at moments, for St. Theodore Christ is like form imprinting matter in the Aristotelian analogy of the wax and its imprint, elsewhere icons are like shadows:

> If every body is inseparably followed by its own shadow, and no one in his right mind could say that a body is shadowless, but rather we can see in the body the shadow that follows, and in the shadow the body which precedes: thus no one could say that Christ is imageless, if indeed He has a body with its characteristic form, but rather we can see in Christ His image existing by implication and in the image Christ plainly visible as its prototype. From the simultaneous existence of both, it follows that when Christ is seen, then His image is also potentially see, and consequently is transferred by imprint into any material whatever.[51]

Here is no signifier ruptured from its signified, no absence to which representation points vainly and endlessly. Rather, visual and material contiguity govern the relationship between Christ and his icon.

It is not that Spenser was a student of Byzantine history or an avid reader of St. John of Damascus and St. Theodore the Studite. However, the history of debates about icons teaches that there were alternatives to both the hostility to physicality and to the textualization of Christ that coincided with (and helped incite) the astonishing violence of iconoclasm in Reformation England. Byzantine iconophiles still castigated idols because they were purely imaginary; indeed, one might say the idol problematically lacked the possibility of a material connection to Christ's flesh.[52] In the conspicuous absence of that sanctifying touchstone, Spenser sought his own alternative, for in the shadowy realm of pagan cosmogony and monstrous flesh he relocated the sensuous, affective heft associated with Byzantine icons and Christ's flesh.

Gaston Bachelard conceived of the imagination as fundamentally material, not visual. Bachelard sought to describe "images that stem *directly from matter*. The eye assigns them names, but only the hand truly knows them."[53] Just as an idol is more than dead matter or false image, so too must imagination be more than its visual etymology suggests. As O'Connell argues, iconoclasm emerges as a result of a "long-standing epistemological dialectic of image and word" and "this tension becomes conflict when technologies of representation are in a state of transition."[54] If the imaginative work of poetry has a relationship to representation in *The Faerie Queene*, it occurs in the shadow of Christ, where the true threat is not the monster but the machine that deadens the flesh and replaces it with the dull hum of a textualized Christ endlessly circulating, as if reproduced on the very printing presses that brought Europe the news of the Reformation.

Given the tendency to align Spenser with Reformation politics and poetics, it is no surprise that the first monster of the Legend of Holiness, Error, the paradigmatic creature of romance, has been read as both the horror of fleshy generation and as a figure of the machine. Monsters not only threaten divine order but their genesis also foregrounds questions of shaping and generation. As Jeffrey Cohen argues, "The monster's body is the raw material of cosmogenesis."[55] In the matter of creation, the monster is as necessary and useful as it is horrifying, explaining Spenser's obsessive interest in the evil creatures that threaten true holiness. This signals, too, his interest not so much in cosmology—the precise ordering of the world—as in cosmogony—the ceaseless generation of the material world. If the monster figures the danger of a perceived chaos of substance, the machine figures the danger of utter and deadening instrumentality. Martin Heidegger has explored the extent to which modernity is constituted by its technology, a technology based on a "system of science [that] consists in a solidarity of procedure and attitude with respect to the objectification of whatever is."[56] The science that founds machine technology "sets upon the real" and produces an "entrapping representation, which secures everything in that objectness that is thus capable of being followed out."[57]

Before the reader encounters the first monster of the Legend of Holiness, the differing portraits of Redcrosse and Una witness this displacement of the burden of materiality. In the previous chapter I revealed the ways in which Redcrosse and Una represent different relationships to the lived embodiment of pain. Una is not merely above the experience of corporeality endowed with the capacity to suffer; she is, in contrast to the physically vigorous knight "pricking on the plaine" (I.I.I) at an airy remove from earthly concerns. Una cannot, however, distance herself entirely from material substance. Redcrosse's fair companion brings with her her own companion:

> Behind her farre away a Dwarfe did lag,
> That lasie seemd in being euer last,
> Or wearied with bearing of her bag
> Of needments at his backe.
>
> (I.I.6)

It is easy to identify Una's dwarf as reason trailing behind faith or flesh dragging down spirit. Yet he is also a weary figure, a figure of labor, and, to be sure, the "needments" he bears are not his own. Despite being the embodiment of beauty, faith, and truth (and thus aligned with the spiritual, rather than the material), Una carries substantial baggage that is, here, outsourced: dumped in the hands of the dwarf so as not to be a burden to the ethereal exemplar of the true religious way. That Spenser coins the term "needments" indicates something about the dwarf (his labor, the materials he bears) necessary to Una. The word also suggests palpability: need made even more substantial. For anyone with a body, there are, always, "needments" to be borne. For Una, matter is what Heidegger calls equipment: substance exhausted in its utility with respect to human purposes such that "it disappears into usefulness."[58]

Yet it is more than just the contrasting portraits of the spiritual Una and the fleshy Redcrosse Knight that indicate the extent to which these meditations on holiness are intimately concerned with poetry's fundamental materiality. The opening encounter with the forest and dragon of Error and the following encounter with the crafty Archimago stress an ultimately substantial if shadowy basis for poetry—the former in a language of grotesque physicality, the latter in the refined and only seemingly insubstantial elements of air and dream. In the case of the former, it is fecundity itself that drives Una and Redcrosse from the clarity of the plain (its lack of subterfuge) to the profusion of the romance forest. The two, indeed, seek shelter from a sudden storm described as follows: "angry *Ioue* an hideous storme of raine / Did poure into his Lemans lap" (1.1.6). Holiness seeks shelter from the violent sexuality of the generative world only to be driven deep into the dark forest of error in search of "Faire harbour" (1.1.7). In the sheltering space of the "wandring wood" (1.1.13), a wood of delight and beguilement, we encounter the much noted catalogue of trees, for the wood is a place not merely of pleasure but of matter, the Greek word *hyle* being the word for both *matter* and for *wood.* That the forest is a safe harbor perhaps refers not merely to the nautical metaphor but also to the great epic catalogue of the ships and crews waging war on Troy in the second book of the *Iliad.* The ship might be said to be made of the most usefully shaped and fully instrumentalized forms of wood. Most of the trees in Spenser's epic catalogue are useful ("the sayling Pine" or the "warlike Beech" for example) or indicate physical properties ("the Poplar neuer dry" or "the Patane round"), qualitative associations, or ceremonial uses such as "the Cypresse funerall" (1.1.8). Near the close of this catalogue, we note a different type of tree: "The Mirrhe sweete bleeding in the bitter wound" (1.1.9), which presents a tree connoting pain and pleasure at once. The details remind us of physical properties (a sweet fragrance and a bitter taste), but they also evoke the memory of another suffering tree. In Ovid's *Metamorphoses,* the incestuous Myrrha, after tricking her father into sleeping with her, flees pregnant from his court. Weary of running and of living, she prays to be killed or transformed and becomes the tree from which her unborn son, Adonis, rips himself free. The tree writhes and bucks with the pain of labor before its bark splits and the child emerges.[59] Suffering, the grief of Myrrha's plight and the pain of her labor, emerges as the product of a compacted mythopoeic history, which *The Faerie Queene* returns to, culminating in the spectacular cosmogony presented in the Garden of Adonis.

These trees are home not only to the intimations of the suffering Adonis but also to the highly memorable creature Error, who adumbrates the shadowy cosmogony of monsters as well as the specter of carnal sin: evil in its most physical and female of embodiments. She is "Halfe like a serpent" and half woman, with a tail of "knots" and "folds" and "many boughtes vpwound." She suckles horrible offspring of "sundrie shapes" with her "poisnous dugs" (1.1.15). In a dark, womblike cave in the midst of a labyrinthine forest, Una and Redcrosse encounter not merely an embodiment of the grotesque materiality of sin but also the intensely material manifestation of romance itself, which is feminine, twisting, and carnal. Error is at once the spiritual transgression opposed by Holiness and the central feature of the genre that makes Spenser's *Faerie Queene* possible. Romance portrays the straying of bodies from narrative telos, and these twistings and turnings also convey a sense of substance in motion or even run amok. While Una shifts the burden of materiality to her accompanying dwarf, Error figures the revenge of substance, which must be cast down by Protestant virtue. It is thus no surprise that Redcrosse defeats Error under the influence of Una, who encourages him to add "faith vnto [his] force" (1.1.19). Is there a difference between faith and force here?

In her death throes, Error adumbrates an image of the organic materiality of poetic production. As Redcrosse strangles the life from her body, the reader and Redcrosse alike are treated to an explosion of the visceral horror:

> Therewith she spewd out of her filthie maw
> A floud of poyson horrible and blacke
> Full of great lumps of flesh and gobbets raw,
> Which stunck so vildly, that it forst him slacke,
> His grasping hold, and from her turne him backe:
> Her vomit full of bookes and papers was,
> With loathly frogs and toades, which eyes did lacke,
> And creeping sought way in the weedy gras:
> Her filthie parbreake all the place defiled has.
>
> (1.1.20)

In addition to the extensive annotation of this moment's religious contexts and implications, Lawrence Rhu has argued that this episode "culminates in a nightmarish image symptomatic of the Reformation in one of its traditionally definitive features. . . . Errour, in her death throes, discloses an unsettling affinity with one of the enabling technologies of the new epoch, the printing press."[60] For Rhu, Error points not only to the circulation of heretical (Catholic) texts but also to the desire for order, similarly expressed by Spenser's Italian precursor Torquato Tasso when faced with the material profusion of romance, a profusion that resists both the classical unity of plot mandated by neo-Aristotelian aesthetic critics of the Renaissance and the requirement of a unifying Christian telos for any heroic poem. In this way, according to Rhu, Spenser displays disgust for theological error and for the dissemination of such error by means mechanically enabled by the technology of the time.

Despite this suggestively mechanistic valence, there is, however, more to Error than the horror of matter shifting registers from the monstrous to the mechanical. She is not, in fact, mechanical in appearance. In her death the resulting products are not multiples duplicated endlessly nor images coined by the mechanisms of print technology. Living creatures, toads and frogs, leap from her mouth and escape the wrath of the Redcrosse Knight. She also spews books and papers. The sum total of her projection is defiling, filthy "parbreake"—that which literally bursts through. Expressed in the language of the abject is the product of an ancient fecundity, as suggested by Error's similarity to the monstrosities contemporaneous with or prior to the Titans, who themselves constantly threatened the civilized order of the Olympian deities. According to Zakiya Hanafi, in *The Monster in the Machine*, early modernity witnesses the translation of monsters into machines amid the rise of secularization that accompanies developing scientific knowledge.[61] But Error contradicts mechanical denaturalization, for it is not metal that takes over but flesh in its elemental forms.

Inasmuch as the mechanical indicates the violent grinding of Protestant allegory, bursting through that machine is a disturbing cascade of generative matter as Error expires and sends her brood into the world:

> She poured forth out of her hellish sinke
> Her fruitfull cursed spawne of serpents small,
> Deformed monsters, fowle, and blacke as inke,
> Which swarming all about his legs did crall,
> And him encombred sore, but could not hurt at all.
> (1.1.22)

These creatures are likened to the monstrous fecundity of the Nile, which overflowing produces "fertile slime" out of which

> breed
> Ten thousand kindes of creatures partly male
> And partly femall of his fruitful seed;
> Such vgly monstrous shapes elsewher may no man reed.
> (1.1.21)

In these horrific scenes of generation, matter is that which burdens; Redcrosse is not injured; he is "encombred," just as Una's dwarf is. The children of Error, "blacke as inke," are like words swarming on a page. Like the creatures of the Nile, they, too, are subject to reading, making them not merely objects of knowledge to be read in some scientific or encyclopedic account of the Nile but also, as is emphasized by the rhyme scheme ("breed," "reed," and "seed"), representatives of a generative, if abject, sensuality.

Error's fecund materiality depends on ancient mythic associations as well as on contemporary religious ones. Error's children are not only like swarming creatures of the Nile; they also, as has been noted, suggest the legend of the brood of the pelican, whose children feed from her blood, a legend used to express the ingratitude of children but also the relationship between Christ and humanity. Error is devoured by her own offspring:

> Her scattred brood, soone as their Parent deare
> They saw so rudely falling to the ground,
> Groning full deadly, all with troublous feare,
> Gathred themselues about her body round,
> Weening their wonted entrance to haue found
> At her wide mouth: but being there withstood
> They flocked all about her bleeding wound,
> And sucked vp their dying mother's bloud,
> Making her death their life, and eke her hurt their good.
> (1.1.25)

Error's body, devoured by her offspring, suggestively if abjectly reintroduces not only Eucharist theology; it also introduces the idea of a textuality rooted in the life of flesh rendered abject by Protestant theology. Error lingers like all flesh in the wake of the Reformation, in the shadow of Christ. Elizabeth Spillers links this abomination to the gendered concerns of poetic production: "Errour exemplifies bad literary procreation. . . . When Redcrosse destroys this female procreation, he makes possible a male procreation which supplants erroneous ideals of bad reading with new forms of moral knowledge."[62] Spillers's gendered schematic—bad (female) procreation versus good (male) procreation—seems less persuasive when one considers the role Una plays in the defeat of Error. Moreover, the very depiction of Error, one of the most visceral and disturbing passages in *The Faerie Queene*, makes the poet more like Error, fashioning dark and squiggling blots of life in the form of words. The incident ends with a victory for Redcrosse and Una, but their emergence from the den of Error leaves one with the sense that, in reading *The Faerie Queene*, one never leaves the wood of Error.

Error, a creature of cave and forest, expresses the abject materiality of the shadowy earth from which Redcrosse springs. Archimago presents as much a portrait of a popish evil-doer working in insubstantial images as a maker who fashions works from the invisible but not ineffable substance of air. Critics such as Terry Eagleton and Susan Buck-Morris have reminded us that the word *aesthetic* derives not just from a concern with beauty but, originally, from a concern with sensory perception. That is, the aesthetic is ultimately a "discourse of the body."[63] In a suggestive, if disputed, etymology, Robert Broxton Onians ties the aesthetic not to the Greek *aisthesis* (to see or perceive) but to *aio* (to breathe), linking breath to all forms of sensory perception.[64] That Archimago possesses an affinity for invisible materiality, of which air is a special case, indicates that moral evaluations of Archimago may have blinded us to his real artistry. Archimago's initial appearance, following hard on the heels of Error's defeat, marks him as ambivalently Catholic. At first he seems to be little more than a harmless hermit dressed in the "blacke weedes" of isolated, penitential life (1.1.29). He is sage, sober and seemingly without malice, though with Archimago everything depends on seeming:

> For that olde man of pleasing wordes had store,
> And well could file his tongue as smooth as glas,
> He told of Saints and Popes, and euermore
> He strowd an *Aue-Mary* after and before.
> (1.1.35)

Archimago presents the carnal papist: with the idolatrous trappings of devotion (the glib words, the Catholic prayers, the cut of saints, the rosary, and the penitential practice) he "often knockt his brest, as one that did repent" (1.1.29). Like Abessa, whom Una encounters later in her iconoclastic spree, Archimago embodies the contradictory nature of the object of iconoclastic attack, at once everything and nothing—the desiccated, dead stuff of false devotion and the negative matter or immateriality of falsehood. But glass, like air, is no less a substance.

Archimago's materialist poetics expresses itself in a mixture of images of earth and images of air. While it is clear that Archimago summons sprites and asks for "a fit false dream, that can delude the sleepers sent" (1.1.43), his interaction with Morpheus emphasizes not the veracity or falsity of dream but rather its efficacy, which appears as physicality. Morpheus, who can barely be roused, finds a dream for Redcrosse in "his prison darke" before lying down his "heauie head, deuoide of careful cark, / Whose sences all were straight benumbd and starke" (1.1.44). Morpheus's recalcitrant physicality is of note here, and while he experiences a kind of pleasurable, anesthetizing sleep, the dream he sends Redcrosse emphasizes a painful cognizance of improper sensation. Archimago draws Redcrosse deeper into his own body by waking sluggish materiality in the form of Morpheus; Spenser does the same for his reader. The summoning of Morpheus and the sprites suggests the dark matter of the earth, while the actual matter of Archimago's *poiesis* is air. Morpheus sends an "idle dream" (an active pun on idol) while Archimago fashions, or refashions, a summoned sprite:

> Who all this while with charmes and hidden artes,
> Had made a lady of that other Spright,
> And fram'd of liquid ayre her tender partes
> So liuely and so like in all mens sight,
> That weaker sence it could haue rauisht quight.
> The maker selfe, for all his wondrous witt,
> Was nigh beguiled with so goodly sight.
>
> (1.1.45)

This creature of false seeming is, like Duessa, so effective in her dissembling as to nearly fool her maker. As is the case for Duessa, false appearances possess a material base. She is "borne without her dew" (1.1.46), suggesting an improper but not an inorganic or insubstantial parturition. Here the sprite appears as a body of air, translucent but palpable, making Archimago not merely a worker of images, a stage manager of deceptive visuality, but one who works in the medium of embodiment. He not only refashions this sprite; he also engenders it, giving it a woman's "tender partes" (1.1.45), which, it is interesting to note, becomes the focus of this body's powers of fascination, just as Duessa's filthy nether parts provide an object of revulsion. Mingling nature and nurture, Archimago teaches the sprite "to imitate that Lady trew / Whose semblance she did carrie vnder feigned hew" (1.1.46). For a ploy whose intent is supposed to be the temptation of Redcrosse with carnal sin and the separation of knight and lady, we encounter some oddly excessive details (how the sprites are summoned, sexed, and trained to play their feminine and masculine roles), just as the summoning of an evil dream hardly required such a detailed trip to the realm of Morpheus. Like the seemingly unnecessary doubling of temptations on Redcrosse's first night in Archimago's hermitage (he is assailed from within by an "ydle dreame" *and* from without by a "faire-forged Spright" [1.1.46, 1.2.2]), the details of this scene of moral import betray an interest in the fleshiness of the earth, the dynamic substantiality of air, and the possibility of shaping and reshaping the gendered body.

Redcrosse's moral lapse begins with airy sprites but soon delves into the vulnerable flesh of the masculine body. This lapse leads to his capture by Orgoglio, whose name conveys the pride of Redcrosse's downfall. Pride is really an expression of preference as Redcrosse relies on his own flesh instead of heavenly grace or Una's guidance. Orgoglio himself is a creature of earth and air:

> The greatest Earth his vncouth mother was,
> And blustring *AEolus* his boasted syre,
> Who with his breath, which through the world doth pas,
> Her hollow womb did secretly inspyre,
> And fild her hidden caues with stormie yre,
> That she conceiu'd; and trebling the dew time,
> In which the wombes of women doe expyre,
> Brought forth this monstrous masse of earthly slyme,
> Puft vp with emptie wynd and fild with sinfull cryme.
> (1.7.9)

Orgoglio unites the elemental matter of the cave of Error and the cave of Morpheus, of the womb of earthy female substance and the subtle substance of air. Monstrous as Orgoglio may be, he emerges from the fecund earth. As in the cave of Error and the cave of Morpheus, Spenser's interest in rooting a poetics in physically generative forces draws him into shadowy matter, visceral detail, and genealogical accounts unnecessary for the narrative plausibility or moral lucidity of the episode. Earth, with its secret, seductive cosmogony, constantly attracts Spenser, just as the Redcrosse knight strays from the disembodying violence of duty, called by the lure of physicality. Orgoglio delivers the shock of embodiment to a knight, whose dedication to spiritual violence leaves him surprised by his own physicality. The giant savagely attacks, mirroring the force with which faith is allied. Although Orgoglio misses his target, his blow topples Redcrosse indirectly: the concussion of Orgoglio's club striking the earth "with the wind it did him ouerthrow, / And all his sences stoond" (1.7.12). Redcrosse responds not to the impact of violence itself but to the peripheral vibrations of sound and air. The startling epic simile describing the side effects of Orgoglio's club evoke a cannon:

> As when that deuelish yron Engin wrought
> In deepest Hell, and framd by *Furies* skill,
> With windy Nitre and quick Sulfur fraught,
> And ramed with bollet rownd, ordaind to kill,
> Conceiueth fyre, the heauens it doth fill
> With thundring noyse and all the ayre doth choke,
> That none can breath, nor see, nor heare at will,
> Through smouldery cloud of duskish stincking smok,
> That th'oenly breath him daunts, who hath escapt the stroke.
> (1.7.13)

That Orgoglio fells the once mighty Knight of Holiness without touching him remains a commentary on his lapse of virtue, although "heuenly grace" still prevents Redcrosse from having "beene poulderd all, as thin as flowre" (1.7.12). Yet despite the figurations of obliterating violence that reduce flesh to almost nothing, our attention is directed to the material displacements of air and sound that accompany violence.

Spenser's cannon activates epic history, referring to Ludovico Ariosto's *Orlando Furioso* where, in the ninth canto, Orlando must defeat enemy forces supported by such a device. Monstrosity links Orgoglio and the cannon, for it is described by Ariosto less as a mechanical device than as an iron beast: "The monster, with a flash of lightning, mumbles, / Spewing a charge of metal from its bore."[65] Orlando defeats his foes and captures the cannon, which he takes as his sole share in the booty in order to destroy the "Accursèd and abominable tool" (9.91) that offends the laws governing chivalrous battle. The cannon delivers the shock of the new in the form of violent technology, while romance converts the cannon into a citable literary convention, domesticating its mechanical novelty. In a genre committed to war and love—and in which, often, the two can be scarcely distinguishable—this mechanical apparatus of destruction crystallizes and exposes something about the system in which combat is valorized. In some sense, the cannon is radically coextensive with the nature of heroic poetry; the device exposes and de-idealizes reified masculine violence. Orlando, as such, consigns the cannon to destruction, sinking it deep into the demonic, Tartarean abyss from which the metal was first disgorged.[66]

Spenser's interest in Ariosto's cannon has everything to do with the mechanization of matter, which is one way in which violence acts upon wayward physical substances such as bodies. To control the body one may destroy it or render it a machine, make it a lump of mute stuff or a useful puppet. Here the overwhelming sensory cascade provides that effect. Yet the passage remains primarily interested in the fluid mechanics of sound, air, and dust that constitute the periphery of obliterating violence. If the cannon deafens, blinds, and, when it strikes, ultimately destroys, to escape the stroke of such violence is to suffer the "smouldry cloud of duskish stincking smok" that matter casts up. In some sense, any form of matter neither destroyed nor mastered (that is, mechanized) is a cloud of wave formations threatening to choke out the piercing force and light of truth. Redcrosse is no longer part of an economy of violence; he has loosened his body from the strict confines of martial holiness and left himself vulnerable to fluid, airy matter, which is always drawn up from the abject womb of earth and which must be cast back down to preserve order.

Monstrosity displays the unbounded and abject generation associated with physicality. Machines constitute the monster's antithesis: matter reduced to technological function. Error, Archimago, and Orgoglio adumbrate that generative, organic principle that resists or appropriates mechanical process in order to foreground the materiality abjected by iconoclastic zeal. The final creature of the Legend of Holiness represents the ultimate collision of the principles associated with monster and machine. The great dragon threatens Una's kingdom and her helpless parents, the as-yet-unsaved Adam and Eve who are king and queen of a realm held hostage to the dragon's violence. The beast appears characterized by its sheer heft and bulk:

> His body monstrous, horrible, and vaste,
> Which to increase his wondrous greatnes more,
> Was swoln with wrath, and poyson, and with bloody gore.
> (I.II.8)

The swollen bulk of the dragon stretches out awkwardly in the closing alexandrine of this stanza. Like Orgoglio, the dragon's body is puffed up. His "stinking gorge" is stuffed with masticated substance ("trickling blood and gobbets raw / Of late devoured bodies") and exudes "smoke and stench" (I.II.13). Like the smoke of the cannon, the dragon signifies the overwhelming and undifferentiated nature of substance. The mouth of the beast is likened to "the griesly mouth of hell," a "darke abysse" in which subjects and objects are torn into bits of flesh (I.II.12). Yet when the narrative approaches the beast and renders the dragon in greater visual specificity, many of the details suggest mechanical articulation. The eyes are like lamps or beacons (I.II.14), while the scaly skin is composed of seemingly metallic plates, as are the dragon's stings and his rending claws (I.II.9–12). These body parts "the sharpest steele exceeden farr" (I.II.II). Even the snaky folds of flesh reminiscent of the twisting, organic body of Error are "bras-scaly" surfaces; they are "entangled knots, . . . Bespotted as with shields of red and blacke" (I.II.II). Is the dragon gross, organic flesh or a metal monster of sin?

A third figure, between undifferentiated substance and mechanized matter, emerges as the narrative figures the dragon as a ship:

> His flaggy winges, when forth he did display,
> Were like two sayles, in which the hollow wynd
> Is gathered full, and worketh speedy way:
> And eke the pennes that did his pineons bynd,
> Were like the mayne-yardes with flying canuas lyned,
> With which whenas him list the ayre to beat,
> And there by force vnwonted passage fynd,
> The clowdes before him fledd for terror great,
> And all the heauens stood still amazed with his threat.
> (I.II.IO)

Wings, like the sails of a ship, are designed to catch wind and make matter dynamic, which is, perhaps, what terrifies the heavens. One might be reminded of Spenser's catalogue of trees that reprises the Aegean ships of Homer's *Iliad*. *Hyle*, matter (as wood), may be instrumentalized and made useful (as ship or any other masterable object). The dragon's suggestive pens, the quills and pinions of the body, are lifted into motion by wind, rendering the materiality of the beast a tempting analogue for poetic inspiration conceived as subtle materiality. Although, in defeat, the dragon is killed and thus reduced to "so huge and horrible mass," a "heaped mountaine" of flesh, we see from the "darksom hollow maw" the spurting life blood, his life breathed out "into smoke and cloudes swift" (1.12.53–55). Redcrosse, one might think, stabs his sword into the dark cave of matter, killing it as he killed Error. The wind is "hollow" or insubstantial, but so are the quills with which one writes, and we have already seen Archimago shape shadowy but substantial bodies of air. The dragon is the shadow of matter banished before the light of Protestant truth, but it is also the shadow of the abjected body of Christ from which Spenser draws the materials by and of which the poem called *The Faerie Queene* is inscribed.

The figure of the ship that returns as the framing device of the closing, celebratory canto of the Legend of Holiness, further emphasizes that poetic communication is at stake in these final episodes. Canto 12 begins:

> Behold I see the hauen nigh at hand,
>   To which I meane my wearie course to bend:
>   Veere the maine shete, and beare vp with the land,
>   The which afore is fayrly to be kend,
>   And seemeth safe from storms, that may offend;
>   There this fayre virgin wearie of her way
>   Must landed bee, now at her iourneyes end:
>   There eke my feeble barke a while may stay,
> Till mery wynd and weather call her thence away.
>
> (1.12.1)

Una's happy homecoming ends painful wandering, but the coincidence of poet and dragon as mariners remains peculiar. The moral telos of the Legend of Holiness may require the defeat of the dragon; the mechanization of the dragon indicates a fantasy of how easily abject matter can be mastered by the imperatives of holy violence and religious knowledge. But to approach harbor and home is to move with the wind toward land, which is "fayrly to be kend." That is, after long wandering in the fluid ways of wood and water, the solidity of the land appears fair and welcome. At the same time, to "ken" the land—to know or to perceive it—is to realize the twisting Anglo-Saxon roots of the word, which spawns also the verb *can* and thus refers both to mental cognition and physical capacity. In the deepest sense, and even in its defeat, the Legend of Holiness comes to know the earth that composes knight and dragon, forest and plain. Redcrosse may defeat the dragon, but to catch with skin or sail the drafts of inspiration one must neither destroy nor master the shadowy earth but know it through experience. Even the ship that enables the journey of the poem must be cared for. The "iolly Mariners" must "strike their sailes" to attend to needs of the ship:

> we must land some of our passengers,
> And light this weary vessell of her loade.
> Here she a while may make her safe abode,
> Till she repaired haue her tackles spent,
> And wants supplide
>
> (1.12.42)

Like the dwarf saddled with Una's material "needments," the ship too must be divested of its burdens. Central to the narrative journey of *The Faerie Queene* is the physicality of the ship, the tackles and wants of which the stuff of poetry is composed. This, here, is no mere equipment, as Heidegger might define it: matter that "disappears into usefulness." The "needments" of Spenser's language in *The Faerie Queene* never recede into docile utility. The sensuous physicality of poetry, like the ship described above, constantly solicits attention, care, use, and repair.

Spenser's call to the poem as ship and to readers as jolly mariners is a call to community, a coming together into one body in communion. This union is secured by the marriage between Una and Redcrosse, at which all solemn rites are performed:

> all the while sweete Musicke did apply
> Her curious skill, the warbling notes to play,
> To driue away the dull Melancholy
>
> (1.12.38)

After "sweete Musicke" comes a heavenly "Angels voice" of some mysterious source, which leaves each person "refte of his sences" and "rauished with rare impression in his sprite" (1.12.39). Coming into a religious community requires a particular vision of communication; here, the hearer is "refte" of senses and flesh. The voice of the angel ravishes matter, drawing it in as impressed spirit.

Yet what is this "Melancholy," with all of its bodily associations, which must be banished for the holy and heavenly communion of this ending? The music that cures melancholy is a transcendent force that ravishes the body of its material burden of affect. Prior to the completion of the ceremony, however, the wedding grinds to a halt as a messenger comes bearing a message of disturbing import, with all the weight that "import" bears etymologically. The messenger turns out to be Archimago, sent by Duessa to interfere with the union. While the moral narrative of this episode emphasizes the exposure of falsehood and the capture of Archimago, the episode itself foregrounds communicability. Archimago, as messenger, runs in "like a man dismayd" (1.12.24) just after the narrator confesses to an inability to capture with his "rude" and "ragged rimes" (1.12.23) the beauty of the heavenly Una, who has at last laid aside the black stole of mourning that, throughout the book, keeps her veiled, much as truths are veiled by allegory. If Una figures the violent clarity of heavenly revelation, Archimago's "dismayd" appearance is much more like the Spenserian narrator of "ragged rimes." To be dismayed is to be stripped of courage, energy, or force (as Archimago will be later), but it is also to be misshapen, literally dis-made, as Spenser uses the word in the Book of Temperance.[67] In addition, the dismaying of Archimago seems to be exactly the opposite of what happens to Redcrosse knight when, though a simple ploughman's son, he is "prickt with courage" (1.10.66) and gallops off in search of adventure. Likewise, "ragged rimes" may not aspire to ravishing transcendence, but they do foreground poetry as a composition of substance and motion, as in a rough-hewn object or an uneven gait. That this messenger played by Archimago is concerned with the opacity or difficulty of his transmission is clear in repeated references to the modalities of communication. He is "a Messenger with letters, which his message said" (1.12.24). When he is ready to deliver the message, "Then to his handes that writt he did betake, / Which he disclosing, read thus, as the paper spake" (1.12.25). The physicality of the letters, the ruffled appearance of the messenger, the references to hands and speaking paper, the repeated use of the word "disclose"—all these foreground the materiality of communication as an encounter with speaking things.

Yet Duessa's message is heard, evaluated, and dismissed on the basis of its veracity alone, as is Archimago's role in the episode. Una spies out the "crafty messenger with letters vaine" and makes sure the guards seize Archimago, the "false footman" (1.12.34). Una manages to "discouer" Archimago in the crudest of senses, revealing an identity that inheres only in falsehood. Of course, Archimago *is* in fact a messenger, though that is not all he is. Archimago's capture is violent; he is compared to a "chained beare, whom cruell dogs doe bait," and here he is dismayed in another sense of the word, possessing (the pun is no accident) "ydle force" (1.12.35):

> But they him layd full low in dungeon deepe,
> And bound him hand and foote with yron chains.
> And with continual watch did warely keepe;
> Who then would thinke, that by his subtile trains
> He could escape fowle death or deadly pains?
> (1.12.36)

Archimago resembles the shifting treacheries of language the king brutally immobilizes.

One critic describes holiness as a virtue predicated on Augustinian precedent, "the quest for the transcendent referent in a world of slipping signifiers."[68] If the voice of the angel that follows the capture of Archimago is the voice of transcendence, what do we make of Archimago's capture? If bondage to material signs is a sign of sinful idolatry, how does the violent materialization of Archimago not also represent a bondage to the material? And what do we make of the fact that matter, in the form of Archimago, escapes forceful capture with his subtle "trains," a word that refers to guile and treachery (especially traps to catch animals) but also to sequences of material objects yoked together. Language, one might say, is a subtle train, pulling with it an irrepressible materiality that is all too easily read in the language of iconoclasm as an insubstantial lure, an empty promise, or a trick of the eye or mind. What of the message itself? Duessa claims that Redcrosse has promised his love to her, which is not so much false as it is out of date. She claims the errant Redcrosse as ineluctably hers, "free or bond, / Or false or trew, or liuing or else dead" (1.12.28). If Duessa is not merely the call of false religion or duplicitous practice but the call of the sensuous particularity of the physical world, her claim has some truth. She closes her letter with the signature "Thy neither friend, nor foe," placing herself beyond the dualisms of good and evil, true and false, matter and spirit. For Redcrosse has in some sense wed himself to Duessa, despite his violent conversion back to the path of Protestant truth in the House of Holiness.

Those works of the imagination and those works of matter that seemed so suspiciously like idols constitute the elemental substrate of poetry. In his incisive essay "Archimag: Between Text and Countertext," Harry Berger Jr. examines habits of reading particular to *The Faerie Queene* and he bases his argument on a distinction between "two orientations, two differently accented modes of sign use." He argues, "On the one hand, there is a set toward the message, the story, whatever is being referred to or talked and written about. On the other hand, there is a set toward the possibility that the text may generate a message about the message."[69] I have tried to suggest here is that what is missing in accounts like Berger's would be a sense of the materiality that grounds poetry. Poetry communicates by means of its imaginative evocation of textures of physicality, and the difficulty in conveying this aspect of poetry results in part from ultimately religious conflicts over representation even as terms like *representation* and *textuality* seem increasingly inadequate to describe poetry and its effects.

One might remember in this final moment of the Legend of Holiness, another sense of communication: the joining of the community of Christ by ingesting his body, a taking in of Christ's body that brings the body of the eater into Christ's body. Jean Calvin in his *Four Godlye Sermons against the Pollution of Idolatries* links the consumption of the Eucharist to idolatrous speech. On both the title page and the first page after the introduction, we discover translations from Psalm 16: "I wyll not take the names of the ydoles in my mouth" and "I wyll not communicate with their bloody sacrifices, neyther wyll I take their names in my mouth."[70] Hovering in the background here is the Protestant revulsion for Catholic transubstantiation; as Prescott puts it, "To insist that Christ is literally on the altar from Cracow to Canterbury is to disperse and mangle him. Catholics are cannibals, or at least they think they are, if they eat God's literal flesh."[71] The danger of poetic speech, like the danger of the Eucharist, is that highly communicable collision of sensory experience and imagination; the intensely felt heft of the physical draws bodies together into subtle trains of association. Though Calvin figures this as pollution, early modern England retained the memory of an incarnational imaginary, the veritable shadow Christ's body cast not only over Byzantine icons but also over post-Reformation aesthetics. Even for our "Protestant" Spenser, who might indeed sympathize with Calvin's pronouncements on the dangers of communication, Duessa and Archimago in their final escapade suggest the same power attributed to words by their connection to the living Word consumed as sacrament. Calvin's understanding of communion, where body, word, and truth are to be concerned, is a stunning combination of monstrous flesh and saving mechanization. He asks of the idolater, "Shal the bodye then wherein the mark of Jesus Christe is printed, be polluted and defiled with so contrary, so repugnant, and so wicked abominations?" Human flesh is the substance in which "hath god engrauen . . . the armes and badges of his sonne."[72] The suffering savior becomes now the searing brand by which God marks the flesh of his flock. Skin is yet another surface printed by the machine of Reformation, as attitudes to bodies and things come under the sway of an iconoclasm eager to banish to the shadows the textures and experiences of matter.

The Legend of Holiness deploys its fascination with dark, abject matter—in spite of the moral orientation of Error, Archimago, Duessa, Orgoglio and the dragon—to tell us something about what it is to be *georgus*, a worker of and in earth. Redcrosse's virtue is not his struggle against the flesh but his struggle to *be* flesh and not an empty allegorical body: an emblem of righteousness. At the close of the legend, Duessa and Archimago have something vital to tell us: the medium is the message. By this point, Redcrosse has been assimilated to the moral triumph of his quest and Archimago's "idle force" has been momentarily defeated, so the message appears to be a melancholic disposition banished by the matrimonial festivities celebrated by the voices of angels. Appearances can be deceiving. By turning to what might have seemed to many Protestants an idolatrous tendency in poetry, Spenser turns back to what Foucault calls that "enigmatic, monotonous, stubborn, primitive being," the "ancient solidity of language as a thing inscribed in the fabric of the world." Poetry's elemental properties convey this sense of substance, which lived in Renaissance England in the shadow of Christ, in dark forests, deep in the earth, or in the flesh as the experience of vulnerability.

PART II

The Legend of Temperance

CHAPTER 3

On Not Defending Poetry: Spenser, Suffering, and the Energy of Affect

The history of poetry is a history of apology. Early modern English writers, faced with a brave new world of anxieties about the value, validity, and cultural uses of poetry, produced myriad literary apologies. Philip Sidney and Thomas Lodge defended poetry, while Thomas Heywood, Philip Massinger, and George Whetstone defended drama. In his translation of Ludovico Ariosto, John Harington not only defended poetry but also appended to *Orlando Furioso* (1591) a moral allegory. Rhyme, imitation, and classical meter were attacked and heartily defended, as were religious poetry, difficult poetry, and tragicomedy.[1] Sidney easily defends poetry against the claim that it is less true and less useful than sciences such as geometry and astronomy and professions such as law and medicine.[2] But he sees a greater challenge to poetry (one requiring a stronger defense) in the claims for the superiority of philosophy and history, which he appropriates in his defense of poetry. Poetry provides a "perfect" or "speaking picture," a clear rhetorical image that illustrates the moral lessons of philosophy and history.[3] The simultaneous publication of Sidney's work as *A Defence of Poesy* and *An Apology for Poetry* (1595) may have been an accident of history, but the slippage between apology and defense is no mere accident of usage. To defend poetry, for Sidney, is to define it as capable, by virtue of a moral force, of beating back a crowd of imposing rival claimants, each asserting a privileged access to truth and a greater capacity to represent reality. Out of this historic ethos emerges the real work of poetry: the creation of clear rhetorical images of moral truth.[4] Sidney divorces poetry from the energies in language that such clear rhetorical images never capture.[5] Such iconic, moral clarity appears ideal only when language is divorced from what makes it resonate so powerfully with bodily experience: its recalcitrant physicality, its vulnerability to time and change, and its capacity to excite and transmit affect.[6]

By not defending poetry, Edmund Spenser exposes the consequences of Sidney's heroic rhetoric of defense. In a literary tradition full of apologies, confessions, and retractions, Spenser seems never to have written one.[7] To be sure, a number of texts might appear to reflect the apologetic tone of the day: *The Shepheardes Calendar* (1579)—especially the October eclogue—with its ambiguous commentary by E. K.; the "Letter of the Authors"; and the proems to books 2, 3, and 4 of the *Faerie Queene* (1590, 1596). Yet these various metapoetic commentaries question the cultural status of the poet or discuss aspects of poetic representation; they neither defend nor excuse the practice of poetry. Spenser does respond to criticism of his own poetry at the opening of the Legend of Friendship, which begins the 1596 continuation of *The Faerie Queene.* But instead of describing or defining poetry, he defends and describes the nature of love, the misapprehension of which, he claims, has provoked his opponent's unjust remarks.

Why does Spenser deflect a defense of poetry into a defense of love? Eros was one way of disarming aggressive masculinity, as the proem to the first book of *The Faerie Queene* makes clear; the poet invokes Cupid and Venus to help him cool the rage of Mars. The heroic Sidney defends poetry at the price of restricting it to a narrow band of moral effects associated with the clarity of visual form. Spenser foregrounds what is most vital and moving about poetry by turning away from forceful visuality and locating an energy in intense experiences of physical and affective pain. This demilitarization of poetic practice releases a communicable energy rooted in the experience of human corporeality, an energy that resonates with the body and between bodies, giving poetry both its feeling of reality and its capacity to move.

Poetry has been a problem at least since Plato precisely because its reality was as questionable as the morality of its depictions; its practice was subject to charges of irrationality, irrelevancy, and immorality. Criticism was born from the act of apology provoked by such responses. "As a consequence," M. H. Abrams argued nearly half a century ago, "literary criticism had been maneuvered into a defensive stance from which it has never entirely recovered."[8] Margaret W. Ferguson, in her subsequent study of early modern defenses of poetry, takes issue with Abrams's position, yoking his desire to free literary criticism from the burden of self-explanation to an "ideal of existence in a realm where one can avoid explaining oneself to foreigners—those who may not understand, much less approve of, one's words or deeds." Her claim rests on the conviction that "only those who possess absolute power, or absolute confidence in their power and their right to it," can exempt themselves from the discourses of defense, apology, and excuse.[9] If the danger of Abram's position is that it tends toward an insular view of poetry, the danger of Ferguson's position is that it assumes an innate difficulty and indirection that make poetry the property of the more ethically aware literary critic. Despite this difference and others, both Abrams and Ferguson assent to the proposition that poetry is a problematic discourse while they also constitute its ambivalent status as a problem for critics.

What about poets or other readers? Abrams may, in his essay, link the apologetics of poetry to "the perennial concern about the clash between what poets say and what their readers believe to be true."[10] Yet he remains concerned for the status of literary critics and their criticism, as does Ferguson, although the authors she considers (including Sidney and Tasso) were poets and critics alike, as were so many practitioners of New Criticism. Abandoning the language of violence implicit in the language of defense need not lead to the isolation of poetry, poets, and literary critics from wider arenas of public concern; indeed, it may facilitate their participation in those arenas. Abrams's desire that poetry be considered "poetry and not another thing" responds to a history of rivalry stretching from Sidney's defense to New Criticism, in which poetry must vie with philosophy, history, morality, or science to claim privileged access to "truth."[11] Robert Matz reminds us that recent "skepticism about the literary could cut more than one way, that its effects are not necessarily only politically progressive, and that whatever value is still accorded the signifiers 'Renaissance' or 'literature' might need to be capitalized on as well as demystified."[12]

Of the more recent attempts to grapple with the problem of poetry's place in the world, Dana Gioia's "Can Poetry Matter?"—published first in the *Atlantic Monthly* (1991) and later in an eponymous collection of essays—contains some of the defensive tone that Abrams deplores and Ferguson requires. Gioia's effort to steer a course for poetry in a time of apparent isolation from the general public provoked controversy. The release of the second edition of his collection on its tenth anniversary coincides with his appointment as the first poet to chair the National Endowment for the Arts. For Gioia, poetry can matter if it combats the specialization and segmentation of literary audiences. It is critical, then, to maintain poetry's civic function, which lies in "improving the health of the language" of a nation by keeping it "clear and honest."[13] Citizens must not lose the "power of language" lest they become "slaves" to those who possess it.[14]

The language of defense in Abrams, Ferguson, and Gioia typifies the way the efficacy of poetry has been traditionally tied to a concatenation of power and clarity. As in Sidney's *Defence*, this notion of poetry's power already disposes us to an understanding of literature determined by a language of force linked to the privileging of iconic visuality as a signifier of rational clarity and moral self-possession. This contemporary understanding of poetic language taps into a historical ambivalence in both rhetoric and poetics about the relation between visuality and vitality. The often-cited Horatian dictum *ut pictura poesis* says that poetry derives its power from a crystalline visuality.[15] In his *Ars Poetica*, Horace claims that "less vividly is the mind stirred by what finds entrance through the ears than by what is brought before the trusty eyes, and what the spectator can see for himself."[16] Precisely this understanding of poetry's ideal visual clarity governs John Hughes's description of poetic invention in the introduction to his 1715 edition of *The Faerie Queene*.[17] Hughes refers to the "principal part of poetry" as the power of raising images or resemblances of things, giving them life and action and presenting them as it were before the eyes," and says that this power has "something in it like creation."[18] Hughes participates in the Horatian tradition that conflates "the power of raising images" and the attempt to convey "life and action," which in the rhetorical tradition are denoted by the frequently conflated terms *enargeia* and *energeia*.[19]

The triumph of Sidney's defensive poetics, with its taste for moral and visual clarity, has so colored the language of criticism as to distract us from Spenser's interest in poetry's capacity to communicate the painful vitality of lived experience. Ironically, the overflowing energy of poetry is most powerfully felt in *The Faerie Queene*, where the poem dwells on temperance, the virtue of moderation. This interest in energy, its lack and excess, appears particularly as a problem of masculinity, for if *The Faerie Queene* is a moral work, it is one to the extent that virtue, as masculinity, is of primary concern. Spenser's unique insights prove vital in a time when the dehiscence of recent approaches to early modern literature and culture makes particularly tense the rivalries that have come to define the truth of literature and its relation to other cultural forms. *The Faerie Queene* suggests that what is most real about lived experience—pain, affect, and carnality—can be best conveyed by poetic language when that language is not confused with or subjected to the language of science, history, or philosophy. I do not suggest that early modern poetry or today's criticism should have no traffic with science, history, or philosophy. Rather, I challenge the assumption that we must defend poetry by locating its value in the clarity of greater external truths, as if to save poetry from irrelevance in acts of critical rescue.

As Spenser shows us repeatedly in *The Faerie Queene*, acts of rescue are themselves complex expressions of force that affirm an ultimately destructive heroic ethos. The danger of rescuing or defending poetry, he knows, is that violence might become naturalized as a species of clarity or truth. Spenser abandons the ideal of violent clarity common to both the literary defense and to Sidney's heroic aesthetic. The rhetorical tradition provides the terms *enargeia* and *energeia* to name a distinction between visuality and vitality, between clarity and energy. A chain of association stretching from Aristotle and Quintilian to George Puttenham and Sidney reveals how an emphasis on visuality, *enargeia*, renders poetry a system of representation that restrains the energy of physical and affective experience in order to establish a moral clarity rooted in appeals to *ēthos*, or reasonable and moderate emotion. *Energeia* appeals to *pathos*, or intense and painful affect, and would become the basis of Spenser's poetics.

The Faerie Queene explores how language communicates the phenomenological reality of corporeal experience, which emerges most dynamically in the energy passing between bodies in moments of intense suffering and sympathy. Attending to the energy of affect in the experiences of suffering and sympathy in *The Faerie Queene* offers new ways of approaching Spenser's poetry, just as Spenser's poetry offers new ways of thinking about poetry's capacity to resonate with what is most material and real about experiencing ourselves as bodies living in dense social networks of affect and obligation.

The conflation of *energeia* and *enargeia* characteristic of Sidney's Horatian poetics occludes the immediacy, the physicality, of affective and bodily experience because it defines visuality as the source of a lifelike clarity that guarantees the persuasive power of language. Neither Sidney nor Horace was first to locate in the image the source of poetry's persuasive appeal. Aristotle's *Rhetoric* describes the usefulness of metaphors, or "smart sayings" notable for proportion and wit as well as for a quality he names *energeia*, which refers to activity, action, performance, force, and vigor. Yet as Aristotle introduces the term *energeia*, frequently translated as *actuality*, he evokes a similar notion, *enargeia*, which refers to clarity, distinctness, vividness, and self-evidence: "We have said that smart sayings . . . set things before the eyes. We must now explain the meaning of 'before the eyes' and what must be done to produce this. I mean that things are set before the eyes by words that signify actuality [*energeia*]."[20]

What possesses actuality, or *energeia*, sets things "before the eyes." In defining *energeia* in language (what one might call *vitality*), Aristotle conjures vivid, visual appearance, though he never uses the term *enargeia*. Thus, the efficacy of language depends solely on visual appearance.[21] Aristotle's conflation of the concepts informing the terms *energeia* and *enargeia* conditions the history of rhetoric, as reflected by later writings. The difference in spelling between *enargeia* and *energeia* is slight, and it in part explains the confusion of commentators from Aristotle to the present. The conceptual difference, however, between vitality and visuality is critical. At stake in the confusion of visuality and vitality is not merely the value of poetry but also the way we imagine language to affect an audience—either as the forceful imposition of clarity or as the evocation of a sympathetic resonance.

Like Aristotle, Longinus and Quintilian emphasize the visual qualities of language, but they also locate a fundamental sympathy at the center of effective rhetoric. In *On the Sublime*, Longinus describes *energeia* as an immediacy of urgency in language that "introduce[s] events in past time as happening in the present moment" and "makes the audience feel themselves set in the thick of danger."[22] *Energeia* turns a narrative of distant events into the experience of present immediacy. According to Quintilian, "The heart of the matter as regards arousing emotions, so far as I can see, lies in being moved by them oneself."[23] While both Longinus and Quintilian stress the value of sympathetic participation, Quintilian requires that this emotional state be evoked solely by visual means, for by bringing a scene before the eyes, one can not only harness powerful emotion but also put to good use the "mental vice[s]" of idle daydreaming and wishful thinking. Only by harnessing powerful affect and presenting clear images does one assuage anxieties about the capacity of language for idle daydreaming and wishful thinking. Yet Quintilian also admits, "Emotions after all are not in our power."[24] Successful speakers must be moved in order to move, but they must harness the potentially overwhelming energy of affect, bending it to their will. The iconic visuality of rhetorical clarity enables the conversion of unbounded vitality to effective spectacle, of *energeia* to *enargeia*.

The visuality prized by Aristotle, Horace, Quintilian, and Longinus provides the means by which the vitality of affect is harnessed, and this visual clarity is more compatible with reasonable, moderate *ēthos* than with the disturbing energies of *pathos*. This conversion of energy to force and of vitality to visuality is characteristic of ways of thinking about poetry in early modernity, ways from which Spenser deviates. Though Puttenham's *The Arte of English Poesie* (1589) distinguishes between two varieties of "ornament"—*enargeia* ("outward shew") and *energeia* (what is "inwardly working a stirre to the mind")[25]—both terms are overdetermined by the framing visual concept of ornament and by the notion of force, what Puttenham calls "strong and vertuous operation."[26]

Masculine power, the "forcibleness of the writer," would define *energeia* for Sidney, too, and would be linked necessarily in his *Defence* to an understanding of poetry as essentially visual: a "speaking picture—with this end, to teach and delight."[27] "Heart-ravishing knowledge" comes of poetry, which is the "first light giver to ignorance" and allows one to overcome the limitation of nature and escape the morally degenerating "clayey lodgings" of the human body. Sidney celebrates the way truth may be "figured forth by the speaking picture of poesy," noting in particular the way in which good writing produces iconic figures: "wisdom and temperance in Ulysses and Diomedes, valour in Achilles . . . and, to fall lower, the Terentian Gnatho and our Chaucer's Pandar so expressed that we now use their names to signify their trades."[28] He imagines poetry as a force that produces vivid figurations, near personifications, which solidify mobile affects and desires into character types designed to instruct readers in moral virtue. Poetry, in Sidney's paradigm, evokes the persuasions of Quintilian's *ēthos*, which are "recommended primarily by goodness: not only mild and calm, but usually attractive and polite, and pleasing and delightful to listeners."[29]

Spenser struggled to develop a poetic style that would resonate with affective and bodily experience and tap the energies of *pathos*. He could do this only by circumventing anxieties about the legitimacy of poetry that restricted the range of poetry to defensive rhetoric, moderated affect, visual clarity, or moral rectitude.

One of the more recent manifestations of anxiety about the function of poetry coincides with the critical return to the distinction between *enargeia* and *energeia* in the influential work of Stephen Greenblatt. Greenblatt associates *enargeia* with rhetoric, with which "only a reality-effect is conjured and nothing more."[30] *Energeia* gives birth to the term *energy*, which Greenblatt describes in his influential *Shakespearean Negotiations*, subtitled *The Circulation of Social Energy*.[31] In this scheme, the social provides the animating energy for a literary work otherwise composed of mere surface reality effects.[32] Though Catherine Gallagher and Greenblatt's *Practicing New Historicism* reserves a good deal of "piety" for the literary,[33] the literary is only ever that through which the "sweet familiar light of the everyday" shines.[34] Even the modernist poets to which *Practicing New Historicism* has recourse conflate vitality and visuality: Ezra Pound's "Luminous detail" and William Carlos Williams's interest in "the strange phosphorous of the life" seem to find *energeia* only in *enargeia*.[35]

Attuned to the seductions of luminous clarity, Spenser turned his attention from *enargeia*, which is aligned with the moral clarity of *ēthos*, to *energeia*, which is aligned with the affective resonance of *pathos*. For him, the value of poetry derives neither from its moral and mimetic properties nor from its ability to reflect or refer to social experience but, rather, from its capacity to convey the vitality of bodies endowed with pain, affect, a vulnerability to change, and a capacity for motion. This concern for the economy, or flow, of energy that lends materiality its feeling of reality Spenser called temperance.

While Spenser opens the Legend of Temperance (book 2 of *The Faerie Queene*) with what appears to be a defense of poetry, he veers away from the pleasing poetic surfaces that lead to moral education and that Sidney justifies in his *Defence*. Spenser's proem stakes a larger claim for the material reality of the poetic imagination. Faced with those who deem his "antique history" little more than "th'aboundance of an ydle braine" or a "painted forgery," Spenser shifts from a strategy of defense to one of redefinition. The problem of the believability of this poetic endeavor rests in its failure to appear as a visual object of knowledge. Thus, he may "vaunt" the "happy land of Faery . . . yet no where [does it] show"; he may "vouch antiquities," but "no body can know" them (2.proem.1). The veracity of Faeryland is fallaciously tied to visual verification, according to this proem: "Why then should witlesse man so much misweene / That nothing is but that which he hath seene?" (2.proem.3). The much noted examples of "great Regions" that, like Spenser's Faeryland, the reader will also have never seen in person are "Indian *Peru*" and "fruitfullest *Virginia*" along with the "*Amazons* huge riuer," which the reader will not have "in venturous vessell measured" (2.proem.2). These exotic locales appear as objects of novelty and discovery but refuse to come fully into view despite being subject to conquest. They are, rather, likened to other such worlds, whether on the moon or elsewhere:

> What if in euery other starre vnseene
> Of other worldes he happily should heare?
> He wonder would much more, yet such to some appeare.
>
> Of faery lond yet if he more inquyre,
> By certeine signes here sett in sondrie place
> He may it fynd; ne let him then admyre,
> But yield his sence to bee too blunt and bace
> That no'te without an hound fine footing trace.
> (2.proem.3–4)

"Faery lond" defies precise location and measure; to approach it, one must seek with different senses. Spenser here asks his reader to abandon the desire for visually objectified knowledge—the real as what is seen and empirically verified. Whereas visuality is tied to the violent discovery of the New World, hearing and scent offer an approach to the imaginative landscapes of Faeryland, which is palpable in the rhymes that echo through the third and fifth stanzas ("heare," "spheare," "appeare," and "eare").

Even as Spenser compliments Elizabeth, describing his Faeryland as the "faire mirhour" in which she might see the "antique ymage" of her "great auncestry" (2.proem.4), he swerves away from the paralyzing visuality of her appearance. His task is to "enfold / in couert vele, and wrap in shadowes light" the violent brilliance of Gloriana, by which one might be "dazled" (2.proem.5). This gesture might well seem to be little more than the parlaying of a defense of allegory into a compliment to the queen. On the contrary, I suggest that the shift away from violent visuality toward the slender substances of covert veils and shadowy light ("clowdily enwrapped" is one description of allegory in the "Letter of the Authors") signals an interest not only in the subtle materiality of poetic language but also in poetry of a different sense.[36] In *The Faerie Queene*, antique images are always in danger of resolving into painted forgeries or idle portraits, which is a concern, as critics have pointed out, for Protestant iconoclasts.[37] More important, however, is that objectified, reified images lack the vitality of what Spenser describes earlier as poetry's ideal: the "matter of iust memory" (2.proem.1). Memory, here, is not a frozen portrait of the past, like the monuments and images that will be referred to frequently in the Legend of Temperance. It is something much more like Augustine's *memoria*, which refers equally to the cognitive activity of consciousness and to the mobility and physicality of memories that swarm about, forcing themselves into consciousness.[38] Spenser's antiquity contains Henri Bergson's *élan vital*, which is simultaneously "the continual elaboration of the absolutely new" and "a persistence of the past in the present."[39] Faced with the age of the new science and the New World (both emblematized by discovery—the violent visuality of knowledge, cognition, and exploration), Spenser seeks a different futurity in an occluded mythic past, one neither historical nor empirical, known as antiquity. This past is what he refers to as Faeryland. He locates there a vitality that poetry, working with different senses, can convey when it is free of the organizing violence of moral clarity.

Yet the seemingly even-tempered poetics of *ēthos* recommended by Quintilian's rhetoric and Sidney's *Defence* has governed almost exclusively the reception of the second book of Spenser's *Faerie Queene*, which is also the section of *The Faerie Queene* most explicitly concerned with the problem of aesthetic experience. The Legend of Temperance seems to present itself as a work in which moderation and moral rectitude govern our understanding of the role of poetry. Here we apparently find Milton's "sage and serious" Spenser,[40] whose patron of temperance, Guyon, experiences the moral dangers of this world in two primary manifestations: the Cave of Mammon and the garden of Acrasia. Critics, tending to take Milton's directive, have been captivated by the state of Guyon's soul in his temptation by Mammon, by the care and detail in Spenser's allegory of the temperate body at the House of Alma, and by the temperate treaty making between Medina and her extreme sisters, Elissa and Perissa. Mostly, critics have been preoccupied with the Bower of Bliss—perhaps the most famous episode in *The Faerie Queene* and, as Greenblatt puts it, "one of the great cruxes of English Renaissance literature."[41] But to the extent that the Bower of Bliss narrows our understanding of the aesthetic to the pleasure of fashioning or appreciating images, it reflects, too, the limitations of present-day discussions of aesthetic work, which fail sufficiently to displace beauty, pleasure, and truth as the central components of aesthetic experience. The spectacular violence and visuality of the Bower of Bliss, its position as a great crux of Renaissance literature, distract us from darker and more powerful poetic possibilities, which are like the "couert vele" to which Spenser turns as, in the proem to the Legend of Temperance, he turns away form the blinding brilliance of Elizabeth.

When we move beyond images of moral rectitude or immoral excess and attend to expressions of a quantitative language of energy and enervation, we discover that the true concern of this book is not with rectitude or with abstinence but with economy, or the regulation of energy. The concerns of monetary economy are certainly present in the Legend of Temperance, not least of all in the distribution of property in Guyon's encounter with Medina or in the temptations of the cave of Mammon. But the primary operations of economy in the book occur at the level of the body, where the distribution of pain, energy, and affect are of central concern.

As Max Weber has remarked, the early modern period shows a surprising "combination of religious control of life and an extremely well developed business sense."[42] The call to work that Weber identifies as central to Protestant theology and practice, with its "negative attitude . . . toward all sensual and *emotional* elements in culture and subjective religiosity" and its "fundamental rejection of every kind of culture of the senses,"[43] indicates that the work of primitive accumulation, the activity that for Marx characterized the transitional period after feudalism when massive social and political changes prepared the way for modern capitalism,[44] also occurs at the level of the flesh. If *ēthos* is to be maintained, bodily affect and energy must be available for practical use, and pain must be made to signify and converted to usable labor. That is, pain and affect remain a problem for the notion of economy. Weber notes that "emotion *can* experience such a heightening that religious feeling can take on a truly hysterical character and then achieve precisely the opposite *effect* of that sober and austere discipline into which the systematic 'holy life' of the Puritan takes a man, namely a weakening of those 'inhibitions' which support the rational personality of the Calvinist against 'emotional states.' This emotional heightening occurs through the alteration . . . between semi-sensuous states of religious exaltation and periods of nervous exhaustion when God seems 'remote.'"[45]

The problem of painful affect is the problem of vitality, most notable in states of excess energy and extreme enervation, both of which disturb the stable economies that allow the Protestant subject to serve the spirit of capitalism. The Legend of Temperance stages the failure of this poetics of *ēthos*, which, in accordance with Sidney's dictates, would work in the service of this economic agenda. We see the flesh anatomized and scoured of the taint of carnality in the House of Alma. We see pleasure annihilated in the Bower of Bliss. We see Guyon chain and bind the personifications Occasion and Furor, which are, respectively, the trigger of intense affect and its extreme manifestation. In each case, allegorical representations, founded on the principle of *enargeia*, visually and violently objectify affective and bodily experience.[46] Yet specters of perverse sensation, Meleager and his army, assault the House of Alma and nearly overrun the castle. The destruction of the Bower of Bliss is extreme in its intemperance and presents a famously dissatisfying conclusion to the Legend of Temperance. The binding of Furor and Occasion presents a desperate doubling: they are first objectified as personifications and then bound in chains by Guyon, who later learns the futility of attempting to contain them. Like alternating currents, pairs of male characters—Mordant and Verdant (whose names mean "death-giving" and "life-giving") and Pyrochles and Cymochles (who represent fiery irascibility and watery uxoriousness)—suggest an exchange of energy, as does the culminating scene of the Bower of Bliss, which finds Acrasia hovering over Verdant, sucking "spright," or energy, from his eyes (2.12.73). Spenser's concern for energy as it materializes in a poetics of painful affect is especially evident in two episodes: Guyon's encounter with the dying Amavia and the sojourn in the cave of Mammon, which causes Guyon's subsequent collapse.

In the explanatory "Letter of the Authors," Guyon's call to work is clear. The Palmer appears at Gloriana's court with the babe Ruddymane (red or bloody hand), seeking a knight to defeat the foul enchantress Acrasia, who is responsible for the deaths of the child's parents. In the actual Legend of Temperance, however, Guyon's calling is less clear. First Guyon is distracted by a spectacle of false suffering engineered by the recently escaped Archimago and Duessa. The former narrates a tale of woe and rape that the latter acts out in spectacular fashion, complete with sobbing and "garments rent" (2.1.13). Guyon's zeal for righteous combat nearly ends with a battle with Redcrosse, the Knight of Holiness, in a well-known and nearly disastrous passing of the torch from one titular knight to the next. But Guyon's encounter with real and unbounded suffering (as opposed to a prepackaged narrative or a striking image) comes as the surprise of a voice echoing in the wood. In two stanzas of complaint, we learn, with Guyon and the Palmer, who merely wait and listen, of the woe of Amavia, who has lost her husband, Mordant, to the wiles of Acrasia, who seduced and then poisoned him. Amavia is left with a corpse, a child, and unmanageable grief. Following this complaint, Spenser offers a startling aural portrait of her suicide:

> With that a deadly shrieke she forth did throw,
> That through the wood reechoed againe,
> And after gaue a grone so deepe and low,
> That seemd her tender heart was rent in twaine,
> Or thrild with point of thorough piercing paine;
> As gentle Hynd, whose sides with cruell steele
> Through launched, forth her bleeding life does raine,
> Whiles the sad pang approching shee doth feele,
> Brayes out her latest breath, and vp her eies doth seele.
> (2.1.38)

The details of the passage derive from what is heard, not from what is seen. The sealing of the eyes that here signifies death also signifies the shift to senses other than the visual, a shift that the proem foregrounds.

Once again, the figure of the trail to be followed by scent appears; in the proem, readers must abandon their sight and rely on the sensitive nose of the hound to find their way to Faeryland. Just previously in this canto, however, Archimago promises to show Guyon the way to the purported rapist Redcrosse, "as sure, as hound / The stricken Deare doth chaleng by the bleeding wound" (2.1.12). Just a few cantos later, Belphoebe encounters the foolish pair Trompart and Braggadocchio as she pursues her wounded quarry, "a bleeding Hynde, / Whose right haunch earst [her] stedfast arrow strake" (2.3.32). Archimago and Belphoebe present figures of violent predation, but Belphoebe is the most visually iconic figure in the book (her blazon, the longest in *The Faerie Queene*, takes up eleven stanzas) as well as a figure of militant virginity whose violence is unerringly precise (she strikes the "right haunch").

Opposed to Archimago's lust for violence and deception or Belphoebe's commanding visual appearance (a force as potent as her bow), Amavia's suffering unleashes a cascade of sensory experience that resounds through the Legend of Temperance. Her pain echoes throughout the episode despite the efforts of Guyon and the Palmer to contain the flood of affect that pours forth like gore from her wounds. The two men, presenting a stern masculinity, remain most concerned with how the iconic qualities of the scene can be used to construct vivid moral portraits. Indeed, though sound draws Guyon down from his horse, "rush[ing] into the thick," he only seems to see the scene before him, noting not even a woman or person but a "sad pourtraict / Of death and dolour." While the blood of her wound ("from which forth gusht a stream of goreblood thick") suggests the liquidity and tactility of affect, the visual returns repeatedly to contain the overwhelming grief of the scene (2.1.39). This containment is particularly evident in the stanza that depicts the babe Ruddymane, who rests in the dying Amavia's lap, innocently sporting in blood as his mother exsanguinates. The stanza begins with the phrase "Pittifull spectacle of deadly smart" and closes with "Pittifull spectacle, as euer eie did vew" (2.1.40). It is as if, faced with the babe's grim and bloody game, the stanza constructs a charm to ward off its horror. The gush of affect is organized into a spectacle that is thus more bearable, even though it is also the most "Pittifull spectacle, as euer eie did vew." The assertion of the spectatorial "eye" is also the assertion of the subjective "I," as the aural pun suggests. Guyon attempts to organize himself psychically as he attempts to contain, visually, Amavia's overwhelming experience.

As the narrative struggles to convert Amavia's *energeia* into a sentimental spectacle of *enargeia*, Guyon holds a firm eye (and I) before the scene and remains oddly unmoved by this wounded woman. He responds more to the visual scene of the dead Mordant, in a moment of perilous identification. This "dead corse of an armed knight" (2.1.41) displays a smiling, cheerful vitality. Mordant is described in the same stanza as possessing "ruddy lips," "rosy red" cheeks, "the freshest flowre of lusty hed," and the very "blossome of his age." Guyon seizes up, faced with a figure of masculinity that alternates uncannily between life and death, between ruination and vitality, between masculinity and effeminacy. In response, Guyon's "hart gan wexe as starke, as marble stone" and "all his sences seemd berefte attone" (2.1.42). Mordant's alternation between energy and enervation paralyzes Guyon. Indeed, the specter of vulnerability to pain seems more threatening here than the potentially effeminizing nature of pleasure present in Mordant's flowery appearance. Guyon struggles out of his paralysis when "ruth and fraile affection did constraine, / His stout courage to stoupe, and shew his inward paine" (2.1.42). This concession to vulnerability is, however, also an attempt to externalize and "show" or objectify "inward" pain visually.

Guyon's attempt to objectify and neutralize suffering prompts an odd act of rescue, as he draws the blade from Amavia's heart and encourages Amavia to divest herself of her grief in a narrative that will make sense of her otherwise incomprehensible pain. Amavia, whom he addresses as "the ymage . . . of ruefull pitty" (2.1.44), will presumably gain from this act of rescue, for "he oft finds present helpe, who does his griefe impart" (2.1.46). Guyon furthermore promises "to compas [her] reliefe, / Or die with you in sorrow, and partake your griefe" (2.1.48). Despite this promise of heroic action, what he actually offers her is the cleansing power of narration. After he hauls the half-dead woman back to life to tell her story, she obliges him with a narrative and a swift death, which leaves plenty of time for the Knight of Temperance and his guide to clean up.

As if the elimination of Amavia and Mordant were not enough to chase the disturbing taint of *pathos* from the Legend of Temperance, Guyon begins to moralize furiously, addressing the Palmer. "Old Sire," he begins, "Behold the ymage of mortalitie, / And feeble nature cloth'd with fleshly tyre" (2.1.57). The moralizing tag aids the visual objectification of what was once a vitally flowing scene. One must avoid "melting" in pleasure or "frying" in pain, that alternating current Sigmund Freud describes as "mysterious" to the principle of economy.[47] According to the Palmer, we must instead champion temperance, with its power to "measure out a mean." After tears, vows of revenge, and the "due rites and dolorous lament," the Palmer and Guyon believe they have "The end of their sad Tragedie vptyde" (2.2.1). This phrasing ambiguously translates the pain of Mordant and Amavia into a tidy tragedy, a narrative now possessed by Guyon and the Palmer.

The painful matter of Mordant, Amavia, and Ruddymane soon becomes a moral exemplum presented for the pleasure of its clarity. In the following canto, once Guyon has helped make peace among Medina and her sisters and their consorts, Medina requests the "dolefull tale" so "that we may pitty such vnhappie bale, / And learne from pleasures poyson to abstaine" (2.2.45). Guyon obliges this request for a moral exemplum and in so doing delivers more pleasure than pain:

> When of his pitteous tale he end did make;
> Whilst with delight of that he wisely spake,
> Those guestes, beguyled, did beguyle their eyes
> Of kindly sleepe, that did them ouertake.
>
> (2.2.46)

Amavia and Mordant are barely in the grave by the time they have become a bedtime story to delight the sleepy guests of Medina's castle. Does this "delight" stem from the narration or from the wise, moral conclusion? From what does this beguilement derive, the enchanting powers of narration or the comfortable shelter of the castle? The closing moment crystallizes a critique of Sidney's temperate poetics of *ēthos*, which delights and instructs, coating a galling moral lesson with the pleasurable veneer of poetry. For not only does this tactic grossly use the suffering of others, it also encourages a sentimental pleasure in compassionating others for their suffering, which is perilously close to a sadistic pleasure *in* their suffering. As Max Horkheimer and Theodor Adorno argue, "Amusement has always meant putting things out of mind, forgetting suffering."[48]

The painful affect that pours from the wounded heart of Amavia and stains the tiny hands of Ruddymane appears deep in the subterranean world of Mammon, god not only of wealth but also of the "world and worldlings" (2.7.8). Worldly economy is and is not of concern in the cave of Mammon, for while the trappings of that economy are everywhere, wealth and ambition are never real temptations for Guyon, who does little in this episode but disapprove.[49] Mammon's periodic offers of wealth, power, and the hand of his daughter, Philotime ("love of honor"), are punctuated blandly and sententiously by Guyon's steadfast refusals. Of the many strange experiences of Mammon's underworld, the most important for Guyon present the temptation of intense affect.

In the cave of Mammon, the desire to damn the flow of affective energy appears in a series of personifications. Guyon first encounters ones of dark affect: Pain, Strife, Revenge, Despite, Hate, Sorrow, Shame, and others. If the point of personification is both to embody and to contain mobile affect, one pair is of particular note for remaining mobile and affecting:

And ouer them sad horror with grim hew,
  Did alwaies sore, beating his yron wings;
  And after him Owles and Night-rauens flew,
  The hatefull messengers of heauy things,
  Of death and dolor telling sad tidings;
  Whiles sad *Celeno*, sitting on a clifte,
  A song of bale and bitter sorrow sings,
  That hart of flint a sonder could haue rifte:
Which hauing ended, after him she flyeth swifte.
(2.7.23)

Despite the aversiveness of this pair, something strangely touching remains in the suggestion of an erotic narrative, as if they reprise the plot of Mordant and Amavia. Celeno's song opens out of wrenching grief, like Amavia's "rent" heart, to break even the sternest "heart of flint." The two figure the persistent physicality ("heavy things") and mobility ("after him she flyeth swift") of affective energy.

While Celeno and Horror present the circulation of painful, bodily affect, Disdain presents a portrait of Guyon's virulent temper and his apparent invulnerability to affect. Disdain is a "sturdie villein":

> And he himselfe was all of yron mould,
> Yet had both life and sence, and well could weld
> That cursed weapon, when his cruell foes he queld.
> (2.7.41)

The impressive figure of Disdain combines invulnerability ("For nothing might abash the villein bold, / Ne mortall steele emperce his miscreated mould" [2.7.42]), anger, and need for restraint ("*Mammon* did his hasty hand withhold" [2.7.42]), making him another Guyon. At the opening of the Legend of Temperance, Guyon appears as "A goodly knight, all armd in harnesse meete, / That from his head no place appeared to his feete" (2.1.5). Even as he resists immoderate affect, his sojourn demonstrates that the temptation of the cave of Mammon is *pathos* and that Spenser succumbs willingly.

While Guyon, preferring emotional abstinence and militant temperance, may refuse to participate in the active, physical energy of affect, his much noted collapse outside the cave (after three days without food, drink, or rest) conveys negatively, as deprivation and exhaustion, the fundamental physicality of his body, which he studiously ignores. His "vitall powres gan wexe both weake and wan" (2.7.65) as his "life" "flit[s] away out of her nest" like a sad Celeno (2.7.66). Spenser demonstrates his interest in the flux and flow of energy, which endows the body with vitality and motion, rather than in the triumphant exercise of force. Indeed, deprivation renders the otherwise violent Guyon a site of compassion, as a glorious angel manifests over his prone body like a pulse of lyric energy:

> Beside his head there satt a faire young man,
> Of wondrous beauty and of freshest yeares,
> Whose tender bud to blossome new began,
> And flourish faire aboue his equall peares;
> His snowy front curled with golden heares,
> Like *Phoebus* face adornd with sunny rayes,
> Diuinely shone, and two sharpe winged sheares,
> Decked with diuerse plumes, like painted Iayes,
> Were fixed at his backe, to cut his ayery wayes.
> (2.8.5)

In the angel coexist *energeia*, in his youthful, flowery vigor, and *enargeia*, in his spectacular appearance as a figure of Apollonian brightness and martial prowess. The violence of *enargeia* is amply figured in the angel's form as well as in his mission. Like the angel who defends the aged Raimondo in Torquato Tasso's *Gerusalemme liberata*,[50] Spenser's angel has been sent by God "Against foule feends to aide vs militant / They for us fight, they watch and dewly ward" (2.8.2). Angels demonstrate a selfless love that occurs here in a defensive posture.

But just as the angel arrives, seeming to embody a heroic *ēthos*, he abandons his militancy. Though the angel bristles with armaments, he is also likened to a figure that echoes throughout the 1590 *Faerie Queene*, an unarmed Cupid:

> When hauing laid his cruell bow away,
> And mortall arrowes, wherewith he doth fill
> The world with murderous spoiles and bloody pray,
> With his faire mother he him dights to play.
>
> (2.8.6)

In a passage reminiscent of the proem to the Legend of Holiness, which seeks to disarm the violence and cruelty of Mars, the angel shifts from holy warrior to Venus's darling. He vows "euermore [to] succour, and defend" Guyon (2.8.8) yet departs immediately after making this promise, leaving the comatose Guyon in the care of the Palmer, who proves useless against the Saracen knights charging to despoil the vulnerable body.

Despite the assigned role of angels in the Legend of Temperance, their function encompasses compassionate witness rather than militant defense. Even as they are introduced at the opening of the eighth canto, their mission is suffused with *pathos*:

> And is there care in heauen? and is there loue
> In heauenly spirits to these creatures bace,
> That may compassion of their euilles moue?
> There is: else much more wretches were the cace
> Of men then beasts.
>
> (2.8.1)

While God's mercy provides human beings with the protection of angels, angels display a capacity to be moved, through compassion, to manifest materially. One might translate this canto's question, "And is there care in heaven?" as "Do angels have bodies that experience affect?"

The answer is emphatically yes. Without compassion, men would be worse than beasts, and it is the beastlike nature of Guyon, reduced to a lump of barely vital flesh, that evokes the care of the angel that hovers over him in sympathetic vibration. When Guyon is least active, most prone, he is most human in his vulnerability to the experience of being flesh. He is, briefly, a location of sympathy rather than a personification of moral disdain.

What else might this angelic apparition signify? The questions one might ask of his manifestation in this startling scene are those one might ask of poetry. Is the angel the blinding light of a truth that shines thought the limited body? Is he the force of truth of poetry? Is the angel, as poetry, useless beauty, transcendent spirit, or cloying sentimentality? Is the angel, like the lyric in Adorno's modernity, a fetish that, at best, exposes the workings of a fetishism? Is poetry a violent compulsion or a decadent spectacle? Or is poetry really the prone body of Guyon in need of defense from those who rush to despoil it? Does Arthur's violent magnificence defend or supplant the compassionate *pathos* of the angel and the vulnerable physicality of the collapsed Guyon?

Like questions about the nature of angels, questions about the nature of poetry are more easily posed than answered. Their difficulty makes the attempt to address them all the more necessary in the shadow of a new millennium, when we ask ourselves, yet again, how poetry matters to and functions in a world of violent action where clarity and force are valued over complexity and experience. Spenser's angel may function most usefully in being heroically useless to Guyon. Despite his militant trappings, the angel serves no heroic function, as if he could draw poetry away from the language of offense and defense, in which one must choose among equally unsavory roles: the moralistic Palmer, the despoiling infidels, or even the magnificent Arthur, whose virtue in *The Faerie Queene* is as blinding as it is violent. The angel hovers over Guyon as an embodiment of the sympathy one piece of flesh may feel for another—a sympathy that resonates at the frequency at which poetry also resonates.

In the landscape of the Legend of Temperance, the angel manifests the vitality and physicality of *pathos* and thus must be apprehended by those other senses that designate the difference between Spenser's Faeryland and Spenser's England. Spenserian poetics makes available a vitality of material experience otherwise occluded by the clarity and truth that violence comes to be known as. In the midst of the most temperate domain in the Legend of Temperance, the Castle of Alma, Spenser makes this apparent. Before dinner, Guyon and Arthur are given books—a history of Britain for Arthur and a history of Faeryland for Guyon. The former takes up a narrative in which the chaos and brutality of history resolve occasionally into stability: "Braue moniments remaine, which yet that land enuies" (2.10.21). Yet the heroic history of England proliferates violence. The narrative Arthur reads asserts consistently and defensively that memory lives on "though carcas sleepe in rest" (2.10.43). Faced with the warring instability and "doleful" monuments of Arthur's England, Spenser turns again to Faeryland (and I think here we learn why Guyon is a fairy):

> But *Guyon* all this while his booke did read,
> Ne yet has ended: for it was a great
> And ample volume, that doth far excead
> My leasure, so long leaues here to repeat:
> It told, how first *Prometheus* did create
> A man, of many partes from beasts deryu'd,
> And then stole fire from heuen, to animate
> His worke, for which he was by *Ioue* depryu'd
> Of life him selfe, and hart-strings of an Ægle ryu'd.
> (2.10.70)

Spenser's Faeryland is best experienced with senses that do not rely on the violence of moral or rational clarity. Prometheus represents what Adonis will represent in the Legend of Chastity: not clanging, continual war but the experience of a painful and creative vitality providing the spark that turns an endless monument into a living book, leaving behind community rather than corpses. Spenser's poetry asks us to participate in the painful experience of animation and in the vitality that inheres in the opacity of living flesh, which resists the clarity we would bring as we define and defend poetry.

In *The Faerie Queene* we are continually invited to feel the physical sympathy, the affective resonance, awakened whenever we make a contact with a vitality central to lived experience, a vitality Spenser found most palpable in moments of intense suffering. This vitality cannot be perceived as an object, as something separate from experience; it can be known only when felt materially as the pain of animation that produces sympathetic resonance. *The Faerie Queene* offers its readers what early modern rhetoric and poetics referred to as *energeia*, which Spenser conceived of as the energy of experiencing human corporeality in pleasure and in pain: an experience embodied in a physicality uniquely available to poetry. Poetry imagines its way to the real so as not to objectify it. Efforts to define what poetry is and to defend it as useful have, in the tradition of Sidney's *Defence*, often looked for *enargeia*, proceeding on the assumption that the "power" of poetry persists in clear perception and expression. But if poetry, as Spenser would have it, runs beneath all clear perception and resonates with the connective tissue of affective and corporeal experience, then all efforts to defend poetry must, fortunately, fail.

CHAPTER 4

Boy Toys and Liquid Joys: Pleasure and Power in the Bower of Bliss

Early in Edmund Spenser's *The Faerie Queene*, the Redcrosse Knight, just having departed the House of Pride, rests by a fountain "Disarmed all of yron-coted Plate" (1.7.2). The duplicitous Duessa will soon discover him in this vulnerable state, as will the giant Orgoglio, who defeats Redcrosse largely as a result of his separation from Una. Though his companion dwarf warns him away from the House of Pride, with its parading vices and rotting foundations, Redcrosse's moral and psychic states justify his defeat at the hands of the giant, who finds him "Pourd out in loosnesse on the grassy grownd" (1.7.7). Spenser, however, takes the extra time to explain Redcrosse's lassitude. The fountain from which he drinks bubbles up from a mythic substrate, for in these waters dwells a nymph suffering from the curse of Phoebe. Having wearied during a hunt and rested, she was fixed to the spot: "her waters wexed dull and slow / And all that drinke thereof, do faint and feeble grow" (1.7.5). After Redcrosse drinks his "chearefull bloud in fayntnes chill did melt" (1.7.6).

It would be easy to read this upwelling mythographic moment as a concretization and a condemnation of Redcrosse's moral situation. However, the fountain remains, as either a narrative or allegorical detail, superfluous. Superfluity is precisely its point, in as much as these episodes are concerned with the excess and scarcity of flows of pleasure and energy. That is, the fountain adumbrates the larger network of watery signifiers at the heart of the Legend of Temperance. Before Redcrosse drinks of the fountain, he sits by its waters, and

> Hee feedes vpon the cooling shade, and bayes
>   His sweatie forehead in the breathing wynd,

> Which through the trembling leaues full gently playes
> Wherein the chearefull birds of sundry kynd
> Doe chaunt sweet musick, to delight his mynd
>
> (1.7.3)

The site of the fountain becomes a *locus ameonus* prefiguring the Bower of Bliss, the destruction of which is the apparent moral telos of the book. Redcrosse at the fountain becomes the site of an exchange of fluids at once erotic and poetic. At the moment of his greatest moral lapse, his greatest susceptibility to dangerous pleasures, Redcrosse is also most receptive to aesthetic experience. As wind passes through the branches of trees and the throats of birds making song, water passes through Redcrosse's body, making his body like a poetic instrument. Redcrosse's experience of liquidity requires him to set aside the signifiers of heroic masculinity that confirm the labor of his quest and convert the energies of his body to violent force; his enervation exposes this appropriation and his abandoned armor serves to concretize the process. As he disarms and experiences this morally questionable liquidity, Redcrosse experiences his body as sensuous and sensible flesh.

This chapter examines the pleasurable liquidity that confounds Redcrosse in the Legend of Holiness and that appears with increasing prominence in the Legend of Temperance, which is that part of *The Faerie Queene* most explicitly concerned with the validity of aesthetic and sexual enjoyment and which features extraordinary figures of excessive pleasure. While James Carscallen has pointed out the way "water tempering wine" constitutes one of a number of emblems of appropriate temperance, we encounter more frequently characters who embody the sensual and censurable qualities of water: the uxorious Cymochles whose heroism is diminished by his lust, the loose Phaedria who ferries knights among the wandering isles, and the enchantress Acrasia who seduces men and appears quite vividly in the poem soaked in the sweat of her sordid play.[1] "Wanton toys" and "lascivious boys" lurk behind almost every bush against a backdrop of "liquid joys" and a host of tempting nymphs and sirens. Given Guyon's quest, the defeat of the irrationally intemperate Acrasia, it is easy to dismiss these liquid figures as obvious villains in the reductive moral landscape of allegorical romance. Yet the Legend of Temperance lingers over a series of disarmed, pleasured male bodies, forcing the reader to ask why Spenser explores masculine pleasure so expansively in a work of apparently unwavering moral purpose and what governs the relationship between the pleasures of poetry (and the pleasured male body) and the imperatives of moral, heroic poetry. Such questions lead us inevitably to the legend's infamous conclusion, the destruction of the Bower of Bliss, which serves as a controversial touchstone for understanding the relationship between aesthetic pleasure and the exercise of power in *The Faerie Queene*.

Although Guyon never experiences Redcrosse's vulnerability to pleasure at the fountain, such capacity for corporeal experience is critical for Spenser's understanding of Temperance. Indeed, for all that such vulnerability contradicts the moral rectitude of Guyon, the titular knight of Temperance who destroys the Bower of Bliss, it is openness to the transformative powers of pleasure that Spenser emphasizes in his account of Temperance. Joshua Scodel distills the representative critical view of the Bower of Bliss when he argues that "Spenser depicts laborious struggle against one's fallen nature and the temptations to which it is prone as a necessary part of virtue." Indeed, such Spenserian "temperance demands laborious action inimical to pleasurable idleness and the erotic excess with which it was so often associated."[2] Guyon and the Palmer become, in Scodel's view, representatives of Spenser's "eclectic synthesis of classical and Christian elements," one that elides Aristotle's distinction between continence (experiencing but resisting pleasure) and temperance (not experiencing pleasure, which is contrary to reason) by struggling heroically against all pleasure as incontinent excess. Once we disentangle Spenser's poetic perspective from the wrathful Guyon and the moralistic Palmer, we can see that the concern of the Legend of Temperance is neither the heroic struggle against pleasure nor the reasonable moderation of pleasure. Spenser's true interest in temperance is in championing the capacity to be vulnerable to experience, a capacity under siege due to the perception that such vulnerability connoted an immoral and effeminate failure to assume the mantle of proper masculinity. We witness, then, in the Legend of Temperance a thorough critique of an ideology of temperance embodied by Guyon and the Palmer, who model the moderation of affect and the expropriation of energy by which heroic subjects are alienated from their own bodies and dedicated, quite violently, to the cause of virtue. Such a critique enables Spenser to ask how the energies and impulses of the body might appear in the abeyance of the shaping force of martial violence, which secures the stability of a civilized order represented by heroic masculinity. Pleasure, which counteracts masculine martial violence, is critical to Spenser's sense of the lived experience of corporeality, and the key to understanding the transformative possibilities of such experience was the intimate interlacing of poetic and corporeal pleasure in the history of literature. Spenser intervenes in this history by creating and destroying the Bower of Bliss in order to witness how the dangerous and unacknowledged pleasures of heroic violence (articulated as the laborious struggle for virtue) occlude a Spenserian sense of the aesthetic that fuses the vitality of lived corporeal experience with the liquidity of sensory experience.

Although the language of delight and delectation saturates the history of poetry, responses to literary pleasures are characterized by obvious ambivalence. For all the seductive allure of enjoyment, pleasure has been primarily defined by moral dispositions that not only censure but more importantly obscure its experience. For Aristotle, "moral excellence," often the articulated goal of classical and early modern works of literature and rhetoric, was intimately tied to "pleasures and pains." Indeed, "it is on account of the pleasure that we do bad things, and on account of the pain that we abstain from noble ones." As such, Aristotle argues, "we ought to have been brought up in a particular way from our very youth, as Plato says, so as both to delight in and be pained by the things that we ought; this is the right education." Moreover, "the man who abstains from bodily pleasures and delights is in this very fact temperate, while the man who is annoyed at it is self-indulgent, and he who stands ground against things that are terrible and delights in this or at least is not pained is brave, while the one who is pained is a coward."[3] True virtue, acquired through education and maintained through action, requires that pain and pleasure be experienced counterintuitively (pain as pleasure and pleasure as pain) or not at all.

Given the heuristic function that pleasure and pain often share with works of rhetoric and literature, it is no surprise to see literary pleasures consistently and dangerously associated with the sensual pleasures of corporeal experience. The fear was that poetry might incite improper desires and affects capable of altering habits of body or mind. Plato warns of the contagious power of imitation in youth, who should avoid poetic representations of "things unbecoming the free man . . .

nor yet any other shameful thing, lest from the imitation they imbibe the reality. Or have you not observed that imitations, if continued from youth far into life, settle down into habits and (second) nature in the body, the speech, and the thought?"[4] Like an irresistible infusion, poetry might insinuate itself disastrously, working in ways "unbecoming" to the young boy who would be a "free man." Liquidity provides Plato with a figure of the overwhelming affective energies that both corporeal and literary pains and pleasures share: "And so in regards to the emotions of sex and anger, and all the appetites and pains and pleasures of the soul which we say accompany all our actions, the effect of the poetic imitation is the same. For it *waters and fosters* these feelings when what we ought to do is dry them up."[5] Poetry was not just a means of representing the problems of immoderate desire; rather, poetry and sexuality were partners in crime, and their common pleasures threatened the constitution of masculine agency. The solution to this problem was either the restriction of poetry to hymns in praise of the gods or to poems in praise of morally salubrious heroic action or the exile of poetry, which Plato finally and famously recommends later in *The Republic*. Horace's *Ars poetica* would later influentially yoke pleasure and virtue, profit and delight, in a way that allowed later writers to cast pleasure as an enticement to virtue, the sweet coating of the bitter pill of moral truth.

The peculiar and discomfiting coexistence of literary, sensory, and often sexual pleasure bequeathed to early modernity a particular conundrum. What was most appealing about literature was, not surprisingly, potentially most ruinous, especially for young readers. Stephen Gosson's 1579 *Schoole of Abuse*, which inspired Philip Sidney's heroic *Defence of Poetry*, casts the dangerous lure of poetry in the language of pleasurable liquidity. Whereas Gosson imagines himself as the true physician prepared to excise the rank flesh that is poetry, the poet is "the deceitfull Phisition" who "giueth sweete Syrropes to make his poison goe downe the smoother." The poet's song is like the "*Syrens* song [that] is the saylers wrack." Continuing the alimentary metaphor, Gosson compares "Poetes to Cookes [for] the pleasures of the one winnes the body from labor and conquereth the sense; the allurement of the other drawes the mind from virtue, and confoundeth wit."[6] Sidney's defense against Gosson debunks but reiterates the notion that poetry is "the nurse of abuse, infecting us with many pestilent desires, with a siren's sweetness drawing the mind to the serpent's tail of sinful fancies."

Moreover, Sidney defends (and thus inadvertently reinforces) the notion that the pleasures of poetry wreak havoc on the project of an assertive nationalist masculinity: "In other nations and in ours, before poets did soften us, we were full of courage, given to martial exercises, the pillars of manlike liberty, and not lulled asleep in shady idleness with poets' pastimes."[7] As Walter J. Ong has argued, "The Renaissance humanist could be disturbed by the plausibility of the charge that literature, and poetry in particular, was actually soft or effeminate, so that, being purveyed to youngsters at the very age they should be maturing in manliness . . . it actually only weakens them."[8] Indeed, Roger Ascham condemned romance for just this, worrying, "What toyes, that dayly readyng of such a booke . . . may worke in the will of a yong jentelman?"[9]

The very properties of poetry (its depictions, its sounds, and, more precisely, its rhymes) were sensuous, infectious, erotic, and potentially compromising. Ascham's fear of the effects of literary "toyes" (such as Arthurian romances) coincides with the use of the word *toy* to suggest, as Patricia Parker argues, that early modern men had reason to be concerned about "the potential impotence or irrelevance of the poetic vocation."[10] Like all works of the imagination in early modernity, poetry might be worse than merely a misleading imitation (a "nurse of lies, a pleaser of fools," in John Harington's paraphrase of Cornelius Agrippa) in being also "a breeder of dangerous errors, and an enticer to wantonness."[11] Poetry and pleasure alike are emptied of content, reduced to "vaine toyes," as they were often called;[12] for, in order to defend against the pleasurable liquidity of aesthetic experience, which threatens to turn men into boys and boys into toys, early modern commentators rendered literature little more than a toy to begin with. Rhyme was paradigmatic in this regard. For George Puttenham, rhyme ("proportion in concord" or "symphonie") consisted of "the eare taking pleasure to heare the like tune reported and to feele his returne," which "breedeth to th'eare a great compassion."[13] If Thomas Campion was, to the consternation of Samuel Daniel, to despise what he perceived as the frivolous and facile nature of rhyme ("childish titillation" he called it), George Gascoigne, no mere opponent of rhyme, did warn his readers "to beware rhyme without reason." William Webbe, too, recommended "good and sensible rhyme" as opposed to poems in which words "be wrested contrary to natural inclination" or "disordered for the rhyme's sake," thus hindering the sense. Campion warned, more sternly, of the capacity of rhyme to force "a man . . . to abjure his matter, and extend a conceit beyond all bounds of art."[14] Rhyme can be dismissed as "childish titillation" precisely because it also provokes in men responses contrary to reason and virtue, thus rendering them boys or toys.

The term *boy toy*, or *toy-boy*—referring to "a young and attractive man regarded as the plaything of an older, often wealthier woman (or occas. man)"—would not enter into usage until the early 1980s.[15] But while *boy toy* holds no currency as a phrase in early modernity, *boy* and *toy* (often along with words like *coy* and *joy*) do associate significantly, forming a thematic, rhyming pair, especially in the landscapes of romance. Of course, boys were not merely potential victims of literary pleasure; they were also its emblem. If the boy actor, with his suggestion of gender transitivity and his participation in networks of homoerotic appeal and homosocial power, was central to the erotic politics of the early modern stage, the boy, as a potential subject or object of literary pleasure, was central to an understanding of early modern poetics. Catherine Belsey argues that "for more than a century" in early modernity "boys were involved, implicated somehow, incorporated into female seductiveness" and that "boys, and the pleasures they represent and enact, are included . . . in the material of poetry at its most seductive."[16] Like other Horatian apologists for poetry in early modernity, Sidney led the way in grounding poetry's validity in the masculinity and the forcefulness of its moral teachings and pleasure's validity in its ability to render attractive the sternest of virtues. Poetry may be "the first light-giver to ignorance, and first nurse whose milk by little and little enabled [readers] to feed afterwards of tougher knowledge."[17] Poetry is designed to teach and delight, to draw the otherwise unwilling reader to tough and bitter knowledge by intermingling gall and honey. Indeed, poetry "giveth so sweet a prospect into the way, as will entice any man to enter into it."[18] Once again, poetry's pleasure must be experienced in spite of itself: the expendable experience of sweetness enables the digestion of tough knowledge. Sidney's more or less representative view of literary pleasure leaves contemporary readers to ask: Does the articulation of literature's moral function impoverish the language we have for discussing early modern aesthetic experience? What might the experience of pleasure, free of the confines of morality, tell us about the intersection of literary and corporeal enjoyment?

Rather than exiling pleasure, restricting pleasure to its most conventional of early modern manifestations, or rendering pleasure the mere handmaiden of morality, Spenser helps us inquire into what Michel Foucault influentially refers to as the uses of pleasure. Of classical culture Foucault remarks, "Foods, wines, and relations with women and boys constituted analogous ethical materials. . . . They all raised the same question: how could one, how must one 'make use' (*chrestai*) of this dynamics of pleasures, desires, and acts?"[19] Foucault examines the creation of "arts of living . . . and of 'using pleasure' according to austere and demanding principles"[20] ruled by a struggle familiar to the landscape of Edmund Spenser's Legend of Temperance, a struggle between *enkrateia*, or self-restraint, and *akraisa*, or incontinence. "*Enkrateia*," Foucault argues, "with its opposite, *akrasia*, is located on the axis of struggle, resistance, and combat; it is self-control, tension, 'continence'; *enkrateia* rules over pleasures and desires, but has to struggle to maintain control."[21] If for Foucault's Greeks the pleasures that could lead to *akrasia* were to be mastered but utilized, Spenser's Acrasia, the architect of the Bower of Bliss and the principle of perverse, feminine sexuality, appears at first to be the unambiguous target of the heroic force and moral ire of Guyon and his guide, the Palmer.[22] Harry Berger describes Acrasia not only as "the enemy of Christian temperance" but also, more strikingly, as "an enemy of God, competing with the Divine creation."[23] Spenser was, however, less interested in the question (or the problem) of the mimetic nature of poetry as exemplified in Acrasia's bower. He was, instead, interested in how pleasure might still be used, as Foucault argues, "to stylize a freedom."[24] That is, Spenser deploys the manifold pleasures of the Bower of Bliss to release the masculine body from the constraining rhetoric of heroic, virtuous labor. The Legend of Temperance highlights flagrant displays of sensuous liquidity that transform heroic knights into boys or toys. The effeminacy and immorality associated with excess pleasure render masculine subjects susceptible to corporeal experience and demonstrate Spenser's interest in the extent to which a poetics rooted in morally problematic flows of pleasure could address early modern subjects' estrangement from their own bodies. Spenser was concerned with the excitable, vulnerable body, its transmissible energies, and the ethical states that might arise from a vulnerability to carnal experience, which Alphonso Lingis describes when he defines libido as "the flux and reflux of tension and of susceptibility in the carnal substance."[25] As we examine the way pleasure renders the masculine heroic body vulnerable to experience, we see in the Legend of Temperance, first, the emergence of an aesthetics and ethics of vulnerable corporeality and, second, the articulation of fantasies of autoerotic and homoerotic feminine sexualities that model orders of agency unavailable to early modern representations of heroic masculinity. Indeed, both male and female figures in the Legend of Temperance are best understood not as subjects prone to sexual acts, identities, or orientations; rather, all these figures exist as sites of pleasure possessing an orientation to corporeal energy, one most often expressed as mobility (or its lack). While the wholesale reconstruction of heroic masculinity would remain the task of the Legend of Chastity's exemplary figures Britomart and Adonis, the Legend of Temperance provided Spenser the opportunity to examine pleasurable experience. Nowhere is Spenser's investigation of pleasurable experience more obvious than in figures of liquidity woven into the Spenserian stanza in a series of seemingly idle but thematically significant rhymes including boy, toy, and joy.

Readings of the Bower of Bliss have been categorized, as Paul Alpers argues, by "a felt disparity or conflict between moral purpose in *The Faerie Queene* and whatever most fills and pleases the imagination—between, as Grierson puts it, the Puritan and the Poet in Spenser."[26] For W. B. Yeats, Spenser the poet emerges in spite of Spenser the Puritan in the Legend of Temperance. "Spenser," Yeats argues, "except among those smooth pastoral scenes and lovely effeminate islands that have made him a great poet, tried to be of his time."[27] The luscious landscapes of the bower make one wonder, as Arlene Okerlund suggests, if "the sensuous beauty of the poetry is enough to make the reader, if not Guyon, forget about any quest after temperance."[28] C. S. Lewis was to resolve this tension between pleasure and morality by finding in Spenser's depictions of wanton bliss "a picture, one of the most powerful ever painted, of the whole sexual nature in disease." For Lewis, this diseased sexual nature appears in moments of intense voyeurism and in an array of pleasures that fail to attain either dignity or propriety. Lewis finds "not a kiss or an embrace in the whole island: only male prurience and female provocation."[29] Lewis narrows considerably the range of sexuality and the power of pleasure, which are at worst prurience and provocation or at best a kiss and an embrace. While articles reprinted in A. C. Hamilton's *Essential Articles for the Study of Edmund Spenser* do take Lewis to task, they tend to address his view of the relationship between art and nature in the Bower of Bliss and the Garden of Adonis, mistaking Spenser's attempt not merely to provide or depict pleasure but to address the experience of pleasure in poetry for an attempt to address long-standing anxieties over the mimetic nature of poetry. N. S. Brooke does dissent from Lewis's view of sexuality, inasmuch as he argues that "the imagery of the bower is concerned not with a perversion of sex, but with a perversion of order."[30] But in shifting from the problem of sex to the problem of order, Brooke removes pleasure from the conversation entirely. As Roland Barthes remarks, "An entire minor mythology would have us believe . . . this peculiar idea that pleasure is *simple*, which is why it is championed or disdained."[31] The sense that we must either sanction or condemn the pleasures in the Bower of Bliss clearly detracts from (by grossly simplifying) our reading of Spenser.

Although critics have largely departed from the style and concerns of the age of Lewis, recent readings of *The Faerie Queene* have not necessarily challenged the predominantly moral reading of Spenser, leaving pleasure largely unexamined. Critics of early modern sexuality have, for the most part, eschewed pleasure for other interests. Jonathan Goldberg admits in *Sodometries* that, while inspired by the work of Foucault, he also "wanted to see how relations between men (or between women and men) in the period provide the sites upon which later sexual identities could batten."[32] Accounts of Spenser follow suit in detailing the vicissitudes of heterosexuality in *Amoretti*, *Epithalamion*, and *The Faerie Queene*,[33] male pastoral homoeroticism in *Shepherd's Calendar*,[34] male homosocial relations between lords and secretaries in Spenser's life,[35] and female homosexuality in *The Faerie Queene*.[36] Such work seems to confirm David Halpern's assertion that scholars of the history of sexuality have repeated but not responded to Foucault's injunction to take seriously "bodies and pleasures."[37] As another commentator puts it, Foucault sought "the liberation of pleasures from the regime of sexuality and sexual identity."[38] Foucault himself insists that "it is from the agency of sex that we have to free ourselves if . . . we wish to assert against the hold of power bodies, pleasures, and knowledges in their multiplicity and their possibility of resistance. The basis for the counterattack . . . must be, not sex-desire, but bodies and pleasures." Foucault was interested in pleasure as that which might "escape the medical and naturalistic connotations inherent in the notion of desire."[39] Valerie Traub's more recent *The Renaissance of Lesbianism in Early Modern England* takes up the subject of "the existence of a cultural awareness of women in the early modern period" and "the complex and often contradictory modes of representation through which such desire was articulated."[40] If the project seems, at first, to "batten" on later sexual identities (tracing a cultural transition in varieties of affective and physical female intimacy from harmless to objectionable), it takes up more complexly the way such intimacies render visible "the somatic and psychological components of erotic enjoyment."[41]

While scholars of the history of sexuality have not always attended to pleasure, other readers of Spenser have effectively exiled considerations of pleasure in affirming the proposition that we do find in *The Faerie Queene* more of the puritan than the poet. Anthony Esolen argues that Spenser's Legend of Temperance "advocates the energetic will and intolerance of the purest of all Old Testament kings,"[42] while Stephen Greenblatt locates in the bower an alignment of sexual and aesthetic pleasure with the forces that endanger cultural cohesion. "The Bower of Bliss," Greenblatt contends, must be destroyed not because its gratifications are unreal but because they threaten 'civility'—civilization—which for Spenser is achieved only through renunciation and the constant exercise of power."[43] In both Greenblatt and his Freudian pretext, *Civilization and Its Discontents*, pleasure is doubly coded as violent; pleasure violently assaults civilization and must be violently repulsed, leaving little room for the *experience* of pleasure. As pleasure and sexuality are restricted to "the expression of an intense craving for release, which is overmastered only by a still more intense fear of release," the capacities of aesthetic experience are also limited: "Spenser's art does not lead us to perceive ideology critically, but rather affirms the . . . inescapable moral power of ideology as that principle of truth toward which art forever yearns. It is art whose status is questioned in Spenser, not ideology."[44] Many follow Greenblatt's lead, arguing that the Legend of Temperance is, according to Richard McCabe, located "in the common 'land' of colonial opportunity," where the trappings of romance bolster an ideological project.[45] "By employing chivalric metaphors for the colonial enterprise," McCabe argues, "Spenser not only lends it the luster of heroic tradition but effectively elides its mercenary nature."[46] Roland Greene has, more recently, expanded Greenblatt's frame of reference from self to world, claiming larger stakes for the destruction of the Bower of Bliss as "alterity" itself becomes "a danger to Christian temperance."[47]

The price of our awareness of the implications of Spenser's relationship to Ireland or the New World need not be a wholesale dismissal of the way art might provide opportunities to investigate ideology, which remains invisible to us if we fail to consider whether Spenser actually advocates the violent application of temperance, be it in the service of a moral or a colonial agenda. Such readings are typical, as Isobel Armstrong notes in recent conversations about the aesthetic, of a particular "hermeneutics of suspicion." "Productive as this hermeneutics has been," she argues, "the concept of the aesthetic has been steadily emptied of content." Armstrong criticizes this failure "to address the democratic and radical potential of aesthetic discourse."[48] Elsewhere I have argued that we find evidence of Spenser's "radical aesthetic" in transformative patterns of pain in *The Faerie Queene*, ones that ask us to reconsider Spenser's purported commitment to the moral rectitude of heroic masculinity by noticing the corporeal workings of suffering and sympathy.[49] Here I argue that we also find, in Spenser's Temperance, transformative patterns of pleasure that reshape the contours of heroic masculinity by launching an inquiry into the ethical ramifications of experiencing pleasure as a physical and affective vulnerability, an openness, to others.

That sexuality and poetry alike might be defined by the dialectic of violence and pleasure Greenblatt identifies in Guyon's eradication of the Bower of Bliss, Spenser was well aware. In the Legend of Temperance Spenser deploys Guyon and the Palmer to dramatize the disastrous consequences of the attempt to moderate pleasure and to deploy bodily energy as violence in the service of heroic, moral agendas. Guyon's destructive acts represent what Foucault describes as one of two varieties of power, the sovereign power to destroy, which is characterized by the "right of seizure: of things, time, bodies, and ultimately life itself; it culminated in the privilege to seize hold of a life in order to suppress it."[50] The Palmer's acts represent fostering, or the moderating influence that disciplines and organizes the exemplar of temperance by, as Foucault puts it, "distributing the living in the domain of value and utility" and treating "the body as a machine" and concentrating on "its disciplining, the optimalization of its capabilities, the extortion of its forces."[51] Indeed, in the "Letter of the Authors," the Palmer first expropriates

Guyon's labor at the court of Gloriana where he "craued of the Faery Queene, to appoint him some knight to performe that aduenture," that is, the defeat of Acrasia, "which being assigned to Sir Guyon, he presently went forth with that same Palmer."[52] The Palmer then becomes the externalization of the disciplinary techniques by which Guyon's energy is directed and his moral health maintained:

> And with his steedy staffe did point his way:
> His race with reason, and with words his will,
> From fowle intemperaunce he ofte did stay,
> And suffred not in wrath his hasty steps to stray.
> (2.1.34)

This temperate discipline of the body that the Palmer achieves with reasonable words appears nowhere more plainly than in the House of Temperance. The opening stanza of the canto in which we encounter Alma's castle claims:

> Of all Gods workes, which doe this world adorne,
> There is no one more faire and excellent,
> Then is mans body both for powre and forme,
> Whiles it is kept in sober gouernment;
> But none then it, more fowle and indecent,
> Distempred through misrule and passions bace:
> It growes a Monster, and incontinent
> Doth loose his dignitie and natiue grace.
> (2.9.1)

Though a monstrous rabble of intemperate sensations assaults Alma's castle, the castle itself depicts the well-ordered body as a veritable factory of functions, one regulated to produce optimal operating efficiency and motivated by the discourse of moral health deriving from Alma herself, whose name means "nourishing." Michael Schoenfeldt points to Alma's castle as the key to the Legend of Temperance, which exposes stringent self-discipline as the foundation of the self. "Spenser," Schoenfeldt argues, "imagines the self as a fragile and unstable edifice, eternally under construction, and assailed on all sides (including the inside) by insurgent passions." By both repulsing the external assaults of the senses and by consistently monitoring and disciplining internal impulses, one achieves an identity "through the forceful imposition of rational order on energies that tend naturally to the twin poles of tyranny and anarchy."[53] In essence, Spenser's critique of what Schoenfeldt explicates so lucidly in the Legend of Temperance—the mutually constitutive nature of inwardness and bodily continence—reveals how Alma and her castle realize the full disciplinary force of the Palmer's fostering influence. Indeed, when Alma brings the knight into the chamber of the heart, the seat of the passions, she stills the delightful hubbub. Before her entrance the heart is witness to "diverse delights" (including singing, laughing, and gaming, or "toy"-ing) and moody affects (shame and grief, envy and coyness). But,

> Soone as the gracious *Alma* came in place,
> They all attonce out of their seates arose,
> And to her homage made, with humble grace
> (2.9.36)

At the end of the episode, while Guyon journeys on to destroy the Bower of Bliss, Arthur remains at Alma's castle, his labor expropriated for the safety of the keep, as he defeats the monstrous Maleger, who represents the incursion of dangerous, diseased sensations. Alma, Arthur, the Palmer, and Guyon may guarantee order, but at what price to the body? As Fredric Jameson argues, "To discipline [the body], to give it the proper tasks and ask it to repress its other random impulses, is at once to limit its effectiveness, or, even worse, to damage it irretrievably."[54] This limitation Marx referred to as the phenomenon of estranged labor, whereby the worker is alienated not only from the products of his own labor but from the essential energy of his laboring body and mind: "It is activity as suffering, strength as weakness, begetting as emasculating, the worker's *own* physical and mental energy, his personal life—indeed, what is life but activity?—as an activity which is turned against him, independent of him and not belonging to him." Marx describes, then, the alienation of worker from the product of his labor, from the energy of his own activity, and, importantly, from "the sensuous external world."[55] In the literature of epic and chivalric romance, heroic masculinity is that form of estranged labor by which the energies of the human body are deployed as virtue, and the signifiers of that masculinity reflect such estrangement.

The Legend of Temperance may dramatize the attempt to exile the distractions of pleasure, but it also consistently stages moments of failure in the strategies Guyon and the Palmer implement in their quest to deny such pleasure and to employ the estranged energies of masculinity in the service of virtuous labor. The very identification of Spenser's poetics with the perspective of Guyon and the Palmer is remarkable in light of the proem that functions as a preface to both the first book and the entire 1590 *Faerie Queene*. There, Spenser clearly repudiates heroic masculinity, *heros*, in his invocation of the aid of *eros*:

> And thou most dreaded impe of highest *Ioue*,
> Faire *Venus* sonne, that with thy cruell dart
> At that good knight so cunningly didst roue,
> That glorious fire it kindled in his hart,
> Lay now thy deadly Heben bow apart,
> And with thy mother mylde come to mine ayde:
> Come both, and with you bring triumphant *Mart*,
> In loues and gentle iollities arraid,
> After his murdrous spoyles and bloudie rage allayd.
> (1.proem.3)

Eros, or Cupid, is identified by virtue of his unnamed victim, Arthur, who has "suffered so much ill" in his futile quest for the love of Gloriana (1.proem.2). This questing desire, which Greenblatt identifies as the heart of the dialectic of sexuality and violence in *The Faerie Queene*, is indeed perfectly embodied by Arthur, that exemplar of Magnificence, or all virtues.[56] Despite the narrator's compassion for Arthur's plight, that sympathy and the hopeless desire it responds to is superseded in the proem by the desire to disarm Cupid, who must lay down his "deadly Heben bow" so that he might help his "mother mild" to summon the god of war, but this is a Mars whose "murdrous spoyles and bloudie rage" are "allayd." The disarmed Cupid, the mild Venus, and the pacified Mars provide a trinity that displaces Calliope—the epic Muse invoked previously in the proem—the questing Arthur, and the absent Gloriana. Furthermore, this reconstituted erotic trinity forces us to modify our understanding of Spenser's oft-cited intention, "Fierce warres and faithfull loues shall moralize my song" (1.proem.1). If we are to consider *The Faerie Queene* a poem concerned with virtue, we must remember the root meaning of the word, turning our attention from morality to masculinity. Indeed, it is not art that Spenser's Bower of Bliss calls into question as a way of championing morality and obscuring ideology. Rather, it is that ethos of heroic masculinity that Spenser will consistently call into question, making its reconstitution the task of the 1590 *Faerie Queene*. As perverse pleasures distract masculine knights from their quests and combats, they unleash in the landscape of the Legend of Temperance a wholly new relationship to a gendered dynamics of corporeal energy.

As a commodity in the Legend of Temperance, energy is not only precious but gendered, being primarily the province of women and boys. Indeed, men regularly struggle to put themselves in motion, as emblematized by Guyon's loss of his horse early on in the legend (2.2.11). The vain, foolish Braggadochio, who unintentionally parodies the gentility and masculinity of romance heroism, steals Guyon's horse, which Guyon will not recover until late in the Legend of Justice. The horse suggests the restless passion, the erotic thrust of heroic masculinity, as when Guyon is introduced and identified with his energetic steed.[57] Moderation comes from the Palmer, who "euer with slow pace the knight did lead, / Who taught his trampling steed with equall steps to tread" (2.1.7). Guyon's trampling steed, of course, also reprises Redcrosse's "angry steed," who "did chide his foming bitt / As much disdayning to the curbe to yield" (1.1.1). Guyon's loss of the power of locomotion expresses a lack of masculine force. Instead of pricking on the plain, Guyon must walk, bearing the "double burden" (2.2.12) of wrecked masculinity as he carries the dead Mordant's armor "with bloud defilde, / An heauie load" (2.2.11). Mordant is, of course, the first boy toy we encounter in the Legend of Temperance, being the lover and victim of Acrasia. Even in death, Mordant, "the flower of his age," appears oddly vital, as if he were a lingering blossom or a pretty toy, with "ruddie lips" and "rosy red / Did paint his chearefull cheekes" (2.1.41). Even in death, it is clear that Mordant was "in his freshest flowre of lusty hed, / Fitt to inflame" (2.1.41). Mordant displays a pleasurable, seductive energy that distracts from both the pain of his grieving widow, Amavia, and the stern morality of Guyon and his Palmer. Guyon has lost the unthinking force of epic masculinity and must bear material remainders of wrecked heroic masculinity as he carries away Mordant's armor.

The Legend of Temperance does offer reason to wonder if masculinity is not vitalized by pleasure but rather stupefied. Mordant, after all, is dead, and his counterpart at the close of book 2, Verdant, sinks into the embrace of Acrasia. Yet these moments of stupefaction also witness a sexual vitality that emerges only as masculinity is disarmed.

Verdant combines a "sweet" and boyish "regard" with "manly sternesse" but displays only the first signs of that manliness, for "on his tender lips the downy heare / Did now but freshly spring, and silken blossoms beare" (2.12.79). Verdant presents the portrait of the ideal youth, with that particular oscillation between masculine and feminine characteristics so energizing to early modern narrative. To be sure, the narrator pities and decries Verdant's bondage to the pleasures of Acrasia as displayed in his abandoned armaments:

> His warlike Armes, the ydle instruments
> Of sleeping praise, were hong vpon a tree,
> And his braue shield, full of old moniments,
> Was fowly ras't, that none the signes might see,
> Ne for them, ne for honour cared hee,
> Ne ought, that did to his aduancement tend,
> But in lewd loues, and wastfull luxuree
> His dayes, his goods, his bodie he did spend:
> O horrible enchantment, that him so did blend.
> (2.12.80)

Like Aeneas distracted by Dido or like Redcrosse poured out in looseness, Verdant's heroic attributes suffer neglect as he sinks into Acrasia's lap of luxury, a place of immoral but pleasurable expenditures of energy ("his dayes, his goods, his bodie he did spend"). The opening of the stanza displays the concatenation of heroic action and virtuous poetry at the moment of their failure, as the instruments of war, which also may be construed as the instruments of writing, hang idle on a tree. Indeed, Parker finds here an indication of the ambivalence and perhaps resistance of "lyric poets in the era of Spenser, subject to a queen who very much demanded their voices."[58] In response to the anxiety of the potential uselessness of poetry and to the subjection of life under the rule of a woman, Parker argues, poets fashioned means of mastering the powerful beloved through the Petrarchan lyric, which explains, too, the destruction of the Bower of Bliss. Parker states, "As with the dyadic antagonism of Petrarchan lyric, there seems to be here, ironically, no temperate middle way, no alternative to the polarity of subject or be subjected."[59]

Critics have tended, with Parker, to identify the sexual blending we associate with Acrasia and Verdant as the reprehensible suspension of martial force, a lack of mobility that indicates enslavement to pleasure and idolatrous attachment to nature. Esolen argues that Alma and Acrasia comprise representations of Venus and figures of nature *in bono* and *in malo*, respectively, the former nourishing and the latter enervating.[60] Verdant is, of course, wrapped in Acrasia's embrace, surrounded by "Many faire Ladies and lasciuious boyes, / That euer mixt their song with light licentious toyes" (2.12.72):

> And all that while, right ouer him she hong,
> With her false eyes fast fixed in his sight,
> As seeking medicine, whence she was stong,
> Or greedily depasturing delight:
> And oft inclining downe with kisses light,
> For feare of waking him, his lips bedewd,
> And through his humid eyes did sucke his spright,
> Quite molten into lust and pleasure lewd;
> Wherewith she sighed soft, as if his case she rewd.
> (2.12.73)

Much has been made of the easily condemned Acrasia in her seemingly parasitic attachment to Verdant as she draws "his spright" with her "false eyes" through his "humid eyes." Acrasia clearly embodies an immoral liquidity as she melts "into lust and pleasure lewd."

Yet we also note a wholesale reorienting of the power of the gaze in this scene when we compare Verdant and Acrasia to their prototypes in Tasso's Rinaldo and Armida. There, the valiant Christian Rinaldo lies in the clutches of the Saracen sorceress Armida. Rinaldo sinks into the same liquid joy that consumes Verdant, but it is *he* who does the looking: "His hungry eyes upon her face he fed / And feeding them so pin'd himself away."[61] Rinaldo's desire is as active as his gaze and yet reprehensibly effeminate. Verdant, however, displays the disarmed masculinity that Spenser calls for in the proem to book 1 and which he will more fully articulate in the Garden of Adonis. Furthermore, Acrasia might compare somewhat favorably with the aggressive Venus of Shakespeare's closely contemporary *Venus and Adonis*.[62] Despite being the embodiment of evil intemperance, Acrasia retains very human qualities, such as her care for the youth—her "feare of waking him," her sighing "as if his case she rewd." Acrasia's display of compassion seems at odds with her apparent use of Verdant as a disposable source of pleasure and energy, but compassion is one signal of the extent to which the disarming of heroic masculinity opens up the possibility of relationships grounded in mutuality. Just as Tasso cannot bring himself to damn the sorceress Armida (she converts to Christianity in order to marry Rinaldo), Spenser cannot bring himself to wholly damn Acrasia because she renders inflexibly "virtuous" masculinity receptive to experience and vulnerable to care. Moreover, we might remember that Lucretius similarly describes the peace-bestowing effects of Venus on Mars as an erotic exchange of gaze and breath: "Mars, mighty in battle rules the savage works of war, who often casts himself upon your lap wholly vanquished by the every-living wound of love, and thus looking upward, with shapely neck thrown back, feeds his eager eyes with love, gaping upon you, goddess, and, as he lies back, his breath hangs upon your lips. There as he reclines, goddess, upon your sacred body, do you, bending around him from above, pour from your lips sweet coaxings, and for your Romans, illustrious one, crave quiet peace" (1.32–40).

Whereas the portrait of Verdant stresses an exchange of energy and compassion through a shared experience of liquid pleasure, Cymochles's effeminate postures enable his receptivity to aesthetic experience. Like Verdant,

> now he has pourd out his ydle mynd
> In daintie delices, and lauish ioyes,
> Hauing his warlike weapons cast behynd,
> And flowes in pleasures, and vaine pleasing toyes
> Mingled emongst loose Ladies and lasciuious boyes.
> (2.5.28)

Like other masculine "victims" of effeminizing pleasure (including Verdant whose arms are like instruments), Cymochles experiences, in this vulnerable state, a heightened awareness of aesthetic experience. In the architecture of the bower itself is evidence of "art stryuing to compayre / With nature," along with "daintie odours," "bounteous smels," and "painted colors" (2.5.29). Experience is here aesthetic in its root sense, which refers to sensory perception long before it comes to refer to the experience of works of art. Though masculine force naps by the fountain, the body wakes to a different order of sensation. The trickling waters of the bower are often host to "the wearie Traueiler" who quenches his thirst,

> And then by it his wearie limbes display,
> Whiles creeping slomber made him to forget
> His former payne, and wypt away his toilsom sweat.
> (2.5.30)

This hypothetical traveler is no longer absorbed in toil, in the experience of a kind of pain that subsumes the body to the imperatives of labor in the form of a quest. Rather, foregrounded here is a body at rest and in a position to produce, rather than expend, energy. In this grove "mery birdes of euery sorte / Chaunted alowd their chearefull harmonee." The harmony of these sounds energizes the listener, making "a sweete consort, / That quickned the dull spright with musicall comfort" (2.5.31). The quickening of the sprite comes with the surrender of masculine force to an aesthetic or sensory relationship to the body, as signaled by a cascade of auditory, olfactory, and tactile signifiers in the description of the bower. Cymochles's gratuitous experience resonates with Jameson's defense of the pleasures of the body: "Lazy, shot through with fits of boredom or enthusiasm . . . listening for the fainter vibrations of a sensorium largely numbed by civilization and rationalization, sensitive to the messages of throbs too immediate, too recognizable as pain or pleasure—maybe all this is not to be described as self-indulgence after all."[63]

The display of Cymochles's pleasured, unarmed body introduces him into the bower's complex circuits of voyeurism as both the subject and the object of an erotic gaze. Like the traveler, Cymochles's body is laid out to view, "carelesly displaid, / In secrete shadow from the sunny ray" (2.5.32). As Cymochles luxuriates "amidst a flock of Damzelles," who entice, incite, and arouse him with "wanton follies and light meriment" (2.5.32), the women display their bodies in a series of acrobatic games, which "loosely disaray" their "vpper parts of meet habiliments / And shewd them naked, deckt with many ornaments" (2.5.32). Valerie Traub, among others, comments on the "poetics of voyeurism" in Spenser, which fashions "scenes ostensibly in the service of a desiring male viewer."[64] Traub's account complicates masculine voyeurism by locating a female intimacy and homoeroticism in the display of breasts in the Bower of Bliss. The portrait of the recumbent Cymochles further complicates the prerogatives of masculine viewing:

> He, like an Adder, lurking in the weedes,
> His wandering thought in deep desire does steepe,
> And his fraile eye with spoyle of beauty feedes;
> Sometimes he falsely faines himself to sleepe,
> Whiles through their lids his wanton eies do peepe,
> To steale a snatch of amorous conceipt,
> Whereby close fire into his heart does creepe:
> So, he them deceiues, deceiud in his deceipt,
> Made dronke with drugs of deare voluptuous receipt.
> (2.5.34)

The dangerous power of masculine spectatorship, as indicated by the image of the adder, consistently strays from potency to distraction. The formerly valiant Cymochles possesses a "wandering thought" and a "fraile eye," and while he "feedes" upon their beauty, his spectatorship of the alluring women is far from dominant. Cymochles neither inflicts nor suffers the power of the gaze.[65] Looking becomes, in this scene, a game of erotic mutuality in which all parties display and are displayed. Cymochles's purportedly superior position, as one who looks, is tempered not only by the display of his own body but also by the awareness of the feminine "objects" of perception. After all, Cymochles is "deceiud in his deceipt." The use of "deceipt" here certainly indicates moral censure, but Cymochles is, more importantly, "dronk with drugs of deare voluptuous receipt." The state of voluptuous receptivity indicates a relationship to desire in which "to perceive is to become perceptible," to "insert oneself . . . into the field one looks into."[66] Cymochles's surrender of epic force results in a receptivity so reprehensible it disrupts the morality aligned with masculinity's efficacious violence.

Cymochles's visible receptivity to pleasure also renders visible his fascination with the female body and its capacity for mobility as it performs, teases, and toys. Even the scandalous display of nudity derives from a series of ongoing motions, which might have appeared in figures of immobility such as in the static tableaux or disarticulated parts common to the early modern blazon. Cymochles's erotic fascination derives from the spectacle of women in motion who display energy. One of the most famous moments of voyeurism in *The Faerie Queene*, Guyon's encounter with two nymphs in a fountain, confirms this fascination with feminine mobility. Encountering yet another of the bower's liquid joys, Guyon notes "Two naked Damzelles,"

> Which therein bathing, seemed to contend,
> And wrestle wantonly, ne car'd to hyde,
> Their dainty parts from vew of any, which them eyd.
> (2.12.63)

Howard Hendrix argues that this is Guyon's only clear moment of temptation in book 2 and that critics have been "notably reticent and circumspect in discussing how and why this spectacle should possess such particular seductiveness," just as "the fact that the young women are wrestling is conspicuously absent from most discussions."[67] Hendrix sees here the power of Guyon's male gaze to eroticize the scene in a way consonant with patriarchal structures of power and as a defense against feminine agency.

While Cymochles and Guyon do participate in a dialectic of concealment and revelation played out upon a series of feminine bodies, erotic fascination in the Legend of Temperance derives from the appearance of autonomy constituted by the capacity for self-locomotion. Guyon is in constant danger of falling into stasis—as when he loses his horse, when he collapses outside the Cave of Mammon, or when he becomes captivated by the nymphs in the fountain. But of the wanton wrestling of the latter, we learn that,

> Sometimes the one would lift the other quight
> Aboue the waters, and then downe againe
> Her plong, as ouer maystered by might,
> Where both awhile would couered remaine,
> And each the other from to rise restraine.
> (2.12.64)

It is, of course, true that the wrestling reveals the bodies of the nymphs: "th'amarous sweet spoiles to greedy eyes reuele" (2.12.64). Yet, as in Cymochles's encounter with the nymphs of the Bower of Bliss, the revelation of flesh is an aspect of a larger circuit of motion, one in which mastery shifts back and forth, never resting in solely one party. This very circuit of motion might remind us of Guyon's encounters with the fountain's ornamentation:

> Most goodly it with curious ymageree
> Was ouerwrought, and shapes of naked boyes,
> Of which some seemd with liuely iollitee,
> To fly about, playing their wanton toyes,
> Whylest others did them selues embay in liquid ioyes.
> (2.12.60)

Even the static monument here depicted suggests, to Guyon, activity, in the flying, playing, and bathing of the boys in their "liuely iollitee." Movement suggests the aesthetic vitality of the fountain, as does the struggle between art and nature, which is remarkably like the wrestling nymphs and, like them, serves to energize an otherwise static landscape:

> So striuing each th'other to vndermine,
> Each did the others worke more beautify;
> So diff'ring both in willes, agreed in fine:
> So all agreed through sweete diuersity,
> This Gardin to adorne with all variety.
> (2.12.59)

The erotic play of the nymphs is competitive but not conflictual; likewise in the Bower of Bliss, "all pleasures plenteously abownd, / And none does others happinesse enuye" (2.12.58). Art and nature may also compete, "striuing each th'other to vndermine" but their differing "willes" coincide in the same end—"sweet diuersity." The boy toys that attend this fountain attend not only a spectacle of female seductiveness but a variety of aesthetic pleasure that helps us revise our understanding of the body's capacity to expend energy and to exert agency in the absence of heroic violence.

The nymphs that fascinate Guyon form a self-involved, erotic circuit of energy and resistance, motion and stasis. They are, for Guyon, not only an engine of motion but also, in their erotic play, signifiers of a sexuality manifest in the language of motion and distracting because apparently complete in itself. Guyon's arrested progress is remarkably like that of the Lover in the *Romance of the Rose*, yet again delayed from consummation by a spectacle arranged by the figure Distraction:

> In the middle of the carol, Diversion, with great nobility, directed the dancing of two darling young ladies dressed only in kirtles, with their hair in single braids. It is useless to speak of how quaintly they danced: each one came very prettily toward the other, and when they were close they thrust their mouths forward in such a way that it would have seemed to you that they were kissing each other on the face. They knew well how to move their bodies. I don't know how to describe it to you, but I never would have wanted to move as long as I could see these people bestirring themselves to carol and dance.
>
> I stood there motionless, watching the carol.[68]

The precise, alluring motions of the two girls provokes the Lover's experience of stasis. Their "bestirring" motions themselves are provoked by the music of the dance they perform. Guyon, too, stands motionless as he witnesses a distracted erotic, one that has slipped from the driving telos of sexual consummation and narrative conclusion. The figure of Distraction is, himself, a boy toy, for, as we are told, "never among men will you come upon any place where you will see a more handsome man. . . . He had neither beard nor mustache, except for a very little down, for he was a young man."[69] The experience of distraction produces energy precisely by immobilizing the violent will to closure; this act of immobilization releases the energy of a pleasurable vitality. We witness briefly in these respective garden scenes not masculine libido interrupted but the unleashing of an utterly different order of sexuality, a feminine homoerotics rooted in a dialectic of competition and collusion, which provides the energy that motivates the mutual beautification of art and nature in the Bower of Bliss.

As Guyon himself becomes an object of display (not only noticed by the nymphs but noticeably aroused), the Palmer's moral imperatives interrupt the triangle, thus preventing Guyon from succumbing to erotic vulnerability. The Palmer may draw Guyon's eyes from spectacles of distraction, but the sound of pleasure inevitably surrounds them both:

> Eftsoones they heard a most melodious sound,
> Of all that mote delight a daintie eare,
> Such as attonce might not on liuing ground,
> Saue in this Paradise, be heard elsewhere:
> Right hard it was, for wight, which did it heare,

To read, what manner musicke that mote bee:
For all that pleasing is to liuing eare,
Was there consorted in one harmonee,
Birdes, voices, instruments, windes, waters, all agree.
(2.12.70)

An erotically charged experience of mutual participation pervades the bower, bringing all sounds and all things into concord. In the course of the stanza, the "daintie eare," trained to experience delight, becomes a "liuing eare" as pleasure is attuned to a broader harmony. As is the case for Redcrosse, Verdant, and Cymochles—and in spite of his reluctant reassertion of heroic masculinity—Guyon witnesses a kind of sensory plenitude that his own body, by virtue of being a body, is capable of participating in or resonating with in "one harmonee."

We see, in the Legend of Temperance, a progression from a liberating masculine lassitude (that renders the heroic male body vulnerable to experience) to a fascination with varieties of erotic mobility indicative of an attempt to conceive of human agency and bodily energy outside of the framework of violent heroic assertion. Such mobility finds its most dynamic expression in the figure of Phaedria, who provides locomotion in the waterways of Acrasia's domain. She appears, for the first time, in

A little Gondelay, bedecked trim
With boughes and arbours wouen cunningly,
That like a little forest seemed outwardly.
(2.6.2)

Like the bower that mingles art and nature, Phaedria's boat suggests a cleverly constructed camouflage, yet it also suggests that in recreating the topos of romance, the "little forest," Phaedria has created her own self-contained world, one that moves around like one of the wandering islands around which she navigates. Phaedria exhibits an utterly self-sufficient relationship to pleasure and locomotion:

And therein sate a Lady fresh and fayre,
Making sweete solace to her selfe alone;
Sometimes she song, as lowd as larke in ayre,
Sometimes she laught, as merry as Pope Ione,
Yet was there not with her else any one,
That to her might moue cause of meriment:

Matter of merth enough, though there were none
She could deuise, and thousand waies inuent,
To feede her foolish humor, and vaine iolliment.
(2.6.3)

Despite the dismissive moralizing tag in the closing alexandrine, the stanza, like Guyon, remains fascinated with the spectacle of a creative, self-moving feminine presence whose pleasure provides a source of mobility for others. Phaedria and her boat constitute the main form of public transport in the waters that surround Acrasia's Bower of Bliss, providing passage for Cymochles and Guyon, who, stranded at the edge of the Idle Lake, are at once in need of and distracted by her services. Cymochles, having been spurred into violence by the shaming rebukes of Atin (who calls him "a womanish weake knight" [2.5.36]), is once again pacified by the influence of Phaedria, for

Her light behauiour, and loose dalliaunce
Gaue wondrous great contentment to the knight,
That of his way he had no souenaunce,
Nor care of vow'd reuenge and cruell fight.
(2.6.8)

Although Phaedria may be described as a "weak wench" who has caused Cymochles to "yield his martial might," she also has the power to quench "his flamed minde." Indeed, "sensuall delight," despite its shady reputation, seems to have a beneficial effect, proving that "easie is, t'appease the stormie winde / Of malice in the calme of pleasaunt womankind" (2.6.8). Pyrochles suffers notably from being inflamed by Furor, or fury, as does Guyon on a few occasions; while Guyon fails in his attempt to bind in chains and to dominate with sheer force Furor and Occasion, Phaedria cools the "malice" incited in Cymochles by the troubling Atin. She lulls Cymochles to sleep with a song borrowed from Tasso's *Gerusalemme liberata*, in which the valiant Rinaldo is lulled to sleep by Armida and thus further distracted from his quest. Spenser redeploys the song that emblematizes Tasso's threatening feminine, liquid pleasures, rendering those pleasures an antidote to uncontrollable masculine aggression as he makes song an antidote to violent action. Similarly, when Cymochles and Guyon meet on Phaedria's island, a vicious fight breaks out, which Phaedria, again, pacifies. Throwing herself at their feet, she reproves their cruelty and appeals to any kind of love or pity that could "find place" or "empierce" their "iron breasts." Phaedria woos the men away from the vicious, mechanical masculinity they enact by invoking, too, the wooing of Mars by Cupid and Venus that opens *The Faerie Queene*:

> Mars is Cupidoes frend,
> And is for Venus loues renowmed more
> Than all his wars and spoiles, the which he did of yore.
>
> Therewith she sweetly smyld.
>
> (2.6.35–36)

Phaedria envisions a world of demilitarized love. While such an ethos appears in association with seemingly reprehensible experiences of lewd pleasure, she once again receives narrative approbation for her success: "Such powre haue pleasing wordes: such is the might / Of courteous clemency in gentle hart" (2.6.36).

Phaedria embodies energy unconstrained by notions of virtuous force. Quests govern the actions of Redcrosse and Guyon, which set the knights tasks demanding that their energy be converted to masculine force that is expropriated as labor. Furthermore, a whole metaphysics of desire attends the quests, assigned as they are by Gloriana, whose elusive lure incites a desire to capture and obtain, as emblematized by Arthur's search for Gloriana, a search which also suggests that Magnificence, the encompassing virtue of *The Faerie Queene*, is only complete when the knight obtains his lady. Unlike Guyon, or even the more susceptible Redcrosse Knight, Phaedria does not employ the violence of masculine quest that propels so many knights so disastrously through the landscape of *The Faerie Queene*. She has no particular quest, and even her distraction of various knights seems to adhere to little pattern; she is not a Duessa or an Archimago, attempting to systematically defeat the virtuous knights. Yet to the extent that figures of feminine agency, self-sufficiency, and pleasure, such as Phaedria, the fountain nymphs, and Acrasia, threaten the masculine power that provides the engine of epic action, they are opposed by Guyon's violence and the Palmer's rectitude. Indeed, although in Tasso's *Gerusalemme liberata* the knights who save Rinaldo are ferried to her secret island by a powerful woman who stands in for the near magical might of reason, Guyon and the Palmer employ a boatman of great masculine force who "strongly he them rowes" through the perilous waters that he strikes, drives, strives against (2.12.5). Whereas Phaedria glides easily through the water, masculine locomotion can be brutal:

> So forth they rowed, and that *Ferryman*
> With his stiffe oares did brush the sea so strong,
> That the hoare waters from his frigot ran,
> And the light bubles daunced all along,
> Whiles the salt brine out of the billowes sprong.
> (2.12.10)

Masculine energy is not only vehement but, interestingly, again the object of appropriation. Although they all are in motion ("they rowed"), the only one expending energy at this point is the laboring ferryman. The Palmer quells waves and drives away sea creatures, figures of elemental energy, while Guyon saves his violence for the bower itself. Once again, energy is expropriated and alienated from the laboring body; this expropriation one may call masculinity. Feminine energy, however, evades capture, developing alternate circuits of operation. More than just targets of moral condemnation, Phaedria's tactics (fascination, diversion, distraction, and delay—all characteristic of the genre of romance) enable action. They resist progress when such progress relies on the violence of estranged labor.

Even the spectacle of Acrasia hovering over the body of the sleeping Verdant indicates the mingling of boyish and feminine erotic energies. Acrasia elicits (rather than contains or constrains) that energy. The Palmer and Guyon, however, attempt to appropriate and economize the energies of poetry and sexuality, as figured in their capture of Acrasia:

> That suddein forth they on them rusht, and threw
> A subtile net, which onely for that same
> The skilfull Palmer formally did frame.
> (2.12.81)

Guyon and Palmer, as they reenact the guileful jealousy of Vulcan, reorient once more the governing forces of *eros* and *heros*. Venus and Cupid disarm Mars in the proem to the 1590 *Faerie Queene* and again on Phaedria's island, and here Verdant plays both Mars and Cupid to Acrasia's Venus. The trinity is, however, reconstituted by the insertion of Vulcan, a god lamed and emasculated by his father's violence and later cuckolded by his wife. One might think of Vulcan as the laboring god, a figure working in his forge to create objects and devices for others, objects he does not himself enjoy or use. Vulcan is the figure, par excellence, of alienation: from pleasure, from his body, and from the products of his labor.

Although Guyon and the Palmer share the last word in the Bower of Bliss, sharing too the sententious final stanza, the object of their closing condemnation, Gryll, provides a striking reminder of the energy of pleasure. Most of Acrasia's victims are restored to human form, but one, formerly a hog, "Repyned greatly, and did him miscall / That had from hoggish forme him brought to naturall" (2.12.86). While some of Acrasia's victims experience only hatred for the captured Acrasia, Gryll, like Verdant, experiences regret. Verdant, though lectured at by Guyon and Palmer, is taken away, "both sorrowful and sad," as if restoration were the source of his unhappiness. Gryll, according to Guyon, represents the lowest of the low, displaying "the mind of beastly man / That hath so soone forgot the excellence / Of his creation" (2.12.87). The Palmer remarks:

> The donghill kinde
> Delightes in filth and fowle incontinence:
> Let *Gryll* be *Gryll*, and haue his hoggish minde;
> But let vs hence depart, whilest wether serues and winde.
> (2.12.87)

While Verdant sighs at the necessity of once again punching his virtuous time card, Gryll refuses to participate in the experience of labor governed by Guyon and the Palmer, an experience in "which man alienates himself," and which "is a labor of self-sacrifice, of mortification." Gryll does this not from mere moral depravity but, one might say, as a consequence of his status as a worker of masculinity. In a system in which one's energy is demanded, Marx argues, "man (the worker) only feels himself freely active in his animal functions—eating, drinking, procreating . . . and in his human functions he no longer feels himself to be anything but an animal. What is animal becomes human and what is human becomes animal."[70] While Gryll maintains a hoggish mind, the Palmer and Guyon exit abruptly, without the elaborate ending of the Legend of Holiness, in which a whole stanza announces the need for narrative progress by enlisting the readers as "iolly Mariners" (1.12.42) who help prepare the ship of the poem for its next voyage. Here, the Palmer and Guyon possess a worklike attitude, subject as they are to weather and wind for their own locomotion. And indeed, this reference to the utility of wind and weather is rare, if not unique, thus far in *The Faerie Queene*. Elsewhere weather contributes either to allegorical significance and the progress of plot, as when Redcrosse and Una seek shelter from the storm in the wood of error, or to metaphorical valence, as when the progress of the poem is described as a ship at the close of the Legend of Holiness. At the close of the Legend of Temperance, Guyon and the Palmer risk being stranded by the vital, natural forces they seek to contain. As Marshall McLuhan suggests, in another context, "The price of eternal vigilance is indifference."[71] The moral vigilance that makes Guyon and the Palmer indifferent to physical or affective experience (construed as either pleasure or as pain) threatens to immobilize them.

The pleasurable liquidity of poetic experience, figured in the Legend of Temperance in disarmed masculine bodies and in mobile feminine bodies, satisfies Jameson's understanding of the "proper political use of pleasure." Jameson argues, "So finally the right to a specific pleasure, to a specific enjoyment of the potentialities of the material body—if it is not to remain only that, if it is to become genuinely political, if it is to evade the complacencies of 'hedonism'—must always in one way or another also be able to stand as a figure for the transformation of social relations as a whole."[72] In the landscape of *The Faerie Queene*, the real quest is to defeat varieties of alienation that render pleasure (or pain) a form of stupefaction, which disables the body's vulnerability to the experiential and ethical dimensions available in common corporeality. It is easy to side with Guyon, the Palmer, and the long histories of poetics that violently reject the pleasures of poetry or anxiously subject them to the work of virtue. However, the resistance to the destruction of the Bower of Bliss offers us lessons in the work of pleasure. For Spenser, the pleasures of poetry rest neither in the distractions of beauty and delight nor in their ability to signify virtue but, rather, in a capacity to resist the anaesthetization of affective and corporeal experience that occurs when pleasure serves no other function than to pervert the virtuous or to make purportedly "virtuous" labor palatable. Pleasure disarms heroic masculinity and activates the sensuous vulnerability of laboring bodies alienated from the capacity to experience their own bodies (and the bodies of others) and, in such experience, to enter into a commonality that Spenser imagined as harmony or concord. If the cascade of significant rhymes ("boy," "toy," "joy," "coy") is in part indicative of the use of pleasure to disarm heroic knights to produce vulnerable subjects capable of experience, then we might see the Legend of Temperance not only as an intervention in early modern debates about rhyme but also as a lesson on the way the properties of poetry resonate at the level of lived corporeality and have consequences reaching far beyond the technical aspects of composition. For early modern historians of sexuality, the Bower of Bliss offers us lessons in the uses of pleasure and in the way bodies and pleasures, as opposed to desire and sexuality, might organize our inquiries. Moreover, it remains one of many untapped archives in *The Faerie Queene*, archives in which the pathways of Spenserian romance lead us to imagine those dimensions of corporeal experience on which early modern sexual acts, identities, and discourses rely. For Spenser, the pleasures of poetry (depicted in poems or enjoyed by readers) constitute a form of resistance to an ethos of aggressive moralistic heroism, a way of activating the sensuous capacities of the body and an invitation to consider how from the texture of aesthetic experiences arise ethical dispositions rooted in common corporeality. This explains why we must read the Legend of Temperance—indeed, the entire *Faerie Queene*—against the grain of even the most thoroughly contextualized moral readings. That infamously elusive and potentially heretical comparison of the Bower of Bliss with "*Eden* selfe, if ought with *Eden* mote compare" comes into focus as we understand the bower to be, ultimately, "sweete and holesome." If it is not "sweete and holesome" to the workers of virtue such as Guyon and the Palmer, we must conclude that it is a paradise to workers of pleasure, such as Spenser himself.

PART III

The Legend of Chastity

CHAPTER 5

Vulnerable Subjects: Amoret's Agony, Britomart's Battle for Chastity

In a rare moment of narrative intervention in the 1590 *Faerie Queene*, Spenser's narrator bemoans the plight of the eternally fleeing Florimell:

> So oft as I this history record,
> My hart doth melt with meere compassion,
> To thinke, how causelesse of her owne accord
> This gentle Damzell, whom I write vpon,
> Should plonged be in such affliction,
> Without all hope of comfort or reliefe,
> That sure I weene, the hardest hart of stone,
> Would hardly finde to aggrauate her griefe;
> For misery craves rather mercy, then repriefe.
>
> (3.8.1)

Florimell, who is betrothed to the knight Marinell, bursts onto the scene of the Legend of Chastity chased by "a griesly foster" (3.1.17) and a series of knights, including Arthur, the exemplar of magnificence, the sum total of all virtue in *The Faerie Queene*, and Guyon, the exemplar of temperance. While Arthur and Guyon rush to the maiden's aid, they join the chase "full of great enuy and fell gealosy" (3.1.18), calling into question the distinction between rapist and rescuer. As Guyon and Arthur chase Florimell in the company of grisly foresters, they mark yet another collision of the martial and the erotic. If the Legend of Temperance begins with the fear that the force of heroic masculinity, *heros*, will capitulate to *eros*, erotic temptation, the Legend of Chastity witnesses the opposite problem as love becomes a state of war and desire a form of violence.

When, in the "Letter of the Authors," Spenser claimed his task was to "fashion a gentleman or noble person in vertuous and gentle discipline" he committed *The Faerie Queene* not merely to the advocacy of moral instruction but also to the construction of an ideal subject, one located ambiguously with respect to gender. And when, in the proem to the 1590 *Faerie Queene* Spenser called upon Venus to soothe and assuage Mars, he committed his project to a notion of love that could generate a disarmed or, one might say, vulnerable subject. In the Legend of Chastity, Spenser struggles to realize his twinned goals of reforming masculinity "to fashion a gentleman or noble person" by disarming that masculinity through the forces of love. As a consequence, he had to expand his sense of the nature of love to reveal the new man as a vulnerable subject, one for whom the precondition of emergence of the subject is a state of vulnerability.

And yet, as I have argued, not only do masculine subjects in *The Faerie Queene* seem to depend (and even prey) upon the vulnerabilities of others but they also proclaim their own dubious vulnerabilities, which threaten the capacity to take up subject positions. Indeed, if two of Spenser's "exemplary" knights share, with Florimell's attackers, a vicious appetite (for love or war), what are readers to make of Spenser's seemingly sympathetic narrator, who expresses his compassion after Florimell has escaped, repeatedly, numerous gruesome attacks? Judith Anderson has noted "an irreducible doubleness," a "sense of irony, ambiguity, variety and elusiveness" characteristic of the Spenserian narrator.[1] I have already noted, in the Legends of Holiness and Temperance, a deep ambivalence about experiences of suffering and of sympathy. Yet where previously figures like Duessa (and even Una) constituted suspect *objects* of sympathy, here the *subject* of sympathy is suspect. The narrator, after all, claims a passive role ("as I this history record"), as if he were merely transcribing the tale. While the narrator bemoans Florimell's plight, claiming no man without a heart of stone could "aggrauate" her grief, he himself has "plonged" her time and again "in such affliction." The narrator, contemplating Una's suffering in the Legend of Holiness worries he will wink out of existence ("for pitty I could dy" [1.3.1]); here he claims his "hart doth melte with meere compassion." Later, in the Legend of Friendship, the narrator will claim that the traumas of Florimell and Amoret make him wish his narrative "neuer had bene writ" (4.1.1).

The narrator's attention to Florimell, however, might seem more sadistic than ironic or elusive; his concern perhaps conceals the visceral pleasure of graphic sexual assaults, as her encounter with the old fisherman indicates (3.8.25–27). Certainly, there has been no shortage of recent readers ready to identify Spenserian sadism as a subset of the Petrarchan scene of desire, especially when we consider Amoret's *raptus* and torture at the hands of the enchanter Busyrane. At the opening of the Legend of Chastity, Florimell is a figure of perpetual flight, always already almost assaulted by desire. Amoret, on the other hand, is immobilized by the desire of another. However much Florimell and Amoret, the chased and the captured, seem to constitute before and after portraits of women at the mercy of rampant masculinity, these women perform complicated roles in the tangled scene of desire in the Legend of Chastity. Moreover, the moment the narrator appears to offer sympathy, he threatens to wink out of existence.

In the Legend of Temperance, masculinity alternates between violent motion and helpless inertia. In the Legend of Chastity these positions are occupied, on the one hand, by the appetite of figures like Arthur, Guyon, and the grisly foresters and, on the other, by the pathetic incapacity of Amoret's lover Scudamour ("shield of love"), who weeps and complains outside Busyrane's castle, unable to enter it, let alone rescue, Amoret. Heroic masculinity, however, poses a threat to the vulnerable, often feminine, bodies that circulate in romance landscapes even as it deploys the conventions of erotic frustration generated by a Petrarchan idiom eager to dilate on the subject of masculine powerlessness. Whereas empowered romance masculinity risks turning rescue into rape, subservient Petrarchan masculinity constitutes itself as helpless and victimized (often resentfully so) before the power of a cruel woman. Masculinity, then, oscillates in a dangerous and disingenuous binary, casting masculine subjects either as rapists or as victims, which naturalizes aggression as it obscures the lack of material and symbolic power most women experience.

This crisis presents itself in the overlapping narratives of Florimell, Amoret, and Britomart. Although Florimell must wait for the Legend of Friendship to find ultimate resolution, the bizarre impasse she encounters in the Legend of Chastity illuminates an impasse Spenser seeks to transform. After a number of previous assaults and near captivity, Florimell is "rescued" by the sea god Proteus. This act of rescue is hardly altruistic. Although Proteus is moved to "Deepe indignation and compassion frayle" (3.8.31) at the sight of the grisly old fisherman assaulting the delicate Florimell, he frees Florimell only to imprison her in his underwater bower. There, he woos and tempts her. Discovering that she loves the knight Marinell, Proteus takes on the shape of Florimell's beloved "for euery shape on him he could endew" (3.8.40). Proteus initiates a cascade of transformations, becoming not only Marinell, a wealthy king, and, when blandishments fail, a menacing giant, but also a centaur and a storm. Florimell's steadfast love for Marinell earns her recognition as a paragon of chastity and a stay in Proteus's "Dongeon deepe" (3.8.41). Florimell translates the volatility of flight into a posture of self-continence. Proteus embodies the instability, alternating between rescue and rape, supplication and aggression. This is masculinity in crisis, masculinity in search of a shape.

The solution Spenser offers to the crisis of masculinity in that book of *The Faerie Queene* most explicitly concerned with desiring bodies, the Legend of Chastity, requires a model of subjectivity that emerges not from subjection (or the projection of subjection onto others, domination) but from vulnerability. In a parallel vein, Andrew Escobedo asks of characters in *The Faerie Queene*, "How might someone gain a voluntary purchase on the largely involuntary experience of desire? How might someone be an agent, and not only a victim, of love?"[2]

Yet as Jonathan Goldberg points out, critical tradition in the wake of Greenblatt suggests that Spenser "worships power . . . and such worship is tantamount to the abasement of self and art to an ideology whose ruthlessness is never questioned since it is the very power whose glamour Spenser finds undeniable."[3] This powerful sense of subjection, Jane Tylus has argued, was the source of an experience of vulnerability that many literary authors, including Spenser, explored in their writings and combated, defensively, with the generation of notions of authorship that endow the vulnerable writer with authority. More potently, Cynthia Marshall identifies a kind of Renaissance self-shattering, as attempts to harness readerly "pleasure in reading about violent acts of torture and domination" so as to cause identification with tortured or violated subjects designed "to break down established subjective identities" and "recuperate that shattered subjectivity as the basis for individual dedication to the Protestant cause."[4] The problem, then, is that subjectivity comes to be defined exclusively through violence while vulnerability comes to connote defensiveness, disingenuousness, or a subservient affiliation with crown or church.

Goldberg's approach to subjectivity in the 1590 *Faerie Queene* invokes the late work of Michel Foucault, noting the compatibility between the idea of early modern self-fashioning and the later volumes of Foucault's *History of Sexuality*, which "reflect a change in Foucault's project . . . not forward but backward historically, not in the service of showing subjecthood as subject but rather exploring the activity of the subject in its own self-creation."[5] For Goldberg, this focus on *askesis*, or self-examination, and "practices of self-modification" through "the discipline of spiritual exercise" defines Spenser's project in the 1590 *Faerie Queene*. Foucault came to define practices of self-modification through late classical and early Christian thinking, though particularly the latter. And as Foucault admits, "sexuality became, in Christian cultures, the seismograph of our subjectivity."[6] Moreover, Foucault stresses that by sexuality he is not referring to sexual acts (and their prohibition). Rather, it is "the relationship between one's will and involuntary assertions."[7]

For Foucault a complex understanding of chastity, as shaped by the writings of Cassian, becomes paradigmatic in defining the intertwining of sexuality and subjectivity in Christianity: "We are now far away from the rationing of pleasure and its strict limitations on permissible action. . . . But what does concern us here is a never-ending struggle over the movements of our thoughts (whether they extend or reflect those of our body, or whether they motivate them), over its simplest of manifestations, over the factors that can activate it. The aim is that the subject should never be affected in his effort by the obscurest or the most seemingly 'unwilled' presence of will."[8] Foucault describes a "chastity-oriented asceticism [in which] one can see a process of 'subjectivisation' which has nothing to do with a sexual ethic based on physical self-control."[9] Rather, "the obligation to seek and state the truth about oneself [becomes] an indispensable and permanent condition of this asceticism" as does "confession to others, submission to their advice and permanent obedience to one's superiors are essential in this battle." Foucault's intervention in "the genealogy of the subject in Western civilization" was a strategic attempt to "take into account not only techniques of domination but also techniques of the self" because his own work in asylums and prisons "perhaps insisted too much on techniques of domination."[10] Critics have, however, found

Foucault's turn to the arts of the self to be a retreat from the political project of understanding forms of social oppression. As Jeffrey Nealon puts it, it has been commonplace to argue "that after the mid-1970s, he largely abandoned his work on the social interpellations of power and became instead a thinker of individual, artistic, self-creation as a mode of resistance."[11] And yet in "The Battle for Chastity," the Christian concern about the integrity of the will (with its required forms of confession, obedience, and submission) threatens to reinscribe the very dialectic of domination that Foucault sought to escape. Even if the arts of self prove a more dubious means of considering power and resistance, Foucault sought ways out of the bind of sexual subjectivity, especially through sadomasochism and friendship. So, too, I argue did Spenser as he explored the nature of chastity.

Spenser rescripts the scene of early modern sexual subjectivity to create a vulnerable subject tied in bonds of friendship to other vulnerable subjects. Out of the crisis of post-Petrarchan eroticism, in which purported masculine subservience conceals an aggressive will to power, Spenser generates a figure of cross-gendered identification. That is, the figure of Amoret emerges in the Legend of Chastity, as if from the *Amoretti*, as a figure of masochistic identification for the poet: not an object of masculine, poetic aggression but the embodiment of a will to identify with suffering and thereby reimagine the gendered violence endemic to Petrarchan lyric subjectivity. Out of the crisis of heroic masculinity, in which rape and rescue can be nearly indistinguishable, Spenser generates the female knight Britomart, who emerges into subjectivity to save Amoret on behalf of Amoret's lover Scudamour, and constitutes an exemplar of the ideal of chastity as a form of vulnerable masculinity. Moreover, between Britomart and Amoret arises a model of sympathetic sociality modeled on female homoerotic friendship. To return to the questionable sympathy of Spenser's narrator, as he bemoans the plight of Florimell, we might remember the phrase "misery craves mercy, rather then repriefe." Not only do those who suffer deserve no condemnation (*repriefe* or "reproof") but, given the violence of heroic masculinity, those who suffer require sympathy rather than rescue. Or, one might say, misery loves company.

"For nearly two thousand years," Susan Sontag argues, "among Christians and Jews, it has been spiritually fashionable to be in pain. Thus it is not love we overvalue, but suffering—more precisely, the spiritual merits and benefits of suffering. The modern contribution to this Christian sensibility has been to discover the making of works of art and the venture of sexual love as the two most exquisite sources of suffering."[12] Given Sontag's title, "The Artist as Exemplary Sufferer," and the scope of the essay's indictment, readers might be forgiven for assuming the subject of her essay (the notebooks of Cesare Pavese) to be the legacy of Renaissance culture, from the glorified violence of religious martyrs to the abject devotion of Petrarchan lovers and the erotic complications of errant knights and ladies. The classic problem of the sincerity of the Petrarchan lover, whose poems always seem to be about something other than love or the beloved, offers an opportunity to consider not only the nature of Petrarchan love but also the validity of the suffering the lover expresses. Petrarchan lyric asks insistently what to do with pain that is at once conventional and fervent in its expression. At the same time that fervent performances of pain raise suspicion, they also compel attention. A strain of literary criticism emerges from a history of assumptions about literature and suffering, an exemplary instance of which might be Edmund Wilson's *The Wound and the Bow*, each of whose essays probes literary works to find in their underlying biographies the secret source of suffering that shapes art.[13] No wonder Elaine Scarry cautions us about "the danger that a fictional character's suffering (whether physical or psychological) will divert our attention away from the living sister or uncle who can be helped by our compassion in a way that the fictional character cannot be; there is also the danger that because artists so successfully express suffering, they may themselves collectively come to be thought of as the most authentic class of sufferers, and thus may inadvertently appropriate concern away from others in radical need of assistance."[14]

Skepticism about the legibility and validity of suffering in the literary and cultural scions of Petrarch has encouraged critics to shift their focus from conversations about vulnerability to ones about power and subjection. In both the penitential psalms and the courtly lyrics of Renaissance England's first and perhaps most influential translator of Petrarch, Sir Thomas Wyatt, Stephen Greenblatt identifies "the essential values of domination and submission, the values of a system of power that has an absolute monarch as head of both church and state."[15] The semblance of inwardness developed in those lyrics is precisely the consequence of suffering experienced by the frustration of a sexuality governed by the chastening rule of an absolute monarch imagined as either a wrathful God or a possessive king. Marshall substitutes self-shattering for Greenblatt's self-fashioning as a central characteristic of early modern culture, the longing for self-shattering honed by Petrarchan lyric prepares the way for quite similar ideological uses. Naturally, too, critics have been keen, in the wake of Louis Montrose and Philippa Berry, to identify the particularly gendered politics of the court of Queen Elizabeth (that greatest of Petrarchan beloveds) with the rhetoric of submission and domination in Petrarchan lyric.[16] Roland Greene's *Post-Petrarchism* identifies the rhetoric of submission and domination not merely as the oft-invoked heart of the Petrarchan scene but as a constitutive element of lyric, which Greene identifies as ritualistic: "Lyric is utterance uniquely disposed to be re-uttered. In performance it may be not only compulsory but coercive discourse, for the nature of lyric's ritual dimension, simply stated, is to superpose the subjectivity of the scripted speaker on the reader, and that substitution can entail a kind of violence."[17] Christopher Warley's reading of Petrarchan sequences places power in the hands of the poet attempting "to describe, and to invent new social positions before there existed an explicit vocabulary to define them."[18] Spenser's *Amoretti*, Warley suggests, places its faith in the construction of a social order anchored by the idea of a feudal Irish landlord. To be a subject apparently endowed with agency is to be subject to, or thrown down before, a power over which one holds no mastery. As Judith Butler puts it, in a rather Foucauldian formulation, "Power that at first appears as external, pressed upon the subject, pressing the subject into subordination, assumes a psychic form that constitutes the subject's self-identity."[19]

With lyric itself perpetrating or promulgating violence while slyly enforcing state or religious authority, it was inevitable that the perpetration of violence was to take center stage in readings of Petrarchan sequences. Moreover, it has become a critical commonplace to identify "masculine desire" in early modernity as solely "exercised in the name of conquest, possession, and determination."[20] Sally Minogue, for example, identifies a highly self-reflexive acquiescence to female rule in Philip Sidney's relationship to England's Cynthia. Minogue locates this ironic self-abnegation in his gift to Elizabeth of "a diamond bedecked whip," which indicates "his recognition of Elizabeth's absolute power over him" and constitutes "a witty coded self-abasement."[21] Despite this subjection, Minogue argues, Elizabeth was the only woman to whom the Petrarchan lover was subservient; in all other cases, the lover controls the lady through the power of representation. In this way of thinking, abject masculinity of the Petrarchan variety remains, despite its appearance, a will to power that conceals its longing for domination. A series of critics, following the lead of Nancy Vickers, borrow from Laura Mulvey's classic argument about cinema that features the "determining male gaze [that] projects its phantasy onto the female figure, which is styled accordingly."[22] Male looking is a form of epic domination (an act Mulvey explicitly links to sadism) that "demands a story, depends on making something happen, forcing a change in another person, a battle of will and strength, victory / defeat." Thus, Vickers argues, the poet in the Petrarchan scene "transforms the [lady's] visible totality into scattered words, the body into signs; his description, at one remove from his experience, safely permits and perpetuates his fascination."[23]

The primary myth that governs this dynamic, Vickers argues, is that of Actaeon, whose accidental vision of the naked Diana provoked punishment; he was transformed into a stag and ripped to pieces by his own hounds. Just as Actaeon was fragmented by desire, the Actaeon-like poet compensates for his suffering by breaking the beloved woman into her constitutive parts through blazon and praise. Thus sadistic masculinity conceals itself in masochistic abjection by fragmenting the body of the woman, eradicating the specificity of female subjectivity and voice. Vickers argues, "Bodies fetishized by a poetic voice logically do not have a voice of their own; the world of making texts is not theirs."[24] Ironically, the canzone at the heart of Vickers analysis is the one in which Laura, in response to the speaker's confession of his love, retorts angrily, "I'non son forse chi tu credi" (Perhaps I am not what you believe me to be).[25] Mark Breitenberg, among others, joins the chorus of condemnation, naming the Petrarchan sonnet "a literary form that perpetuates the empowerment of men at the expense of women" because "it constructs and confirms men as looking and writing subjects. Petrarchism sustains male poets in control of the medium of representation, thus denying women any public means of representing their own subjectivity."[26] Abject masculinity that risks effeminate behavior is equally a threat, according to Breitenberg, who argues that this represents "the power of appropriating woman," which "spills over into a form of pleasure in acting as woman."[27] This construction of early modern masculinity creates a particular double bind. On the one hand, to write a masculine "I" is to oppress and erase women. On the other hand, to represent femininity or, even worse, to identify with femininity is to appropriate and erase it. Carol Siegel argues, more generally, that the male masochist attempts to occupy a feminine subject position and, in so doing, evicts the woman and represents a "negation of female specificity."[28]

Early modern lyric sequences enabled poets to rehearse a variety of gendered postures and positions, as critics have increasingly pointed out. The very lyric at the heart of Vickers's analysis, Petrarch's twenty-third canzone, is, as she admits, a lyric of metamorphosis. The speaker is wrung through a variety of changes culminating in the figure of Actaeon. Prior to this, Petrarch's speaker becomes Daphne (a laurel tree), Cygnus (a swan), Battus (a stone), Biblis (a fountain), and Echo (a disembodied voice). Like a Proteus, the speaker of this canzone comes to assume not only all these shapes but also the lineaments of a variety of desires and affects—fear, grief, and incestuous longing, among others. Most importantly, it is interesting that the lyric's speaker's first metamorphic impulse is to assume the shape of the beloved object. Despite his desire for the poetic honor of the laurel leaves and the woman whose name constantly evokes them, Petrarch's speaker finds himself *becoming* what he originally wishes to possess. One might even argue that Petrarch's twenty-third canzone responds to the imaginative crisis of not only becoming the thing he desired but, by virtue of that transformation, experiencing rather than inflicting violence. It is the male speaker immobilized and not Daphne fleeing her rapist. As Cygnus, who grieves for Phaeton, the speaker laments the self-destructive ambitions of masculinity. As Battus, the speaker indicts fickle, untrustworthy masculinity. As Biblis, who desires her own twin brother, and through Echo, who disembodies herself for the sake of the self-absorbed Narcissus, Petrarch indicts the narcissism so easily associated with Petrarchan erotic discourse. As he becomes Actaeon, the speaker admits, "Io perchè d'altra vista non m'appago / steti a mirarla" (Because I could not satisfy myself with any other sight / I stood staring at her [152–53]). Whereas the gaze of Ovid's Actaeon is accidental, here the gaze is culpably obsessive. As punishment, Petrarch's Actaeon notes, "senti' trarmi de la propria imago" (I felt myself torn from my proper likeness [157]). Satisfaction, rather than its frustration, is precisely what rends the speaker, as the rhyme between "imago" and "appago" may indicate. The speaker is torn from the self that cannot tear itself from the desire that provokes its ready violation of the woman's vulnerable body. This canzone indicates a speaker less like the one Vickers imagines and more like the one Barbara Estrin imagines. In her reading of Petrarch, the lyric self is always performative, "always already the other even in those moments when it seems to be more intensively self-assertive."[29] Estrin joins Dorothy Stephens, Gordon Braden, Catherine Bates, Diana Henderson, and Lynn Enterline, whose recent works on Ovid, Spenser, Gaspara Stampa, and Sidney, question the identification of domineering masculinity with the Petrarchan scenario.[30]

And yet many have underestimated the complexities of power in the Petrarchan lyric while, more importantly, conflating these scenarios of subjection with unthinking references to sadomasochism. For some critics the purported sadomasochism of Petrarchan eroticism reflects an entire culture of subjection. But the true masochism of Spenser's poetry resides in its capacity to analyze and even imagine differently patterns of submission and domination. As Gilles Deleuze puts it, the point of masoschism is "not to describe the world, since this has already been done, but to define a counterpart of the world capable of containing its violence and excesses."[31] First, there is a kind of masochistic theatricality in Petrarchan poetry that acts out, to parody and to revise, fantasies of domination. Theodor Reik describes masochism as a phenomenon of strategic deviation, of going "astray in order to reach [a] secret aim by detour."[32] Detour and compromise are the central creative strategies of the masochist for whom desire provokes a particular species of anxiety that interrupts pleasure. He responds first by projecting a world of fantasy, constructing the scene and objects of desire to replace an inhibited world of action. In that setting, the masochist forges new relationships between pleasure and anxiety; pleasure appropriates anxiety, using that anxiety to extend erotic experience and prevent closure. This drive forward, through pain to pleasure, Reik calls "the flight to the future."[33] Experiences of pain and humiliation and the exhibition of such sufferings come to constitute a subversive triumph over, not a capitulation to, authority; rather, the application of violence exposes the futility of punishment as mechanisms of discipline are appropriated for the uses of pleasure.[34]

Secondly, the perverse triumph of this masochistic theater of domination depends on a series of reversals—pain for pleasure, parody for acquiescence, masculine for feminine. As Adela Pinch notes, "Masochism is the name for a structure that involves not only an identification with suffering but also an identification across gender boundaries."[35] Thirdly, Petrarchan poetry may aim at sex as the culminating act of erotic possession, but by forestalling or avoiding consummation, this poetry displaces sexual conquest, substituting for it other pleasures. Foucault, with reference to contemporary sexual communities and practices, describes sadomasochism as "a kind of creation, a creative enterprise, which has as one of its main features what I call the desexualization of pleasure. The idea that bodily pleasure should always come from sexual pleasure as the root of *all* our possible pleasure—I think *that's* something quite wrong."[36] Finally, Deleuze emphasizes masochism's primary recourse to disavowal, which "should perhaps be understood as the point of departure of an operation that consists neither in negating nor even destroying, but rather in radically contesting the validity of that which is: it suspends belief in and neutralizes the given in such a way that a new horizon opens up beyond the given and in place of it."[37] Masochistic fantasy attempts to contain and reimagine the violent excesses of the world using these strategies: the appropriation of mechanisms of discipline, reversals of power and gender roles, the displacement of sexual consummation or possession as a driving goal, and, finally, a disavowal of the status quo and the substitution of an alternative vision to replace it.

Like *The Faerie Queene*, Spenser's *Amoretti* explores states of vulnerability and sets the stage for a masochistic contestation of the discourse of subjection. But as dictated by the Petrarchan tradition, Spenser's *Amoretti*, at first, seems to conform to the disingenuous rhetoric of masculine submission that conceals the will to dominate, presenting a lover at the mercy of the powerful beloved. The lover, unable to obtain his beloved, responds as Reik's masochist might, frustration and denial generating the sonnet sequence as a creative alternative. Having projected a fantasy scene, the lover stages his desire in the dominant metaphors of combat, in accordance with the contract established by Petrarchan tradition. She is a "tyrannes" and "cruel warrior." She takes "hostages" and "ambushes" the speaker. The speaker "sues for peace" and tries to make "treat[ies]" to no avail.[38] All the while the lover displays himself demonstratively, bemoaning his agony. Whereas the lover of Spenser's later Neoplatonic hymns claims a shaping power over the object of his desire, the beloved of the *Amoretti*, elusive and inaccessible, exerts power. The lover claims:

> You frame my thoughts, and fashion me within;
> You stop my tongue, and teach my heart to speak;
> You calm the storm that passion did begin.
> (*Amoretti* 8.9–11)

Desire provokes a reversal not merely of the poet-lover's power to "fashion" the object of his fantasy and desire; it also reverses the power of looking from which derives the power to create. Again and again in the *Amoretti* the speaker stresses the power of the beloved's eyes:

> Fair eyes! The mirror of my mazéd heart,
> What wondrous virtue is contained in you,
> The which both life and death forth from you dart,
> Into the object of your mighty view?
> (*Amoretti* 7.1–4)

In the *Hymn in Honour of Beauty*, the beloved's "wondrous virtue" is extracted and reshaped, and the beloved becomes no more than a mirror to reflect the lover's thoughts and desires. Here, the beloved is the mirror, or exemplar, of virtue that the lover reflects. As such, her eyes possess the power of life and death over the lover, who is no more than a fashioned object.

Dissatisfied with the power the beloved possesses, the lover of the *Amoretti* makes a flight forward, through the anxieties and difficulties of love, a flight from pain to pleasure. The poet asks, "Why then should I account of little pain, / That endless pleasure shall unto me gain?" (*Amoretti* 26.13–14). He remarks, similarly, "All pains are nothing in respect of this; / All sorrows short that gain eternal bliss" (*Amoretti* 62.13–14). Though this gesture is in keeping with the strategies Reik associates with masochism, it is also an attempt to translate pain into pleasure, replacing the former with the latter and making suffering no more than a wayside stop on the route to power and possession. The lover argues, "fondness it were for any, being free, / To covet fetters though they golden be" (*Amoretti* 37.13–14). In renouncing his own abject, masochistic state, the speaker attempts to perpetrate a reversal. He advises the beloved to renounce her liberty in order to procure a new kind of liberty for the two of them:

> Sweet be the bands, the which true love doth tie
> Without constraint, or dread of any ill:
> The gentle bird feels no captivity
> Within her cage: but sings and feeds her fill.
> (*Amoretti* 65.5–8)

By reversing the scenario, the speaker leaves behind his weakness as the beloved abandons her cruelty. However, the speaker's freedom comes at the price of the beloved's freedom. In the *Amoretti*'s poem of capture, the lover at last becomes huntsman rather than prey:

> Like as a huntsman after weary chase
> Seeing the game from him escaped away,
> Sits down to rest in some shady place,
> With panting hounds beguiléd of their prey:
> So after long pursuit and vain assay,
> When I all weary had the chase forsook,
> The gentle dear returned the self-same way,
> Thinking to quench her thirst at the next brook:
> There she beholding me with milder look,
> Sought not to fly, but fearless still did bide;
> Till I in hand her yet half trembling took,
> And with her own good-will her firmly tied.
> (*Amoretti* 67.1–12)

This metaphoric substitution and reversal of roles exposes a sly will to power in the speaker's rhetoric, for concealed within abject suffering is a fierce urge for control. Actaeon catches his prey instead of being reduced to Diana's prey. In order to gain control, the beloved needed to acquiescence rather than be conquered, to refuse her prior lack of sympathy ("she is no woman but a senseless stone" [*Amoretti* 54.14]) for a state of mutual captivity earlier recommended. In reality, however, the lover has simply projected his own impotent vulnerability onto the figure of the beloved who now is "thralléd to his love" and "now captived / So firmly that she never may remove" (*Amoretti* 71.6–8). The fantasized reversal places the beloved in a "sweet prison" of eternal peace.

Spenser's *Amoretti* shows the progress from erotic frustration to a fantasy of self-gratification that reveals a formerly veiled will to power by which the lover assumes poetry's shaping power. The anxiety provoked by the beloved's inaccessibility provokes a *flight forward* through anxiety and pain to pleasure. This suffering represents a parodic victory through defeat but also indicates an attempted *flight out* of masochism by reversing the roles yet again. In the *Amoretti*, then, we see the lover attempt to convert a masochistic compromise into a more conventionally gendered arrangement by compelling the beloved's sympathetic identification with his suffering and then projecting his own captivity onto her. This is, no doubt, the very aspect of masculinity that Breitenberg, Vickers, and others critique and that is amply demonstrated in sonnet 69, which, with a surge of masculine, heroic metaphor, debates how best to memorialize the triumph of the lover's conquest, as in the manner of the "famous warriors of the anticke world" (*Amoretti* 69.1). This triumph represents a grand payoff of his "labour and long toyle" (*Amoretti* 69.14).

This is not, however, the end of the *Amoretti*'s story. Immediately following the reassertion of masculine dominion in the sonnet of capture, the beloved remains oddly elusive as the very notions of both capture and love change irrevocably in the wake of a devotional Easter sonnet that follows hard upon the lover's victory. The sixty-eighth sonnet celebrates the rebirth of divinity through pain and death. Christ may, in this sonnet, be described in triumphant language: "the Glorious lord of lyfe that on this day / Didst make thy triumph over death and sin" (*Amoretti* 68.1–2). Certainly, this is a Christ who "harrowd hell" in order to redeem the "captivity" of tortured souls. As such, this sounds like the ideal Christ for the Petrarchan lover (*Amoretti* 68.3–4) But the "felicity" provided by this triumphant Christ depends on the spilling of blood. In other words, the rearticulation of love through the language of Christ's passion makes the pain of Petrarchan verse similarly transformative. The speaker calls finally to the beloved: "So let us love, deare love, lyke as we ought, / love the lesson that the Lord us taught" (*Amoretti* 68.13–14). Given, as Anne Lake Prescott has argued, that the preceding sonnet of capture contains the elements of medieval ritual (the Easter Eve ritual in which the hart, water, and willing submission are all part), we can see that *imitatio Christi* is no distant memory for this sonnet.[39] Love works through transformative pain that renders lovers "lyke," suggesting a relationship of similitude rather than of domination.

The failure of masculine domination to constitute love in the terms of the paschal sonnet explains, perhaps, why the speaker of the sequence discards his celebratory tone and displays, instead, increasing anxiety about the absence of the beloved in the face of distance, loss of intimacy, or death itself. Acquisition is fleeting; no sooner is the beloved caught (and celebrated) than the beloved is again absent. When erotic capture defines the speaker's love, that absence is palpable. The speaker reverts to an abject position, becoming the "gentle dear" so recently captured:

> Lacking my love, I go from place to place,
> Like as a young fawn, that late hath lost the hind
> And seek each where, where last I saw her face
> (*Amoretti* 78.1–3)

As when the lover seeks refuge in the sheltering bosom of the beloved, so too does he seek the comfort of a physical, maternal presence that eludes him as it does the "young fawn" who seeks the hind. Neither the scattered Actaeon nor the punishing Diana appears; the register of desire shifts from masculine erotic quest to longing for maternal care. The speaker enters a new masochistic contract, one characterized by an understanding of love as likeness:

> But, when mine eyes I thereunto direct,
> They idly back return to me again:
> And, when I hope to see their true object,
> I find myself but fed with fancies vain.
> Cease then, mine eyes, to seek herself to see;
> And let my thoughts behold herself in me.
> (*Amoretti* 78.9–14)

Spenser exposes the desire to capture the beloved as a fantasy that the speaker has previously taken for reality. When the lover stops looking for the beloved, he abandons the masculine gaze that either scatters or is scattered, that fashions or is fashioned by the woman. Just as Petrarch's lover becomes, briefly, the Daphne he seeks, so too here does Spenser's lover attempt an identification with, rather than an acquisition of, the woman he desires. Here, there is no anxiety that the desire for women effeminizes the lover. Spenser suggests that the lover should *be*, rather than *have*, the woman he desires. If we follow the *Amoretti* into Spenser's life, we identify an erotic trajectory that ends with his marriage to Elizabeth Boyle and the writing of his *Epithalamion*, one of the great marriage poems in the English language. However, if we follow the continuing journey of the *Amoretti* into the Legend of Chastity, we follow the struggle to restructure desire by deploying imitative sympathy and mutual vulnerability. Out of the *Amoretti* emerges Amoret, the culmination of the lover's attempt to "behold" the beloved in himself through an imaginative and sympathetic identification, and the attempt to fashion a vulnerable masculinity continues in Britomart's redemption of Scudamour's failed masculinity.

Spenser's "Letter of the Authors" identifies Britomart's rescue of Amoret as accidental. The letter assigns the quest of rescuing Amoret, kidnapped from her own wedding by the enchanter Busyrane, to Sir Scudamour, who is also, conveniently, the lady's bridegroom. Oddly, a nameless groom delivers the news of this *raptus* and the resulting quest to the court where the bereaved Scudamour waits. Scudamour fails but is lucky enough to be aided by Britomart, who happens along. Of the many oddities of Spenser's letter, both the description of a quest's failure *before* its occurrence and the figure of the groom, who seems to distance Scudamour from his bride and from the trauma of his own loss, is notable. The letter presents the structure of masculine quest itself as failed *avant la lettre*. Britomart is deflected from her own quest for successful, dynastic heterosexuality and projected into the detour that becomes her ultimate test in the culminating episode of the Legend of Chastity by an act of sympathetic identification with a spectacle of wrecked masculinity. Britomart stumbles across Amoret's would-be husband Scudamour and trades one erotic dilemma for another as

> she heard with greiuous throb
> Him grone, as if his hart were peeces made
> And with most painefull pangs to sigh and sob,
> That pitty did the Virgins hart of patience rob.
> (3.11.8)

Captivated by his agony, Britomart listens to his tale and promises succor as she sympathizes with the suffering and shattered masculinity before her. Whereas Redcrosse, Arthur, and Guyon in the face of male suffering oscillate between states of paralysis and violent remedy, Britomart offers compassionate witness and promises, "I will with proofe of last extremity, / Deliuer her fro thence, or with her for you dy" (3.11.18). This gesture of devotion elicits admiration, for he claims:

> Ah gentlest knight aliue (sayd *Scudamore*)
> What huge heroicke magnanimity
> Dwels in thy bounteous brest? what couldst thou more
> If shee were thine, and thou as now am I?
> (3.11.19)

Scudamour's gratitude exposes the powerful identificatory contract Britomart has entered, which crosses the tenuous border between sympathy and desire. She will, she claims, die for him in seeking his love, which is both a gesture of desire and a gesture of identification and replacement. Scudamour recognizes Britomart's offer to replace him as a heroic gesutre. In saving Scudamour, the wrecked spectacle of masculinity, Britomart will save herself as well. Thus, through Britomart Scudamour will gain access to Amoret just as through Britomart "Spenser" gains access to masculinity. As a masculine, female Petrarchan lover, Britomart will be the compromise that saves love. She is, however, more than merely a relay between Amoret and Scudamour, since she is also a subject of desire through Scudamour. In the end, she has the chance to win Amoret and accomplish her own masculine identification. As opposed to the erotic scene in which a dominant masculinity rules and ruins all, Britomart veers into a productive, masochistic detour.

Busyrane keeps Amoret captive, thrall to his perverse pleasure. His pleasure is, in fact, not merely torture. Though he controls her body, Busyrane, like Proteus, seeks Amoret's *love*, which she refuses to surrender. As such, Busyrane's various torments, literalize Petrarchan tropes, include the piercing of Amoret's exposed heart with a dart. While there are significant variations in accounts of the significance of the House of Busyrane, of the demonic masque of Cupid that displays the captive Amoret, and of the abduction itself, nearly all the critical accounts maintain particularly limited mappings of desire, rarely straying from heterosexuality. Thomas Roche, for example, affirms a contentious way of seeing Amoret's captivity as a projection of her fear of the cruelties of sexual passion.[40] For Helen Cheney Gilde, Amoret's captivity represents the trauma of a failure to integrate sexual passion and love.[41] Others, rather than blaming Amoret, describe the House of Busyrane as a particular failure of erotic discourse in early modernity. For C. S. Lewis, the scene indicates a problem of courtly love, which, in the reunion of Amoret and Scudamour, is replaced by a model of companionate marriage.[42] Maureen Quilligan reads the scene as a critique of the sterility and misogyny of Petrarchan language. Understandably, critics read Busyrane as the aggressor. He is a "sadistic sonneteer" according to Quilligan;[43] one who perpetrates a "vengeance of male sexuality on the chastely reticent female" according to Roche;[44] a "sadistic torturer" according to Sheila Cavanagh;[45] an exemplar of the "corruption of sexual desire" according to James Broaddus;[46] and a figure, according to Lauren Silberman, whose "mere sadomasochism" Spenser refuses.[47] Although Katherine Eggert has more recently attempted to distinguish between rape and rapture in the Legend of Chastity, the most serious of recent claims posits the capture and torture of Amoret as a rape scene.[48] Cavanagh, for example, deplores what she sees as the constant abuse of women in *The Faerie Queene* and the deployment of representations akin to contemporary misogynistic pornography. Likewise, Susan Frye argues for the scene of Amoret's imprisonment as a rape that enforces a particular vision of married chastity. As such, she identifies "Spenser as a central popularizer, aestheticizer, and enforcer of marriage through the threat of rape."[49] More recently, Chih-hsin Lin complicates the courtly love tropes of Amoret's suffering by introducing notions of married chastity in the writings of Martin Luther and John Calvin, thus rendering heterosexual marriage, newly sacralized by Reformation theology, Amoret's defining condition.[50]

Without disregarding frequent manifestations of sexual aggression in *The Faerie Queene*, we can see that, despite the painful fixity suggested by Amoret's capture, a great deal of ambiguity persists. Scudamour, who has not had access to the castle let alone his would-be bride, describes the heart as "riue[n] in tway," while it appears differently in the Masque of Cupid, "quite through transfixed with a deadly dart," and then in Busyrane's inner chamber only "seeming transfixed with a cruell dart" (3.11.11; 3.12.21, 31). A great deal of criticism has, like Busyrane, attempted to fix the meaning of this most slippery of organs. But sexuality in the House of Busyrane, and in the Legend of Chastity, remains far from easily assimilated to the violent heterosexuality that some critics incorrectly refer to as sadomasochism and that proleptically figures the hermaphroditic union of Amoret and Scudamour excised in the 1596 text; for, despite either Merlin's dynastic narrative of Britomart and Arthegall early in the Legend of Chastity, Britomart's quest takes her through a landscape of complex and non-normative sexualities, from her homoerotic encounter with Malecasta to the lascivious and effeminate Ollyphant, one of a brother-sister pair of giants, whose perversity begins with an incestuous coupling in the womb. Prior to encountering Scudamour, Britomart saves a squire whom Ollyphant kidnapped to satisfy his nefarious tastes; this penchant for sexual abduction he shares with his masculine sister, Argante, who also nabs young boys. In obscuring this sexual diversity, invocations of Busyrane's sadism have a normalizing function, securing the dominance of heterosexual forms of eroticism. As Kaja Silverman has argued, sadism is not only "the perversion which has commandeered most of the literary and theoretical attention" but "also the one which is the most compatible with conventional heterosexuality."[51]

The desiring heart around which the whole scene of Amoret's capture orbits is, as I have mentioned, revealed in three separate moments, beginning with Scudamour's narration of a scene to which he has had no access. Having passed to Busyrane's inner sanctum, Britomart then witnesses the tortured Amoret. Amoret's heart is not, in fact, "riue[n] in tway" but "transfixed." Later, at the end of the Masque of Cupid, she sees

> a wide wound therein (O ruefull sight)
> Entrenched deep with knife accursed keene,
> Yet freshly bleeding forth, her fainting spright
> (The worke of cruell hand) was to be seene . . .
> . . . .
> At that wide orifice her trembling hart
> Was drawne forth, and in siluer basin layd,
> Quite through transfixed with a deadly dart.
> (3.12.20–21)

In Busyrane's chamber we see that heart simply exposed:

> And her before the vile Enchaunter sate,
> Figuring straunge characters of his art,
> With liuing blood he those characters wrate,
> Dreadfully dropping from her dying hart,

> Seemingly transfixed with a cruell dart,
> And all perforce to make her him to loue.
>
> (3.12.31)

Again and again the Legend of Chastity circles back to Amoret's heart. The wound here is, certainly, a wound of love, but despite Busyrane's bizarre coercion, the imagery of the scene suggests that this is not the wound of the idealized woman abused and violated by masculine desire. The wounded heart of the Petrarchan scene belongs, rather, to the *lover* and not to the *beloved*. It is the lover of *Amoretti* who prostrates himself, exposing his heart in the demonstrative throes of his verse. In the first sonnet that speaker identifies his body and spirit with the text of his love as he urges his lady to "read the sorrows of my dying sprite / Written with tears in heart's close-bleeding blood" (*Amoretti* 1.7–8). In sonnet 22 the speaker asserts his desire in the language of religious devotion, promising he will "build an altar to appease" his lady's "ire / And on the same [his] heart will sacrifice / Burning in flames of pure and chaste desire" (*Amoretti* 22.9–12). Just as each sonnet provides a different portrait of the desiring heart, so too is each snapshot of Amoret's heart a different perspective on the scene of desire. One might recognize this essentially Spenserian gesture in a later writer from whom the masochistic nature of writing gained its name. Leopold von Sacher-Masoch's Severin admits, in his diary, "And yet I am writing with no ordinary ink but with the red blood that drips from my heart; and the wounds that were healed long ago have opened up again and throb with pain; now and then a tear falls on the page."[52] Amoret is, then, not so much an object to master but a subject position arrived at; she, Busyrane, and even the weeping Scudamour offer interlocking portraits of self-torturing masculinity immobilized by its own vulnerability and desperate to project that vulnerability onto the flesh of its objects of desire.

The rescue of Amoret by Britomart represents a radical analysis of Petrarchan masculinity, rescuing it from self-immobilizing fantasies in which subjection is experienced and simultaneously projected onto the bodies of desired women. But how, then, is the Legend of Chastity to fashion a subject rooted in vulnerability amidst all of this violence? The answer lies in Britomart, the figure through whom Spenser reformulates masculinity as *female masculinity*, the genesis of which he tracks in an extended portrait of Britomart's entry into subjectivity. Yet at first Britomart seems no solution to but rather part of the problem of the violent competition typified by heroic masculinity in *The Faerie Queene*, as her debut confirms:

> At last as through an open plaine they yode,
> They spide a knight, that towards pricked fayre,
> And him beside an aged Squire there rode.
> (3.1.4)

In this opening scene, Guyon and Arthur mistake the exemplar of chastity for both an enemy and a man. The combat that follows constitutes another bungled passing of the torch, from one titular knight to the next, as Guyon unsuccessfully challenges the incoming Knight of Chastity, Britomart. Whereas at first the context and the pronouns fool knights and readers alike, the reader, at least, is informed that Guyon's mysterious opponent is none other than "a single damzell." Indeed, the narrator teases Guyon with the shame he would experience if only he were aware of Britomart's true gender. At the same time, that narrator also, it seems, attempts to soothe his might-have-been-threatened masculinity: "For not thy fault, but secret powre vnseene, / That speare enchaunted was, which layd thee on the greene" (3.1.7). The narrator's claim seems dubious. Certainly Britomart is not the only knight to wield enchanted equipment; nearly all the knights, not least of all Arthur, have, in accordance with romance tradition, talismanic weapons and arms.[53] Rather than indicating weakness, Britomart's enchanted spear suggestively supplements the phallic masculinity on display in Guyon's attack; as Kathryn Schwartz has argued of the Legend of Chastity, "Masculinity was never male to begin with."[54] Yet the narrator makes amply clear that, though Guyon might have been publicly shamed for his failed performance, he is spared the knowledge of Britomart's gender, the ensuing embarrassment, and the anxiety of having been replaced by a woman. Guyon is spared this humiliation, but as a consequence he passes into narrative obsolescence.

Studies by Schwartz and Valerie Traub, among others, have noted the extent to which the female appropriation of masculinity in early modernity produces anxiety and even violence.[55] While such anxieties may persist in *The Faerie Queene* it is also clear that Britomart's assumption of the mantle of heroism in the Legend of Chastity makes her the culminating figure in his project to fashion a gentleman or, in Britomart's case, a noble person. But is masculinity enacted by the female body necessarily a solution to the problem of creating a vulnerable subject? At first, it would seem that Britomart's instantiation of heroic masculinity is as problematically prone to uncontrollable martial violence as any of the other figures in the poem. Her vision of chastity seems to extend the defensive armature of virginity that the warlike Belphoebe embodies; chastity encases Britomart like her armor and shifts from defense to offense with blinding rapidity.

Moreover, if Foucault is right to suggest that Christianity is typified not merely by confession but also by the battle for chastity, does that battle signify anything, for Britomart, except paranoid defense? Chastity was not only a battle for the autonomy of the will but also, with respect to women, a social phenomenon of substantial force. As the necessary precondition to proper marriage, Theodora Jankowski describes premarried chastity, or virginity, as, "a 'means' toward an 'end' of social integration and conformity."[56] As a quality that ensures lineage, inheritance, and proper class distinctions, "virginity carries the seeds of its own destruction" thus giving way to married chastity. But while "early modern English society expected a virgin to be chaste, silent, and obedient," Jankowski insists, "adult virgin women can be considered a queer space within the early modern Protestant sex-gender system." Jankowski's study rests, in part, on the earlier work of Philipa Berry, who argues that Elizabethan chastity might be construed not as a capitulation to the demand that women be asexual and the sexual on demand for marriage but as "feminine autonomy" from masculine prerogative.[57] Thus chastity was also the landscape of a battle for autonomy from masculine rule and, as Berry puts it, for the representation of women as something other than "a lifeless mirror" of male self-knowledge.

But to what end does the Legend of Chastity deploy this potential space of female autonomy? It seems the substitution of the male world of martial endeavor for an all, or mostly, female world enables a trajectory in which vulnerability comes to be the true test for heroic masculinity. Rather quickly, in the Legend of Chastity, men are rendered more or less obsolete (including the defeat of Guyon and the necessity of rescuing Redcrosse) with respect to heroism as well as chastity, leaving the critical moments in the book, and even Britomart's first "test" of chastity at the castle of Malecasta ("badly chaste"), a matter that occurs among women. Britomart's departure from the scene of Florimell's flight leads her directly to the gates of Castle Joyeous, one of many veritable theme parks of sordid sexuality in *The Faerie Queene*. There, Britomart defends Redcrosse knight from the assault of six other knights, who would compel him to abandon his love for their lady and each of which represents a different step on the ladder of lechery that afflicts the unchaste. After defeating these knights handily, and barely being wounded by one, Garadante (the sin of erotic "looking"), Britomart gains entry for herself and Redcrosse, where they are feasted and shown the "loose demeanure" and "lasciuious disport" of Malecasta. Britomart remains armed, thus obscured, and attracts the attention of her hostess, who develops a loose passion for her "all ignorant of her contrary sex" (III.i.47.1) and crawls into her bed that night to disastrous consequences.

J. E. Hankins and others argue that the scene constitutes a particular test of chastity in which Britomart's sleep allegorically represents the temporary slumber of her chastity.[58] In addition, critics read Malecasta as an embodiment of the particularly dangerous temptations of courtly love. That Britomart does not leave unscathed further indicates that she has, as Roche remarks, "partially succumbed to the beauty of castle Joyeous and thus deserves a slight wound."[59] Should we presume that the "beauty of castle Joyeous" Roche notes would not refer to Malecasta herself? Indeed, few critics seem to notice (or care) that if Britomart is unchaste it would be in relation to another woman. The narrative offers some reason for this; Malecasta, we are told, is "All ignoraunt of [Britomart's] contrary sex" (3.1.47) just as "Britomart would not such guilfull message know" (III.i.51.9). Moreover, Britomart appears as an ambivalently gendered figure in Castle Joyeous:

For she was full of amiable grace,
    And manly terrour mixed therewithall,
    That as the one stird vp affections bace,
    So th'other did mens rash desires apall,
    And hold them backe, that would in errour fall;
    As he that hath espide a vermeill Rose,
    To which sharpe thornes and breres the way forstall,
    Dare not for dread his hardy hand expose,
But wishing it far off, his idle wish doth lose.

(3.1.46)

One might read this scene of desire as "lesbian" in some sense, as Camille Paglia and James Norhnberg do, or as a cross-gendering of the scenario of Petrarchan or courtly love, as one critic does when he suggests that just "as Britomart is a woman disguised as a man, Malecasta is, in effect, a man disguised as a woman."[60] And yet the trading of masculine for feminine is not necessarily the fundamental revision in this regendered quest. The mixture of masculine and feminine qualities appears notably as a mixture of postures that vulnerably solicit ("stird up affectiosn bace") or aggressively dissuade ("rashe desire appall") the sexual will of others. In her very appearance, Britomart enacts or encourages a battle of chastity in which sexual desires evoked by physical appearance are violently quelled.

Certainly, this pattern holds for Malecasta and Britomart's late night rendezvous. Although initially rejected, disconsolate Malecasta sneaks into Britomart's bedroom only to timidly lie in bed next to her. Britomart's reaction, upon brushing up against her, is to assume the presence of a "loathed leachour" (3.1.62). She springs up violently, shocking Malecasta into a shriek and a swoon. Malecasta's knights respond, noting the figure of Britomart, "the warlike Mayd/ All in her snow-white smocke, with locks vnbownd,/ Threatening the point of her auenging blade" (3.1.63). Here, at this moment of vulnerable disarmament, Britomart's appearance assures us of her purity and feminine modesty. But Britomart's reaction to Malecasta's advances seems disproportionately defensive. It is hard not to see the "auenging blade," the "flaming sword" of the lady knight as an odd combination of arousal and aggression. Britomart's fierce over-articulation of militant chastity contrasts quite markedly with Malecasta's less than libidinous advances. She may work her "crafty engins" in sneaking into the bedroom, but little else happens (3.1.57). Indeed, she comes rather sympathetically as one who suffers from the wound of love and even resembles Britomart's pain: "find[ing] no rest in such perplexed plight" (3.1.59). Despite her well-documented looseness, she doesn't touch Britomart. Rather, Malecasta was "Of euery finest fingers touch affrayd; / Ne any noise she made, ne word she spake, / But inly sigh'd" (3.1.61). With an absence of clear lechery, it seems hard to agree with one critic who argues that "Spenser has managed to portray Malecasta's infatuation sympathetically enough so that the reader is more amused than condemning of her loose behavior. The allegorical meaning of the scene is clear: the 'badly chaste woman' lives with fantasy, not love, and her indecent behavior carries with it the seeds of her own outrage."[61] So what it is about Malecasta that so disturbs the imperturbable Britomart?

As Foucault remarks of Cassian, the culminating victory in the battle of chastity was the eradication of not merely voluntary breaches of chastity but of all involuntary concupiscence (as in sleep or dream). Thus it seems the ethical practice of constantly questing for the truth of the self requires "eternal vigilance, a suspiciousness directed at every moment against one's thought, an endless self-questioning to flush out any secret fornication lurking in the inmost recesses of the mind."[62] This self-objectifying vigilance seems quite apt in describing Britomart's paranoid impregnability. She fails not in rejecting the advances of the desiring Malecasta but, rather, in rejecting a kind of vulnerability, an openness to the pain of others, but also to a kind of physical intimacy and social affiliation rooted in friendship and shared pain that later she finds in the arms of Amoret.

Britomart may be the exemplar of chastity, but from her disregard for Florimell's pain to her zeal for combat to her violent rejection of Malecasta, she fails to constitute a heroic masculinity vulnerable to others and receptive to the pain of others. In some sense, this lapse compels the narrative to retrace Britomart's coming into being as a knight and exemplar of chastity by retelling her history in the most extended portrait in *The Faerie Queene* of the prehistory of a titular knight. The images she sees, as a young girl, in Venus's looking glass initiates a transformation that materializes Britomart as both a suffering, vulnerable body *and* masculine knight. A number of critics have associated the complicated play of likeness and difference in Lacan's mirror stage with the genesis of Britomart's quest.[63] The *infans*, "sunk in motor incapacity and nursling dependence," sees an image of him or herself which, in its visual coherence, he or she takes as both a model for and an indication of his or her own stable subjectivity.[64] By wishing to be the stable, coherent object perceived, the child commits a fundamental act of *méconaissance*, orienting the self in a "fictional direction" by mistaking the visual coherence of an image for psychic coherence and bodily capacity. Identification has extraordinary implications as the child enters "a temporal dialectic that decisively projects the formation of the individual into history. The *mirror stage* is a drama whose internal thrust is precipitated from insufficiency to anticipation—and which manufactures for the subject, caught up in the lure of spatial identification, the succession of fantasies that extends from a fragmented body-image to a form of its totality . . . and lastly to the assumption of the armour of alienating identity, which mark with its rigid structure the subject's entire mental development."[65] Misrecognition indicates the fallibility of an empowered, stable self; that self is no more than the projection of an aggressive rationalization. Identity is armor, a rigid, masculine structure, and though it provides only the "illusion of autonomy," it is that illusion that enables "its function as a subject."[66]

Just as what Lacan calls *méconaissance*, or misrecognition, forms the appropriate opening of the Legend of Chastity, so too is the mirror a suitable image to associate with Britomart, who emerges into subjectivity as a mirror, or exemplar, from an exemplary encounter with a mirror. When Spenser first identifies Guyon's mysterious opponent, we learn that:

> Euen the famous *Britomart* it was,
> Whom straunge aduenture did from *Britayne* fett,
> To seeke her louer (loue farr sought alas,)
> Whose image shee had seene in *Venus* looking glas.
> (3.1.8)

Yet before applying Lacan to Britomart, one should ask how Britomart, as a figure of female masculinity, applies to Lacan, whose theory of how subjects are fashioned depends upon a mute, disordered materiality out of which the masculine "agency of the ego emerges."[67] The "motor incapacity and nursling dependence" that Lacan associates with the *infans* remains an aspect of developmental progress, explaining the temporal dialectic of the mirror stage as the subject thrusts forward to a future moment of capacity and independence. Elsewhere in the essay, the alienating armor of identity seems propped on an innate, organic disorder. Lacan locates in humans "a certain dehiscence at the heart of the organism, a primal Discord betrayed by signs of uneasiness and motor unco-ordination of the neo-natal months."[68] While human subjectivity may rest uneasily on an organic, bodily chaos, the mirror stage itself appears to be grounded reductively in biology. Lacan notes casually, for example, that the human infant may be able to recognize an image in a mirror but still will be "outdone by the chimpanzee in instrumental intelligence."[69] Furthermore, the mirror stage itself is based in "homeomorphic identification" of which "the maturation of the gonad of the female pigeon" and the habits of "the migratory locust" are exemplary.[70] Lacan posits an innate bodily disorder that *necessitates* the mirror stage with its organizing armor of identity. Lacan then associates this masculine assumption of subjectivity with the adaptation of the species, as indicated by the biological reality of locusts and pigeons. As a result, Lacan naturalizes the longing of that organic matter to acquire organizing form and the appropriation of matter by that organizing form. Masculine ego may be illusory, but it effectively encases the chaotic, feminine body.

Lacan's allegory of subjectivity reflects the gendered history of both allegory and matter; if masculine self-assertion is only an illusion, it is an effective one. What of Britomart's female masculinity? Elizabeth Bellamy argues, "Spenser's epic chooses androgyny and its threats to the phallus as its central vehicle for chastity and the social construction of gender."[71] Schwartz's reading of the Knight of Chastity's genesis, for all its invocation of Lacan, relegates Britomart to the language of disguise plots and transvestism, a language used in early modern cross-dressing debates of decades past. Britomart's mirror stage reflects neither delusion nor disguise. Rather, it offers her the opportunity to refashion herself by activating, through intense suffering, a body otherwise relegated to feminine passivity.

Of course, Britomart is initially a dutiful and proper child, successfully interpellated as her father's "onely daughter and his hayre" (3.2.22). It is this position that allows her free access to her father's private affairs, "For nothing he from her reseru'd apart" (3.2.22). While not sunk in motor incapacity, as the Lacanian infant, she registers no desires of her own. It is mere "fortune" that she wanders into her father's closet at all. Once there, looking at the magic mirror, it takes some time, for "her to bethinke of, that mote to her selfe pertaine" (3.2.22). Nothing pertains to the subject wholly absorbed in the gender and station assigned to her by birth—except marriage. Indeed, when she does think of what pertains to herself, it is inevitably her future husband, though Britomart, we learn, is not necessarily interested in marriage at all. Using purity as a defense for Britomart's thoughts of matrimony, the narrator informs us,

> Not that she lusted after any one;
> . . . .
> Yet wist her life at last must lincke in that same knot.
> (3.2.23)

Marriage is, at first, an unexamined inevitability for the soon-to-be knight of Chastity.

In Britomart's case, it is the mirror scene that catapults her *into* chaos from her relatively staid and stable existence a daughter and wife to be. In the mirror she views:

> A comely knight, all arm'd in complete wize,
> Through whose bright ventayle lifted vp on hye
> His manly face, that did his foes agrize,
> And frends to termes of gentle truce entize,
> Lookt foorth, as *Phoebus* face out of the east
> (3.2.24)

The action of the Legend of Chastity requires that Britomart fall in love with this knight. Her resulting quest accomplishes multiple other adventures and initiates a dynastic epic narrative common to heroic poetry, as Britomart and Arthegall become the future parents of a line of princes culminating in Queen Elizabeth. However, the desire *for* that masculine figure is swiftly overtaken by the desire to *be* that masculine figure in the mirror, as the summary offered at the beginning of the canto suggests:

> The Redcrosse knight to Britomart
> describeth Artegall:
> The wondrous myrrhour, by which she
> in loue with him did fall.
> (3.2.proem)

Britomart may have fallen "in love" with Arthegall by looking in a mirror, but Arthegall, as a "wondrous myrrhour" also provides the young Britomart a site of identification. As Mikkel Borch-Jacobsen argues, "What triggers desire is mimetic assimilation, identification with a model of desire. . . . Desire, in other words, does not aim essentially at acquiring, possessing, or enjoying an object; it aims . . . at a subjective identity."[72] Britomart's desire aims as much at being as at having, which catapults her into a quandary about the bodily nature of that desire.

The potential rift between desire and identification shatters Britomart's stable self and sends her into bodily convulsions. She experiences "motor incapacity and nursling dependence" as we see her

> Sad, solemne, sowre, and full of fancies fraile
> She woxe; yet wist she nether how, nor why,
> She wist not, silly Mayd, what she did aile,
> Yet wist, she was not well at ease perdy,
> Yet thought it was not loue but some melancholy.
> (3.2.27)

Here we see Britomart in utter disarray. The elemental, repetitive depiction of this "silly Mayd," enacts the infantilization of Britomart's foray into subjectivity. Britomart, in other words, is at the cusp of consolidating a new self and, by implication, renovating the contours of her suffering, disordered body. The painful corporeality she experiences reflects the inadequacy of her current self and demands the generation of a body from which she is not exiled. Painful confusion and tortured desire become that out of which Britomart will construct a viable, mobile self.

Faced with the conceptual mess Britomart experiences as desire, she receives one answer to her dilemma from Merlin: marriage. At the failure of Glaucé's various cures for Britomart's distress, the two seek the maker of the magic mirror for his help in finding the elusive body witnessed in its glass. Merlin attempts to compel the final materialization of Britomart's mirror stage by projecting Britomart into his own brand of anticipation. She is, we discover, destined to marry Arthegall and mother the line of kings leading to Elizabeth. Her desire for Arthegall becomes the key to accomplishing this destiny, and her interpellation includes a reproductive mandate. Yet inasmuch as Merlin is an enchanter who mandates marriage, he is, in some sense, a kindlier Busyrane.

While Merlin provides a master narrative, compelling Britomart's identification as a royal progenitor, Glaucé's erotic machinations provide the ultimately subversive means to realizing her desire. Indeed, she promises her young charge: "I auow to thee, by wrong or right / To compas thy desire, and find that loued knight" (3.2.46). The ambivalence of the word "compas" engenders several narratives. With a particular ruthlessness, Glaucé commits herself to Britomart's desire. The most obvious meaning would be that she will toil selflessly to help Britomart find Arthegall. Indeed, "compasse" means to plan or contrive or devise the means to accomplishing one's ends, though it often connotes less than virtuous machinations. It also, of course, means to surround, encircle, or to get something within grasp. The use of the word in *The Faerie Queene* is somewhat equivocal. Saturne resorts to trickery "when for to compasse *Philliras* hard loue" (3.11.43), implying that to "compasse" another's love is to procure something for oneself. Likewise in the Legend of Justice, the Amazon Radigund speaks of Britomart's captive beau, Arthegall, hoping to "compasse this [her] enterprize" (5.5.48). Even in the Mutability Cantos, Faunus resorts to trickery in order "to compasse his desire" (7.6.43).

Britomart is aware not only of the way in which desire and identification mingle in her mirror scene but also of the potentially disastrous consequences, as her much noted fear of narcissism makes clear. She worries at first that she loves no more than a "shade and semblant of a knight" (3.2.38). Yet while Britomart may fear that the specular image she spies is no more than an illusion, her language reflects a more bodily concern for the object of her desires, as when she admits, "I fonder loue a shade, the body far exyld" (3.2.44). Desire's improbable self-referentiality threatens the materialization of the stable body of Britomart *as* rather than *for* Arthegall. Narcissus becomes the dangerous figure of dis-identification, as Glaucé points out—that "wretched boy" who "Was of him selfe the ydle Paramoure; / Both loue and louer" (3.2.45). Narcissus's problem is as much that he was "both loue and louer" as it is that he was an "idle Paramoure" for inhabiting a kind of desire that exiled him from his own body. Britomart seeks a body that desire may not be able to provide, though she fears sinking into monstrous desires, such as incest and bestiality, like Pasiphae, Biblis, and Myrrah. The danger of Narcissus is exile from the body whereas the danger of Pasiphae, Biblis, and Myrrah is self-destructive bodily fixation. Whereas Britomart fears being exiled from or limited to her body, Glaucé realizes:

> No shadow, but a body hath in powre:
> That body, wheresoeuer it light,
> May learned be by cyphres, or by Magick might.
>
> (3.2.45)

Glaucé's words are more convincing than her charms are effective. Indeed, her cures for lovesickness are as useless as her auguries. However, Glaucé does teach Britomart, as Merlin does not, that the shapes and capacities of the body may be learned. Britomart may be educated, that is, into the body she requires to become capable of action, be it to locate Arthegall or to wander in dark forests.

Glaucé's tutelage witnesses an investment in Britomart's body that is at once erotic and mimetic, mirrors Britomart's desire for Arthegall, and manifests as the care of the suffering body as she nurses the lovesick girl:

> her twixt her armes twaine
> Shee streightly strayned, and colled tenderly,
> And euery trembling ioynt, and euery vaine
> Shee softly felt, and rubbed busily,
> To doe the frosen cold away to fly;
> And her faire deawy eies and kisses deare
> Shee oft did bathe, and oft againe did dry;
> . . . .
> With that vpleaning on her elbow weake,
> Her alablaster brest she soft did kis,
> Which all the while shee felt to pant and quake,
> As it an Earth-quake were.
>
> (3.2.34, 42)

Vigorous massage seems a common practice for fainting ladies. Indeed, Una's dwarf rouses her from a similar spell with similarly vigorous attention (1.7.21) and Redcrosse attends the fainting Duessa (1.2.45). Yet the muscular ministrations that return shape and feeling to Britomart's enervated body mutate into an ambiguous welter of kissing and panting as the two bodies in question, bodies that will later be rematerialized in the interest of new erotic agencies, become barely distinguishable.

Glaucé's erotic activation of Britomart's suffering body opens out into a narrative that encourages her to school herself in a new bodily regime. She says:

> Let vs in feigned armes our selues disguize,
> And our weake hands (need makes good schollers) teach
> The dreadfull speare and shield to exercize.
>
> (3.3.53)

While she uses the language of disguise, Glaucé also notes the extent to which this apparent disguise will alter the texture of the flesh beneath the alienating armor, as weak hands and arms gain strength through exercise. Glaucé posits new bodies and new sites of identification for the pair, citing "many wemen valorous" (3.3.54) as precedent for Britomart's "masculine" assertions—including Spenser's own creation, the warrior queen Angela. Glaucé claims for Britomart the prerogatives of the questing knight and positions herself as the erotic sidekick by playing the part of the female page whose disguise allows her to be close to a traveling or soldiering husband.

Britomart's newfound masculinity exceeds the parameters of Glaucé's disguise plot and Merlin's dynastic plot, which serve no other purpose than to unite her with her absent "husband," Arthegall. Glaucé's descriptions of the warrior queen Angela enchant and inspire the young girl:

> Her harty wordes so deepe into the mynd
> Of the young Damzell sunke, that great desire
> Of warlike armes in her forthwith they tynd
> And generous stout courage did inspyre.
> (3.3.57)

Rather than simply specular, desire's mimetic thrust is also verbal or aural; Britomart identifies with an aural narrative, as the words of her nurse enter both mind and body. Seduced by Glaucé's narration, she is encouraged to complete an identification with Angela: "Therefore faire Infant her ensample make / Vnto thy selfe" (3.3.56). Britomart incorporates the figure of the warrior queen, accepts the charge to externalize that cathexis, and, with her nurse's help, rematerializes her body as a warrior body. Britomart's appropriation of masculinity, once spurred by a specular identification with the mirror image of Arthegall, now proceeds from an aural identification with the female masculinity of the warrior queen Angela.

From the trap of Narcissus, Britomart emerges into masculine mobility through a vitalizing experience of suffering. She is neither in disguise nor cross-dressed. Rather, she seeks a bodily habit compatible with her desires and identifications. The critical language of disguise and transvestism limits Britomart's body to the cultural forms pressing upon it, whereas efforts to read Britomart and the Legend of Chastity as decidedly "female" limit Britomart's cultural performances to an essentialized body. Susanne Lindgren Wofford, for example, claims that Spenser's Britomart marks clear sexual difference by accentuating "the gap between external image and self."[73] Wofford argues that some of the evidence of Britomart's love wound is particularly female, referring to menstruation:

> Sithens it has infixed faster hold
> Within my bleeding bowells, and so sore
> Now ranckleth in this same fraile fleshly mould,
> That all mine entrailes flow with poisnous gore.
> (3.2.39)

If bleeding bowels might suggest menstruation, the entrails flowing with poisonous gore suggest the violent, carnal desire a variety of male figures in the *Faerie Queene* experience, such as the love sickness of the hag's son, later in book 3, in whose bowels "wicked flame . . . shortly grew into outrageous fire" (3.7.16). In fact, Spenser describes Paridell's "false" love for Hellenore with the same physicality that Britomart experiences—weeping, wailing, swooning, and lamenting.[74] Britomart, at first, also imagines her love to be without precedent ("mine is not . . . like others wownd" [3.2.36]). Of course, the longing for that which cannot be realized is the ordinary state of the Petrarchan lover, whose desire depends precisely on the inaccessibility of the object.

The interest of Britomart's experience of Petrarchan love and despair is not that the bodily signifiers of desire are specific to the female body; rather, Britomart restores, through suffering, a bodily component of desire while also appropriating masculine languages of agency to free herself from the abjection of Petrarchan desire. Eve Sedgwick remarks, "No woman becomes less a woman through any amount of 'male identification,' to the extent that femaleness is always (though always differently) to be looked for *in* the tortuousness, in the strangeness of the figure made between the flatly gendered definition from an outside view and the always more or less crooked stiles to be surveyed from an inner."[75] The "tortuousness" and "strangeness" Sedgwick describes apply equally to femaleness as they do to the masculinity Britomart appropriates on her tortuous and tortured quest. Spenser's Britomart gazes into the mirror of masculinity and faces the threat of its narcissism and violence. Of early modern erotic mirror games, Berry remarks, "This figure (the beloved) was usually little more than an instrument in an elaborate game of *masculine* 'speculation' and self-determination, for the philosophical enterprise common to both Petrarchism and Renaissance Neoplatonism used woman as a 'speculum' or mirror of masculine narcissism."[76] Britomart, however, defeats the man in the mirror by replacing him, as she moves from feminine incapacity through erotic torment to masculine self-assertion.

Wound, mirror, and lyric: these are the tropes of subjectivity that Britomart not only appropriates in her quest but also refashions. In the process she becomes a subject capable of telling her own stories. We might turn back to Britomart's conversation with the Redcrosse Knight. Following their escape from Castle Joyeous, and in response to Redcrosse's queries about her "true sex," Britomart claims,

> Faire Sir, I let you weete, that from the howre
> I taken was from nourses tender pap,
> I haue beene trained vp in warlike stowre,
> To tossen speare and shield, and to affrap
> The warlike ryder to his most mishap;
> Sithence I loathed to haue my life to lead,
> As Ladies wont, in pleasures wanton lap,
> To finger the fine needle and nyce thread;
> Me leuer were with point of foemans speare be dead.
>
> All my delight on deedes of armes is set,
> To hunt out perills and aduentures hard,
> By sea, by land, where so they may be met,
> Onely for honour and for high gard.
>
> (3.2.6–7)

The verity of this statement is of little interest. For the first time, Britomart appears as a woman asserting control over her past and her future—momentarily free of both Merlin's destiny and Glaucé's disguise plot. Of note is a certain disdain for femininity, which is described by lazy domesticity and wanton sexuality, for indeed the tools with which Britomart fashions her subjectivity are tainted by a disdain for feminine behavior she will later face in her relationship to Amoret. At this moment, however, Britomart resists being read as feminine following the revelation of her sex.

Rather than returning to a state of docile femininity, Britomart forges on in her quest as a masculine Petrarchan lover, as her use of lyric suggests. The galley of sorrow that sails from Petrarch to Spenser through Wyatt and Surrey embodies Britomart's despair, as when, on a sparkling strand, she cries out:

> Huge sea of sorrow, and tempestuous griefe,
> Wherein my feeble barke is tossed long,
> Far from the hoped hauen of reliefe.
> (3.4.8);

or later when she claims:

> Loue my lewd Pillot hath a restless minde
> And fortune Boteswaine no assuraunce knowes,
> But saile withouten starres, gainst tyde and winde:
> How can they other doe, sith both are bold and blind?
> (3.4.9)

Of the many maritime references in the *Amoretti* we might remember, in particular, sonnet 34, in which the speaker is:

> Like as a ship, that through the ocean wide,
> By conduct of some star doth make her way,
> Whenas a storm hath dimmed her trusty guide,
> Out of her course doth wander far astray:
> So I whose star, that wont with her bright ray
> Me to direct, with clouds is overcast,
> Do wander now, in darkness and dismay.
> (*Amoretti* 34.1–7)

The inaccessible woman of the sonnet, identified through the sequence as a "tyrannes" and a "cruel warrior" must, in the form of Amoret, be released and must, in the form of Britomart, now ride as a warrior with her own pain and her own narrative. Thus, male subjectivity is constituted not merely by means of a narcissistic, masculine speculation (as Berry argues) but also by identification across the gendered, positional logic of Petrarchan desire. That is to say, Britomart succeeds in constituting an exemplary masculinity in ways that Redcrosse, Guyon, and even Arthur do not, making her the means by which Spenser fashions gentlemen and noble persons.

Britomart, in locating herself in the realm of male prerogative, reshapes the terrain of those prerogatives. She presents a site of cross-gender identification for men and women alike, and interestingly the privileged location of this identification is her father's closet. The closet joins sonnet, mirror, and wound as signifiers of masculine subjectivity. Though Bellamy thinks of the closet as a womb,[77] Alan Stewart points out that the closet in Spenser's time "is often associated with the constructions of a new modern subjectivity."[78] It was also, Stewart points out, a space strictly gendered and often eroticized. Wives were frequently forbidden access to the husband and lord's closet because of their purported inability to keep secrets. The closet was, in Stewart's words, "a secret nonpublic transactive space between two men behind a locked door."[79] As Richard Rambuss's account makes clear, Spenser, a secretary himself, was well aware of the networks of anxiety and power surrounding access to a lord's closet.[80] He explains Britomart's entrance as an indication of her father's trust: "For nothing from her reseru'd apart, / Being his onely daughter and his hayre" (3.2.22). The casual nature of the occurrence ("One day it fortuned") emphasizes the regularity with which Britomart gains access to that realm of interiority, subjectivity, power, and male homosociality. Britomart, as heir, is already considered privy to any number of public secrets that constitute her father as lord. Already, she is accorded independence and agency, and, I would argue, it is no accident that her father's closet is the site of the emergence of female masculine subjectivity and the possibility of female same-sex eroticism and friendship, which travels from closet to the beds she shares with Glauce, Malecasta, and Amoret.

James Broaddus argues that Britomart has no real interior life in that "her interior comprises not much more than her affection for Artegall . . . That affection not only impels her quest, but governs her behavior on that quest."[81] Broaddus sees Britomart as a virtual allegory of heterosexuality. Graham Hough points out that Britomart is no "mere embodiment" of chastity, and certainly her narrative suggests more than mere heterosexuality.[82] Despite her predecessors in Virgil, Boiardo, Ariosto, and Tasso, she is neither the typical subject of romance, who can be easily assimilated as a wandering, desiring knight, nor even the typical warrior woman of romance. What kind of subject *is* she? Spenser neither achieves nor even aims for the illusion of interiority, or what some have, following Joel Fineman, called the subjectivity effect.[83] Hough is right to suggest that "however near Spenser may come to 'humanizing' his characters (and he sometimes comes very near) he never touches the confines of incarnational literature—he never embodies his themes in the completely rounded and individual representation of a human person."[84] Incarnational literature finds its acme in Shakespearean drama and is distinct from visionary symbolism, naïve allegory, and empirical realism. "The archetype of incarnational literature," Hough argues, "is the union of the body and soul in the human person. . . . It seeks for the union of theme and image not through the representation of living, acting, and suffering human beings, but through words as talismans . . . or through direct visionary experience."[85] Shakespearean characters may have generated so powerful a subjectivity effect to ensure not only the illusion of interiority but also the preeminence of Shakespeare in the literary cannon. However, Spenser generates a more radical, that is, fundamental, incarnational literature by returning the subjective experience of "living, acting, and suffering" to those characters. What indeed is incarnational about characters denuded of living, acting, and suffering? In Britomart Spenser generates a subject struggling to experience states of painful affect that vitalize and activate her at the level of the body and thus grant her the possibility of agency and expression. Britomart represents Spenser's achievement in fashioning an allegorical or incarnational subjectivity that emerges as Britomart bears, and bares, experiences of vulnerability.

To defeat Busyrane and to rescue Amoret is to address the violence perpetrated as a consequence of the conflation of masculinity and aggression. This is the masculinity figured by the boar entombed beneath the garden of Adonis at the center of the Legend of Chastity: a masculinity that cannot but destroy itself and anything in its path. After this rescue, in the opening canto of the Legend of Friendship, Britomart does, in fact, perform masculinity as predatory and violent, as if she has mastered heroic masculinity but has not accepted her own vulnerability. At first Britomart attempts to convince Amoret of her masculinity by performing "lustfulnesse" and "excesse" and thus terrifies her. Then, she stops attempting to "hide her fained sex" and "maske her wounded mind" (4.1.7). Once that specter of aggression is laid to rest between rescuer and lady, these women transact a bond based on affection and sympathy. They create out of narrated suffering a relationship rooted in female friendship:

So did they all their former strife accord;
And eke fayre *Amoret* now freed from feare,
More franke affection did to her afford,
And to her bed, which she was wont forbeare,
Now freely drew, and found right safe assurance theare.

Wheare all that night they of their loues did treat,
And hard aduentures twixt themselues alone,
That each the other gan with passion great,
And griefull pittie priuately bemone.

(4.1.15–16)

No longer, then, does suffering constitute a threat either to the implicitly masculine subject unable to contemplate pain of any variety or to the woman for whom the only role available in *any* narrative is that of a helpless victim. There is, perhaps, no other moment in the whole of *The Faerie Queene* in which Amoret is allowed to be anything but a placeholder of someone else's desire or a marker of someone else's narrative. The relationship between Britomart and Amoret is as suggestively erotic as it is useful in providing a model of sympathetic sociality predicated upon neither aggressive appropriation nor sentimentality nor the erasure of difference between lover and beloved. Like the nymphs in the fountain of the Bower of Bliss, Amoret, and Britomart translate conflict into collaboration as Britomart learns to inhabit masculinity without succumbing to the urge to establish subjectivity through a dialectic of submission and domination. Sympathetic sociality becomes possible as Britomart admits vulnerability and conflict becomes companionship.

Through the Legend of Chastity, Britomart is armed only to be disarmed by the time she arrives in bed with Amoret. As Judith Anderson traces the arms and armor of this exemplar of Chastity, she reads Britomart as a figure associated with the mythographic complex Edgar Wind identifies in his *Pagan Mysteries in the Renaissance* when he identifies the *Venus armata*, who combines martian and venerean qualities: "Dressed in armour . . . the *Venus armata* signifies the warfare of love."[86] For Anderson, this arming is as enabling as it is inhibiting; indeed, "the danger of containment by the protective armor in the negative sense of suppression and self-enclosure becomes evident."[87] If arming represents an escape from the world of dutiful daughters and marriage plots, disarming represents an escape from the isolating rage and melancholia of unreformed masculinity. In disarming, Britomart has more than flirted with an eroticism encountered between women. One approach to these moments would be to place these relationships in the context of other representations of female same-sex love in the Renaissance, as for example, in Valerie Traub's *The Renaissance of Lesbianism in Early Modern England*. Here I would suggest, with Foucault, that the question of sexuality opens out onto the question of friendship. In an interview titled "Friendship as a Way of Life," Foucault argues that "the development toward which the problem of homosexuality tends is the one of friendship."[88] Britomart's encounters with Malecasta, Glaucé, and Amoret might, like the nymphs in the fountain of the Bower of Bliss, offer locations of same-sex sexual activity, but to understand sexuality through the immediacy of sexual pleasures grated onto sexual identities (or even their precursors) would "cancel everything that can be troubling in affection, tenderness, friendship, fidelity, camaraderie, and companionship, things that our rather sanitized society can't allow a place for without fearing the formation of new alliances and the tying together of unforeseen lines of force. . . . To imagine a sexual act that doesn't conform to law or nature is not what disturbs people. But that individuals are beginning to love one another—there's the problem . . . Institutional codes can't validate these relations with multiple intensities, imperceptible movements and changing forms."[89]

For Foucault, institutions of male affiliation—from the army to the prison—were the unanticipated locations of relations of "multiple intensities, imperceptible movement and changing forms." For Spenser, no stranger to the early modern institution of friendship, which was itself a gendered phenomenon that frequently excluded women, friendship was definitively gendered male *elsewhere* in his writings, particularly in the letters he exchanged with Gabriel Harvey and, more problematically, in the *Shepheardes Calendar*.[90] While I will speculate on the nature of friendship in my conclusion, it remains to be said that the 1590 *Faerie Queene* is unusual, if not unique, in suggesting that the fabric of intimate and social relationships was most ideally constituted among women. As I will show in the next chapter, it is compassionate companionship between female deities, Venus and Diana, that facilitates the final revisionary gestures of the Legend of Chastity. Having used the gendered scripts of Petrarchan lyric and heroic masculinity to elude subjection and domination in generating vulnerable subjectivity in the form of Britomart, Spenser creates a vulnerable materiality that eludes the gendered violence of allegory. That vulnerability rests in the suffering flesh of Spenser's Adonis.

CHAPTER 6

Damaged Gods: Adonis and the Pain of Allegory

The figure of Mars disarmed by Venus represented for Renaissance artists and thinkers a potent allegory of peace, one rooted in the intimacy of erotic vulnerability. If, as I have argued, the 1590 *Faerie Queene* is in fact an allegory of vulnerability, one that disarms and reforms masculinity as a project of ethics, it is the case that the very notion of an allegory of vulnerability requires investigation, as does the mythic complex composed by Venus and Mars. There were, of course, other ways of representing the promise of peace, including Rubens's *Allegory of the Blessings of Peace* (1629), in which the rapacious Mars is not seduced into surrender but warded off by an armed Minerva. Elsewhere, Rubens imagines Hercules, a figure of heroic virtue, defending against the depravities of war. Paradoxically, if predictably, such representations of the bounty of nonviolence depend on both vigilance and a capacity for violence. If this defensiveness poses one problem for conceiving of an allegory of vulnerability, a second arises when one considers the relationship between allegory as a mode of representation and its content. If allegory depends, as Gordon Teskey argues, on gendered violence for its effects, how are readers to understand an allegory of nonviolence? And finally, what relationship does allegory, which accounts for structural and systemic effects, have with the intimate particularity of the vulnerable body that is the locus of moments of erotic disarmament? In this chapter, I will suggest that Spenser recognized a series of structural and formal problems in deploying an allegory of vulnerability. He responds to them by interrogating the systemic violence associated with both allegorical representation and the materiality of which vulnerable bodies are composed. The Legend of Chastity not only reconsiders the intimacy of erotic subjection as I discussed in the previous chapter but also provides a new understanding of the erotics of allegory, which eludes gendered, structural violence, and a recalibrated allegory of vulnerability, which replaces Mars, a figure of war, with Adonis, the principle of vulnerability.

C. S. Lewis describes allegory as a genre that derives from an essential human capacity. "It is the very nature of thought and language," he argues, "to represent what is immaterial in picturable terms."[1] Allegory, the natural union of thought and language in visual form, occurs in what Lewis calls "married pairs of sensibles and insensibles."[2] Lewis's influential study recounts a history of love and allegory culminating in *The Faerie Queene*. Considering the intertwining fortunes of love and allegory, Lewis's description of the union of sensible and insensible in "married pairs" is hardly idle language. For Lewis, *The Faerie Queene*, specifically the rescue of Amoret from Busyrane, witnesses "the final defeat of courtly love by the romantic conception of marriage."[3] Allegory and love, in Lewis's study, tend toward the ideal of heterosexual union, which provides a model of the union of abstract principle and concrete substance.

For Lewis, this erotic metaphysics informs not only works of courtly love and romance, which influence Petrarch and the sonnet tradition, but also allegory as developed by the School of Chartres, including Bernardus Silvestris's *Cosmographia* and Alan de Lille's *Anticlaudianus* and *De planctu naturae*. Allegory, informed by eros, speaks to both the shape of the material universe and the corresponding shape of human embodiment, which is composed of an outer physical form and an inner life. "Hence," Lewis claims, "the development of allegory, to supply the subjective element in literature, to paint the inner world followed inevitably."[4] Allegory, what Angus Fletcher has described as "a protean device" and "a radical linguistic structure,"[5] and what Maureen Quilligan has associated with punning and linguistic play,[6] Lewis takes to be the genre designed to express natural cosmic order reflected in the inner world of subjectivity because allegory is rooted in a stable order based on heterosexual union.

Recent writing on gender and the history of allegory and metaphysics seriously complicates the ideal union of love and allegory that perfectly reflects the created order and the subjective life of humanity expressed in the ideal of romantic companionate marriage. While the "*bellum intestinum*" or "inner conflict" exemplified by Prudentius's *Psychomachia* may be, for Lewis,[7] "the root of all allegory," Angus Fletcher's study finds in allegory "symbolic power struggles," violent tensions, and obsessive desires.[8] Gordon Teskey's more recent study locates a fundamental, gendered violence at the heart of the metaphysics that constitutes allegory. "Allegory's primary work," Teskey claims, "is to force meaning on beings who are reduced for that purpose to substance."[9] Allegory is the literary form suited to a "hierarchical, animated idealism," in which matter, "perversely resisting the desire of the male, must be ravished by form." Lurking in this form of violence is the conviction that "to be ravished is what Matter secretly wants, so that it may bear in its substance the imprint of beautiful forms." Personification represents the successful imprinting of feminine matter by masculine form; the inverse of personification, capture, results from the failure of such imprinting. In allegories, moments of capture are dramatized in scenes of violence against women, who "continue forever to resist being converted into an embodiment of the meaning that is imprinted on her."[10] In Teskey's account, Spenser's Amoret embodies such resistance in her scene of imprisonment and torture in the castle of Busyrane.[11]

As Judith Butler has similarly argued, the concept of matter central to western metaphysics is "*founded through a series of violations*" that emerge from "an exclusion and degradation of the feminine," which is consistently associated with materiality.[12] Developing the work of Luce Irigaray, Butler points out not merely the way feminine matter is shaped violently by masculine form but, more importantly, the extent to which the "feminine" becomes only the space in which masculine self-reproduction occurs, as exemplified by the receptacle or nurse of becoming in Plato's *Timaeus*, which provides the site of the reproduction of masculine form in matter. Thus, Plato witnesses "a disjunction between materiality which is feminine and formless and, hence, without a body, and bodies which are formed through—but not of—that feminine materiality."[13] Matter is subordinated as femininity—the categorically penetrable, submissive partner to masculine form. Similarly, Teskey argues "matter is made pregnant with form by assuming a 'subject' (*sub-iectum* 'cast down') position with respect to the male."[14] Matter is excluded from participation in the process of generation by being the *location of* but not *partner to* the reproduction of form, as in the legacy of Aristotelian physiology in which women's bodies are mere receptacles for masculine seed. The gendered violence Teskey and Butler identify complicates the ideal of harmonious procreative, companionate marriage at the heart of Lewis's *The Allegory of Love*. Indeed, these arguments suggest that Spenser's project of disarming masculinity would require a reconsideration of the fundamental metaphysical contracts described by allegory.

The 1590 *Faerie Queene*, by disarming and reforming masculinity to revise the erotic contract governing masculine and feminine subjects, revises, too, the gendered relationships between form and matter that govern allegory. As I argued in Chapter 5, this project culminates, on the one hand, in Britomart's entry into masculine subjectivity through identifications with both suffering masculinity and captured femininity and, on the other, Amoret's escape into a sympathetic, erotic sociality with Britomart. In the Legend of Chastity, Spenser explores damaged metaphysical orders (represented by divinities) to rework the principle of generation by which matter and form come to be associated with gendered positions. The reader encounters, therefore, a damaged iteration of the Diana and Actaeon myth. With Venus playing the part of Actaeon, the encounter rescripts so as to displace the violent scene of desire witnessed by Petrarchan and Ovidian verse while forcing militant divinity to accommodate vulnerable flesh. And, as Venus and Diana become inadvertent mothers of Amoret and Belphoebe, masculine self-generation, evidenced by the solar generation of Chrysogonee, gives way to a homoerotic maternity that reproduces itself. This exploration of damaged divinity concludes with the reconstitution of abject materiality through Adonis, a figure of vulnerable masculinity whose affiliation with Venus replaces the dyad of Venus and Mars and whose suffering grounds a new understanding of generation that replaces the violent discipline of wayward matter typical of the Neoplatonic cosmologies that locate a systemic, gendered violence at the heart of creation.

Although the gendered matrix of Plato's *Timaeus* witnesses the violent subjection of feminine substance to masculine form, the resulting Neoplatonic tradition of allegory so influential for Chaucer and Spenser was anything but conventionally heterosexual. Bernardus Silvestris's *Cosmographia* features the wayward, chaotic principle, Silva, who embodies the *malignitas* of materiality. Silva, or Hyle, is "a formless chaos, a hostile coalescence," but she "yearn[s] to emerge from her ancient confusion."[15] As Winthrop Wetherbee argues, "One cannot simply say the imposition of order on chaos, for Bernardus is at pains to emphasize the collaboration of the principles involved."[16] Brian Stock describes this impulse as the way "Bernardus introduces the idea of a moral allegory (i.e., the improvement of the cosmos and man) into his drama in primarily physical terms."[17] While Teskey takes this to be an affirmation of the Aristotelian notion that matter desires form as a women desires a man, Silvestris delegates masculine shaping force to two major female figures, Natura and Noys, and a host of ancillary female principles, including Endelechia, Urania, Providence, Physis, Theory, and Practice. As Stock points out, it is Noys, a female personification, who "beats out and refines" Silva's "innate toughness."[18] Likewise, Silvestris's Natura was at the forefront of the twelfth-century "discovery of Nature, a power identified precisely with the preservation of life and order, and the obedience of all creation to cosmic law."[19] While Nature and Noys alike may be representatives or viceroys of divine, masculine force, as female embodiments of their respective principles they mediate and alter the gendered dynamic governing the violence by which form imprints matter. Indeed, Stock sees in the *Cosmographia's* "presentation of the problem of matter" evidence that Silvestris was "fascinated" by an "unusual feature" of Hermeticism, which was "the bisexuality of God and matter."[20]

The perversity of creation in Neoplatonic allegory, straying so quickly and emphatically from the "natural" state of heterosexual union, becomes even more apparent in Alain de Lille's *De planctu naturae.* Like the *Cosmographia, De planctu naturae* begins, as its title suggests, with Nature's complaint, a complaint about the degradations of the created order. Whereas the *Cosmographia* reacts to the ancient, chaotic state of matter, *De planctu naturae* rails against the deformation of created order embodied by perverse sexuality and improper grammar. Disorder reigns "because of a Venus turned monster, when Venus wars with Venus and turns 'hes' into 'shes' and with her witchcraft unmans man."[21] The improper yoking of grammatical subjects and predicates are, like the improper sexual concatenation of two male bodies, unproductive and contrary to the will of Nature. Such a man "hammers on an anvil which issues no seed" and is not only "a barbarian in grammar" but also "disclaims the manhood given him by nature."[22] Later in the plaint the reader learns that the crisis of order began with Nature's delegation of creative power to Venus. Nature describes herself as God's "vice-regent, the mistress of his mint." She confesses that her "writing-reed would instantly go off course if it were not guided by the finger of the superintendent on high."[23] As Alexandre Leupin argues, Nature is identified with a "standard of orthodox writing and coition . . . the venerable order that sodomy so glaringly offends."[24] Yet, despite the aid from "on high" and her staunch reliance on orthodoxy, Nature could not finish the work of creation without her own vice-regent, Venus. Though Venus's husband, Hymenaeus, and child, Desire, assist her with the work of creation, Venus must fit "her artisan's hammer to its anvil." Venus, endowed with a phallic hammer and stylus, "an unusually powerful writing-pen," falls into adultery and spawns sexual impropriety and moral corruption, which remain to be corrected by Nature with the help of Genius. By castigating and correcting perverse sexuality and linguistic propriety, which reflect a deep disturbance in the order of material creation, *De planctu naturae* admits to the possibility of what one might call a queer materiality constituted by joinings unimaginable in the cosmology of *Timaeus*. God and Genius try to stabilize the shaping force delegated to Nature as Venus, endowed with phallic masculinity by Nature, strays. The transaction between powerful female figures and the delegation to them of phallic masculinity result in disturbing but instructive outcomes.

Indeed, the canto in which Spenser describes the Garden of Adonis foregrounds a damaged erotic psychology of reproduction. That canto opens with an address to "faire Ladies" reading the *Faerie Queene*, who must, in the wake of Belphoebe's appearance:

> wonder, how this noble Damozell
> So great perfections did in her compile,
> Sith that in saluage forests she did dwell,
> So farre from court and royall Citadell,
> The great schoolmaistresse of all courtesy
> (3.6.1)

Belphoebe, then, is naturally born to the "ciuile usage" and "gentility" that one might expect would be "far expell[ed]" from the savage woods. But the question of the genesis of Belphoebe's "natural" virtue raises the question of how such virtue could be produced at all when militant chastity, virginity, would contradict the possibility of reproduction. For Belphoebe to be implicated in human reproduction would be to admit to a material taint that besmirches the virginity from which her power derives.

Britomart's militant chastity is, of course, designed to yield to a dynastic imperative as she gives birth to a great line of monarchs. The erotic psychology that governs Britomart's emergence as a subject dictates that her progress through *The Faerie Queene* will be governed by anything but conventional heterosexuality. Similarly, human reproduction, which ought to anchor the potentially disruptive pleasure of sexuality, is, in the Legend of Chastity, anything but conventional in either its erotic psychology or its relationship to the materiality of the human body. Thus while the narrative posits an immaculate conception for Belphoebe and her twin sister, Amoret, one that would escape the taint of sexual reproduction, the elaboration of the birth of these twins consistently queers or deranges the relationship between masculine and feminine positions in the scheme of reproduction. This would be of particular interest to the "faire Ladies" not only because Belphoebe emerges from the wilderness as an untainted exemplar of virtue. More importantly, the Legend of Chastity demonstrates that the "taint" of materiality that reproduction foregrounds becomes the basis of a revision of the gendered positions Spenser's fair ladies may occupy in the scheme of creation.

That Belphoebe's conception, her "whole creation" would be "pure and vnspotted from all loathly crime, / That is ingenerate in fleshly slime" (3.6.3) suggests that she represents the ideal reproduction of masculine virtue from the empty and available womb of her mother, Chrysogonee. The accidental conception took place as Chrysogonee slept "all naked bare displayd" while the "sunne-beames" then "pierst into her wombe, where they embayd / With so sweet sence and secret power vnspide" (3.6.7). The masculine vigor of the sun reproduces itself "in her pregnant flesh," where it is "fructifide." The narrator claims that "antique books" explain Chrysogonee's pregnancy and make "so straunge ensample of conception" comprehensible (3.6.6, 8). "Reason teacheth," we hear,

> that the fruitfull seades
> Of all things liuing, through impression
> Of the sunbeames in moyst complexion,
> Doe life conceiue and quickened are by kynd
> (3.6.8)

The sun, "Great father he of generation / Is rightly cald, th'authour of life and light" (3.6.9), and dominates the process, rendering active the passive potential of substances without suffering their material taint. Belphoebe and Amoret are similarly kept free of this taint,

> For not as other wemens commune brood,
> They were enwombed in the sacred throne
> Of [Chrysogonee's] chaste bodie, nor with commune food,
> As other wemens babes, they sucked vitall blood.
> (3.6.5)

Chrysogonee conceives immaculately, and in this her daughters are to be distinguished from the "commune brood" of women. She gives birth "withouten paine, that she conceiu'd / Withouten pleasure" (3.6.27). Pleasure in sex and pain in labor constitute the tainted, bodily experience of human generation.

Yet, as the narrative asserts and privileges the masculine force of the sun, which pierces and impregnates, activates and endows with life, the taint of matter remains. Thus, though the sun activates all life, those here rise "after *Nilus* inundation" and are the "Infinite shapes of creatures men doe fynd, / Informed in the mud, on which the Sunne hath shynd" (3.6.8). The informing, impressing force of masculinity may activate fertility, but the creatures that rise from the Nile mud appear, elsewhere in *The Faerie Queene*, as manifestations of a monstrous fecundity, as when, in the Legend of Holiness, Error's brood boils forth from her body. Likewise, though masculine sun and seed seem to be independent of the tainted, feminine material in which they reproduce themselves, Chrysogonee is consistently associated with flowers, both when the sun beams fructify her pregnant flesh and, previously, when, because of the heat, she bathes "with roses red, and violets blew, / And all the sweetest flowres, that in the forrest grew" (3.6.6). As is revealed in the Garden of Adonis, the language of vegetation provides a mediating discourse between tainted feminine materiality and immaculate masculine form.

Venus and Diana witness the birth of Amoret and Belphoebe; each chooses a child to foster. Their intersection with the narrative is, however, no accident, as the two goddesses embody, as erotic psychology, the drama of material creation that manifests in Chrysogonee's reproductive narrative. Though reason and ancient authority should provide ample justification for spontaneous solar generation, this variety of masculine self-reproduction seems anything but ordinary when it is embodied in Chrysogonee's conception. In responding as it does to the fear of material taint in human reproduction, this scene of queer conception and birth draws Venus and Diana into its orbit. Having lost track of her wayward son Cupid, the heavenly Venus descends from:

> her heauenly hous,
> The house of goodly formes and faire aspects,
> Whence all the world deriues the glorious
> Features of beautie, and all shapes select,
> With which high God his workmanship hath deckt.
> (3.6.12)

From the House of Venus derive the beauty and shape of heavenly form; this Venus, though she is much like the goddess Nature, sinks into the world of materiality to seek her son in court, in cities, and in the country. She, too, retreats finally to "the saluage woods and forests wyde" (3.6.16), where she encounters the virgin huntress. Diana and her crew, like Chrysogonee, seek relief from the sun (and their exertions) by bathing in a fountain. The goddess appears unarmed and unclothed:

> She hauing hong vpon a bough on high
> Her bow and painted quiuer, had vnlaste
> Her siluer buskins from her nimble thigh,
> And her lanck loynes vngirt, and brests vnbraste,
> After her heat the breathing cold to taste;
> Her golden lockes, that late in tresses bright
> Embreaded were for hindring of her haste,
> Now loose about her shoulders hong vndight,
> And were with sweet *Ambrosia* all besprinckled light.
> (3.6.18)

The virgin goddess appears uncased in a moment of vulnerability that is the inverse of the violent, iconicity of Belphoebe's blazon in the Legend of Temperance. This vulnerability reminds us, too, of Diana's encounter with Actaeon.

Yet in a bold revision of the encounter between an unwitting male viewer and the naked goddess, Venus appears as the invasive principle disrupting the calm of Diana's chaste community. Indeed, "Soone as she *Venus* saw behinde her backe, / She was asham'd to be so loose surpriz'd"

(3.6.19). The shame and surprise of the encounter remains fascinating for the way it translates the heterosexual desire and masculine anxiety of the Actaeon myth. Since the canto opens with an address to the fair ladies reading *The Faerie Queene*, this eroticism passes from Diana and Venus to the imagined female readers who become the privileged spectators of the naked body of the disarmed goddess of chastity and of her tense encounter with the goddess of love. More important, however, is the appearance of Diana's body, which represents more than an object of erotic titillation. Eros becomes not just the experience of pleasure but also the experience of bodily vulnerability. Diana "woxe halfe wroth against her damzels slacke" for having "suffred her so carelesly disguiz'd / Be ouertaken" (3.6.19). Cupid, stanzas before this, proves difficult to find because he is "Disguiz'd in thousand shapes, that none might him bewray" (3.6.11). Disguise, of course, most commonly refers either to false appearances, as in the case of Cupid or Archimago and Duessa, or to sumptuous, excessive clothing, such as that Busyrane wears in the Masque of Cupid. Diana's odd use of the term suggests not only that she is *dis*-guised or *un*-guised but, more interestingly, that nakedness—bare, material appearance—constitutes disguise. If nakedness were not merely shameful but also false in the manner of a disguise, then the vulnerable body would be a false appearance beneath or beyond which lay the higher truth of chastity. This would suggest, ironically, that Diana appears as real and natural only when armed and clothed. When Diana's inattentive nymphs finally protect their mistress they "did like a girlond her enclose" (3.6.19). Instead of being encased in armaments, equipment, or garb, Diana finds cover in the bodies of her nymphs who appear to be flowers. Diana's gesture confirms a disdain for shameful naked matter, but in attempting to conceal her body, the "girlond," composed of nymphs' bodies, only foregrounds the troublesome desires of flesh, which Diana disdains and Venus represents.

Diana's disdain for matter expresses itself as a disdain for Venus's plight, her inability to locate a son who, like substance itself, appears "in thousand shapes." Criticizing her "Faire sister" for a lack of sympathy, Venus claims, "ill beseemes it to vpbrayd / A dolefull heart with so disdainfull pride; / The like that mine, may be your paine another tide" (3.6.21). This plea for compassion asserts a commonality Diana refuses because that compassion would imply a material tie constituted by the common vulnerability of the body to change, to loss, or to desire. Thus

Diana objects violently when Venus, in a witty allusion to the myth of Callisto, suggests an ever more insidious variety of shared, material experience. Cupid, she warns, may "lurke emongst your Nimphes in secret wize" precisely because he may "like one of them him selfe disguize" (3.6.23). Diana, driven by a need to distinguish herself from Venus and by a newfound suspicion regarding her nymphs, is at last calmed by Venus's soothing words that flow forth like the fountain Diana bathes in:

> so her she soone appeasd
> With sugred words and gentle blandishment,
> From which a fountaine from her sweet lips went,
> And welled goodly forth
>
> (3.6.25)

Diana, "well pleasd" with Venus's welling, sugary words, joins the search for the "fugitiue" Cupid (3.6.25–26). Diana surrenders her initial impulse to differentiate herself violently from the earthly Venus and her lascivious son. The sisters join in a pleasurable union, which leads them to the discovery of the sleeping Chrysogonee and her babes, Amoret and Belphoebe. The spectacle of birth astonishes the goddesses, drawing them into deeper sympathy. Diana and Venus are:

> through wonder nigh of sense bereau'd
> And gazing each on other, nought bespake:
> At last they both agreed, her seeming grieu'd
> Out of her heauie swowne not to awake,
> But from her louing side the tender babes to take.
>
> (3.6.27)

Each goddess chooses a babe to foster separately and in a distinct style. Thus Belphoebe is raised "in perfect Maydenhed" in the savage forest and Amoret "in goodly womanhed" in the "ioyous Paradize" of the Garden of Adonis (3.6.28–29).

While in fostering the children they remain distinct, Venus and Diana are similarly cast as mothers to Belphoebe and Amoret, the female figures whose appearances frame this canto. While the sun may have provided the activating energy for this birth and Chrysogonee the hosting body, Diana and Venus endow each "daughter" with character. They not only assume the role of the exhausted Chrysogonee; they also leave their own character, or mark, behind. The goddesses come together as mothers to whom is delegated a task of translation, as the mother, matter, becomes more than just the receptacle in which creation occurs.

The queer pairing of Venus and Diana reflects a reconfigured scene of generation, suggesting a new gendered paradigm for creation, as the goddesses displace the masculine force of the sun represented in the solar generation signaled even in Chrysogonee's name (golden birth). Parental care draws Venus down to the material realm from the heavenly sphere as she seeks her absent son. In surprising Diana, Venus emphasizes the conflict between Diana's vulnerable, material form and her aggressive, divine chastity. Spenser translates the violent dialectic of erotic display and revenge central to the Actaeon myth into the conflict between Venus and Diana, between sexual pleasure and sexual restraint. In spite of their differences, a sweet sympathy springs up between the forlorn mother Venus and the childless and chaste Diana. As Diana and Venus become the "mothers" of Belphoebe and Amoret, their relationship enters a new phase as a parental mutuality develops out of the sympathy that replaced the eroticized aggression of their initial encounter. Diana's transformation into a sympathetic, mothering figure represents a noticeable departure from her defensive chastity and the disdain for matter that it implies.

While Venus initiates the pattern of transformation in this canto, the Venus who appears in the Garden of Adonis appears not merely as a figure of sexual pleasure but also, more important, as a figure of parental care. Indeed, Spenser introduces the Garden of Adonis as the place Venus takes Amoret "To be vpbrought in goodly womanhed" (3.6.28). At first the garden might seem merely decorative:

> In that same Gardin all the goodly flowres,
> Wherewith dame Nature doth her beautifie,
> And decks the girlonds of her Paramoures,
> Are fetcht.
>
> (3.6.30)

One might expect Venus to be concerned only with ornamental flowers and ornamented paramours, but the narrative identifies her with "dame Nature." As such, Venus assumes the mantle of the goddess who governs the process of generation and reproduction dramatized in the Garden of Adonis, that "first seminary / Of all things, that are borne to liue and dye." This concern for reproduction and generation, and not merely for sexual desire or sexual union, constitutes the heart of the allegory in the garden, which is itself the allegorical heart of the Legend of Chastity. "Long worke it were," the narrator admits,

> Here to account the endlesse progenie
> Of all the weedes, that bud and blossome there;
> But so much as doth need, must needs be counted here.
> (3.6.30)

The Legend of Chastity attempts to account not just for "the endlesse progeny" produced by nature but also for the nature of that production. The plants, or weeds, that bud and blossom refer ambiguously both to souls or forms planted in the garden and to the material or "fleshly weeds" those souls wear as their "attire." Souls constantly cycle in and out of the garden in an endless pattern of regeneration; they are plucked from the seed beds of form, clothed with mortal covering or "sinfull mire," sent to live in "mortall state" (3.6.32), returned back to the garden, and:

> They in that Gardin planted be agayne;
> And grow afresh, as they had neuer seene
> Fleshly corruption, nor mortall payne.
> (3.6.33)

Though the garden is Venus's "ioyous Paradize," the garden's lack of "fleshly corruption" and "mortall payne" is only an appearance. For an earthly paradise the Garden of Adonis is unique in its incorporation of suffering and loss, the histories of which are carried in the various vegetative states depicted in the garden. The plants of the garden refer to specific mythic histories (such as those of Adonis, Hyacinthus, and Narcissus) and to the history of matter itself, *hyle*, which is also wood, a vegetative substance. Matter, in the garden, bears a history of pain.

Like Plato's *Timaeus* and Bernardus Silvestris's *Cosmographia*, Spenser's Garden of Adonis still props the whole order of creation on abject materiality. Abject matter enables the cycle of birth, death, and rebirth, for there exists an "euerlasting store" of substance to draw from,

> For in the wide wombe of the world there lyes,
> In hatefull darkenesse and in deepe horrore,

> An huge eternall *Chaos*, which supplyes
> The substaunces of natures fruitfull progenyes.
> (3.6.36)

The "hatefull darkenesse" supplies the "borrow[d]" raw material that provides the metaphysical stability of the whole cyclical process. Though particular incarnations fade and die, "That substance," in the Garden of Adonis as in Aristotle, "is eterne." Eternal substance constitutes the aspect of the cosmological system that conserves its shape and order by preventing loss; substance is that which does not "into nothing goe, / But chaunged is, and often altred to and froe" (3.6.37).

Despite this invocation of Aristotelian substance as change without loss, pain creeps back into the system:

> For formes are variable and decay,
> By course of kinde, and by occasion;
> And that faire flowre of beautie fades away,
> As doth the lilly fresh before the sunny ray.
> (3.6.38)

Flowers grow melancholic as time and death enter the confines of this walled paradise:

> Great enimy to it, and to all the rest,
> That in the *Gardin* of *Adonis* springs,
> Is wicked *Tyme*, who with his scyth addrest,
> Does mow the flowring herbes and goodly things,
> And all their glory to the ground downe flings,
> Where they doe wither, and are fowly mard:
> He flyes about, and with his flaggy winges
> Beates down both leaues and buds without regard,
> Ne euer pittie may relent his malice hard.
> (3.6.39)

The appearance of personification is noticeably intrusive and unnecessary. In a stable metaphysical system, one governed by the birth, death, and rebirth of souls and by the cyclical change of eternal substance, there would be no need for Time embodied as a force exhibiting malice, lacking pity, or flying about with "flaggy winges."

The interjection of this awkward moment of personification indicates a kind of material contagion; it is as if the allegorical embodiment of abstract concepts has contaminated those concepts with the taint of substance. The appearance of Time also serves to alter substantially the role of Venus in the Garden of Adonis. Though the garden is her earthly paradise, and though we will see her enjoy her paramour Adonis, Venus serves to provide care and compassion. Despite Time's lack of pity,

> Yet pitty often did the gods relent,
> To see so faire thinges mard, and spoiled quight:
> And their great mother *Venus* did lament
> The losse of her deare brood, her deare delight:
> Her hart was pierst with pitty at the sight,
> When walking through the Gardin, them she spyde,
> Yet no'te she find redresse for such despight.
> (3.6.40)

Venus, as mother, suffers for the pain of her creations. She is neither the perverse Venus nor the wounded Nature of *De planctu naturae*; nor is she the powerfully active Nature of the *Cosmographia*. The influential Renaissance Neoplatonist Marisilio Ficino conceived of two Venuses, one heavenly and one earthly. The former was "born of Uranus without a mother, because *mother*, to the physicists, is matter" and "is a stranger to any association with corporeal matter," while the earthly, vulgar Venus "is thought to have commerce with matter."[25] If, for Ficino, the earthly Venus follows the lead of the heavenly Venus, here, the heavenly Venus has followed the earthly Venus, descending to the world of matter as a mother whose sole purpose is the display of care. Ideality in Venus's garden exists in the conditional:

> But were it not that *Time* their troubler is,
> All that in this delightfull Gardin growes,
> Should happy bee, and haue immortall blis.
> (3.6.41)

Of course, time does trouble. Rather than fantasize a perpetual summer or capitulate to an endless winter, this garden compromises: "There is continuall Spring, and haruest there / Continuall, both meeting at one tyme" (3.6.42). The simultaneity of verdant growth and mature harvest disarms but does not deny deadly *Time*, for without time there is neither desire nor its realization, let alone ripening and fruition.

As the compassionate Venus disarms *Time*, she also creates a haven for Adonis and, in so doing, alters the erotic psychology of their relationship. Adonis, one might say, is Venus's Actaeon. The story of Adonis provides a cautionary tale for the disastrous forces associated with eros—compulsive desire, violent masculinity, jealous rage, cyclical revenge—all of which are handily emblematized by the boar that gores Adonis. Whereas Actaeon loses his life by inadvertently occupying the position of masculine desire in surprising the bathing Diana, Adonis loses his life in preferring *heros* to *eros*. Unable to refuse the thrill of the hunt, Adonis dies proving his masculinity and thus completes a cycle of aggression and revenge. Ovid's Venus, we may remember, falls for the youth because her own son Cupid wounds her inadvertently as he embraces her. Adonis, so beautiful at his birth that it is said he might be mistaken for a cupid, becomes the object of Venus's obsession and keeps her away from the heavens and on earth.[26] Venus may indeed play Adonis's second mother when one remembers his birth mother's story. Myrrha, having conceived an unnatural passion for her own father and having consummated that desire, flees her home, begs to be transformed, becomes a tree, and then gives birth to Adonis. Of Myrrha's incestuous desire, Ovid's narrator claims, "Cupid himself denies that his dart wounded you, Myrrha, and that his firebrand vindicates you from your crimes" (Ipse negat nocuisse tibi sua tela Cupido, Myrrha, facesque suas a crimine vindicat isto).[27]

Adonis's own death appears to be the consequence of a cycle of revenge, for in drawing Venus's interest he "avenges the passion of his mother" (matrisque ulciscitur ignes).[28] To warn Adonis away from the dangerous creatures of the hunt, Venus recalls the story of Atalanta and Hippomenes. The latter, seeking the hand of the athletic maiden Atalanta, receives Venus's help, and wins the girl by beating her, unfairly, at a foot race, which, had he lost, would have cost him his life. Hippomenes and Atlanta, forgetting to thank Venus properly, suffer her wrath and, through her machinations, offend Cybele, the ancient earth mother, and are transformed into lions. The creatures of the forest embody a savage and self-destructive cycle of sin, resentment, and revenge as they "bear their breasts for battle" (pugnae pectora praebet).[29] Even in monumentalizing the slain Adonis, Venus remains trapped in an economy of resentment and competition. As she decrees that Adonis's blood will become a flower, she compares her power to memorialize to that of Proserpina, who wrought a transformation on the nymph Menthe, who gives her name to the herb. She asks, "Will the transformation of my hero, son of Cinyras, be envied of us?" (nobis Cinyreius heros invidiae mutates erit?).[30]

The psychology of Spenser's Venus and Adonis and the physical landscape of the Garden of Adonis alike work to suspend the cycles of aggression and revenge that dominate Ovid's tale. At the heart of the garden and "in the middest of that Paradise," there is "a stately Mount" that embodies the *mons veneris,* which provides shelter from the "sharpe steele" of cultivation, from the savagery of "wicked beasts," and from the elements. Both "*Aelous* sharp blast" and "*Phoebus* beams" remain barred from the "gloomy groue of mirtle trees" (3.6.44–43). The mount is a place of heady sexuality, where trees drip with "sweet gum" and "pretious deaw" and exude "dainty odours, and most sweet delight" (3.6.43). This conflation of the shape of paradise with female genitalia revises the expectations set for the destructive, wanton sexuality associated with the filthy nether parts of Duessa in the Legend of Holiness or with the Scylla and Charybdis imagery of the Legend of Temperance, which suggests the devouring *vagina dentata* of early modern misogyny. This *mons veneris* also constitutes a rewriting of the womb as a receptacle, as in both Chrysogonee's birth (indeed, the *mons veneris* is sheltered from the sun) and in the hateful womb of Chaos, from which Genius draws matter to clothe souls.

The sheltering womb of the Garden of Adonis witnesses an erotic mutuality between Venus and Adonis. As opposed to Ovid's Venus, who is violently compelled to love Adonis, or Shakespeare's Venus, who violently compels Adonis's submission to her love, Spenser's Venus finds in Adonis "ioyous company" (3.6.46). Indeed, he lives "in eternall blis, / Ioying his goddesse, and of her enioyd" (3.6.48). She "reape[s] sweet pleasure of the wanton boy," and in so doing shelters him from the violence Ovid's Adonis invites:

> There yet, some say, in secret he does ly,
> Lapped in flowres and pretious spycery,
> By her hid from the world, and from the skill
> Of *Stygian* Gods, which doe her loue enuy
> (3.6.46)

If Venus does try to shelter Adonis from violence, that violence is not excluded, as the hesitation of the verse suggests in "some say." Adonis, who has just appeared at the heart of the garden, is now the subject of a rumor. Similarly of Adonis:

> And sooth it seemes they say: for he may not
> For euer die, and euer buried bee
> In balefull night, where all thinges are forgot;
> All be he subject to mortalitie,
> Yet is eterne in mutabilitie,
> And by succession made perpetuall,
> Transformed oft, and chaunged diuerslie:
> For him the Father of all formes they call;
> Therfore needs mote he liue, that liuing giues to all.
> (3.4.47)

Adonis, the figure at the heart of Venus's ideal, earthly abode, reconstitutes materiality as ever changing but never dying substance. What was drawn from the dark womb of the earth is reconstituted as a figure of suffering masculinity rather than of violated femininity. To claim identity in flux is to be "eterne in mutabilitie." For Adonis the experience of mutability is constitutive, not damaging; he suffers, and as he does so, he suffers mortality and change.

Adonis displays a variety of receptivity to Venus's love that is no mere inversion of masculine and feminine positions. Rather, Adonis reconstitutes masculinity entirely by reconstituting the function of paternity. What Gilles Deleuze asks of the male masochist one might ask of Adonis: "What does 'becoming a man' signify? Clearly it does not mean *to be like the father*, or to take his place. On the contrary, it consists in obliterating his role and his likeness in order to generate the new man."[31] Adonis may be the "Father of all formes," but despite his association with solar force, the role he occupies is nothing like that of the inseminating, celestial sun that impregnates Chrysogonee. Adonis, figure of mutable materiality, completes a reproductive circuit with Venus analogous to the reproductive relationship between Venus and Diana. Adonis as matter (a mother) joins with Venus; the two create between them a garden.

Adonis exemplifies disarmed masculinity; he is the shape of masculinity in the suspension of violent conflict. In the garden, the savage boar fated to gore Adonis has been neither negated nor excluded; rather, Venus imprisons the boar "In a strong rocky Caue, which is they say, / Hewen vnderneath the Mount, that none him losen may" (3.6.48). The boar remains as a reminder of the savage force of violent masculinity. Just as the boar is disarmed so too is Venus's son Cupid, who appears at long last as Adonis's playmate:

> Who when he hath with spoiles and cruelty
> Ransackt the world, and in the wofull harts
> Of many wretches set his triumphes hye,
> Thether resortes, and laying his sad dartes
> Asyde, with faire *Adonis* playes his wanton partes.
> (3.6.49)

Cupid enters the Garden of Adonis having set aside the need for his cruel triumphs or the sharp tools with which he inflicts them. Here, Spenser replaces the opening proem's triad of Venus, the disarmed Cupid, and the mollified Mars with an erotic trio of Venus, Cupid, and Adonis, the latter acting as both son and lover. Adonis, a figure of pain, pleasure, and generation replaces Mars, the figure of temporarily pacified violence. The "new man" of masochistic fantasy is Adonis, who incorporates pain and alteration; Adonis suffers change. The species of allegory whose "essence is violence emerging from chaos to impose schematic order on historical process," Teskey argues, "struggles to bring forth from the union of Venus and Mars, even as they embrace in the grave, a world we can value and a narrative in which we can live. The child it hopes for is Harmony."[32] By replacing Mars with Adonis, Spenser announces that pain is the essence of his allegory, not violence. Rather than the "creative but nauseating drive to force heterogeneities together" that is characteristic of allegorical violence, Spenser's allegory emerges through the sympathy that follows suffering. Indeed, Cupid and Psyche emerge as the ideal, procreating couple at the close of the canto. Psyche, having long labored under and suffered from the wrath of Venus, at last marries Cupid, and the two produce a daughter, Pleasure. Pleasure, rather than the opposite of or antidote to pain, emerges from sympathetic sociality. Pleasure is born from the joy of suffering turning into sympathy.

We might remember that the birth of Adonis in the *Metamorphoses* is also the birth of pain, a birth that transforms the bleeding tree into a birthing tree. Adonis's mother, Myrrha, having sated her incestuous lust and fled into exile, pregnant, begs to be transformed, and so she becomes a tree. But, we learn, "The misbegotten chyld / Grew still within the tree, and from his mothers womb defyld / Sought meanes to bee delyvered."[33] Despite the great pain of her labor, "woordes wherwith to tell / And utter foorth her greef did want. She had no use of speech / With which Lucina in her throwes shee might of help beseech."[34] Though she has no voice, she "often sighes, and shed foorth teares as though shee there should drowne."[35] Finally,

> Lucina to this wofull tree came gently downe, and layd
> Her hand theron, and speaking woordes of ease the midwife playd.
> The tree did cranye, and the barke deviding made away,
> And yeelded out the chyld alyve, which cryde and wayld streyght way.[36]

Myrrha, as the Myrrh tree, produces not only tears, as sap; she gives birth to a beautiful child, whose birth cries take the place of her silence. Adonis embodies and redeems his mother's pain, a pain for which transformation provides only a partial solution.

Perhaps the most provocative and salient detail in Golding's translation of Ovid, for Spenser's purposes, is the birth of the human "chyld alyve" from the body of the tree. Born from a bleeding tree, Adonis embodies, too, a vision of matter endowed with life. If suffering, the quickening experience of pain, served as a reminder of all that was suppressed in the machine of the Protestant allegorizing of the flesh, Spenser's damaged divinities, especially Adonis, introduce that vulnerability into the texture of allegory by disarming its disembodying, hierarchical violence.

Conclusion

And thou most dreaded impe of highest *Ioue*,
Faire *Venus* sonne, that with thy cruell dart
At that good knight so cunningly didst roue,
That glorious fire it kindled in his hart,
Lay now thy deadly Heben bow apart,
And with thy mother mylde come to mine ayde:
Come both, and with you bring triumphant *Mart*,
In loues and gentle iollities arraid,
After his murdrous spoyles and bloudie rage allayd.

(1.proem.3)

The Faerie Queene opens with an act of disarmament. Although the poem confirms its affiliation with the heroic by trumpeting "Fierce warres and faithfull loues," it also lays claim to the power of love to disarm the fury of Mars and set aside that fundamental aggression at the heart of epic violence, even when such violence might be dedicated to apparently virtuous purposes. In so doing *The Faerie Queene* comes to redefine masculinity as an ethical project accessible through the intimate aesthetics of the vulnerable body and through bonds of shared vulnerability that oppose forms of structural violence. With that proem Spenser launches himself into a massive endeavor, one that would outlive him. Although the proem announces a project of disarmament that clearly resonates with mythographic tradition and contemporary political allegory, it may be, at first, difficult to detect this project. That difficulty stems from the complexity of Spenser's poem; from the representation of violence that is, at times, glorified and gratuitous; and from the tendency to construe vulnerability as mere privation.

As I have suggested, the consequences of the Reformation complicate but also enable the task of apprehending vulnerability as an ethical project, a project of transforming the very idea of virtuous work and of the forms of masculinity on which notions of virtue rest. On the one hand, much post-Reformation theology and practice obscured experiences of vulnerability central to a deeply embodied religion with a primary focus on the devotional act of witnessing and contemplating the suffering of others, beginning with Christ and extending outward. On the other hand, because the far-reaching consequences of the Reformation were distributed not solely in the sphere of religion—in battles over icons, idols, sacraments, and rites—it became possible that an ethics rooted in vulnerability could appear widely and obliquely in a range of meaning-making systems, from the sanctioned purposes of poetry and poetics to the intimate urgencies of desire, sex, and sexuality.

Like Spenser, Lucretius invokes a Venus capable of disarming Mars and bringing peace to the land. Yet Lucretius also identifies her as "Aeneadum genetrix" or "mother of Aeneas and his race."[1] As such, it would seem that this Venus would be the mother of empire. But Lucretius describes the mother of life itself: "nurturing Venus, who beneath the smooth-moving heavenly signs fill with yourself the sea full-laden with ships, the earth that bears the crops, since through you every kind of living thing is conceived and rising up looks on the light of the sun."[2] Venus calms the rough seas, charms the wild beasts, and drives "love into the breasts of all creatures" causing them "greedily to beget their generations after their kind."[3] In *De rerum natura*, all life is Venus's empire, and she disseminates the impulse to love as a means of increasing life. Her power to soothe Mars and bring peace saves lives by stopping conflict, but her original function is generation itself. To disarm, to experience vulnerability is merely to return to this original life-giving state. It is fitting that Spenser's project culminates in the central canto of the Legend of Chastity, as the bleeding tree of Reformation trauma becomes a locus of a transformative aesthetics and ethics of vulnerability. Out of the absence of the iconic presence of Christ blossoms Adonis in the midst of a garden that unites generation and mortality. Even Venus and Diana find concord in this garden.

The invocation of Venus by Lucretius indicates that Spenser's quite singular attempt to explore vulnerability had precedent, while the attention Rubens paid to Venus, Mars, and Adonis also indicates that he inherited and struggled with similar mythic constructs in an attempt to explore the possibility that war might be allayed by love. Lucretius lived through shockingly violent times. The forty-four years of his life were punctuated with civil war, public riots, foreign wars, political assassinations, massacres, plots, and conspiracies as the fabric of Roman society was rent by social and economic instability. Spenser and Rubens lived through tumultuous times with the cultural memory of a series of crises of succession, international conflicts, gruesomely public martyrdoms, and the destruction and reallocation of religious sensibilities and properties alike. These artists sought, in their different ways, a solution to violence through the cultivation of a mortality characterized by vulnerability to the painful experiences flesh is heir to.

Like the artists of those eras, many of our own era have had in mind a new sense of vulnerability. It is in this context that Judith Butler attempts to understand how "each of us is constituted politically in part by virtue of the social vulnerability of our bodies."[4] Not only is vulnerability a primary feature of social existence in Butler's account, but it also has the potential to become a virtue when one refuses to allow injury to foment indifference or violence. "Perhaps," she suggests, "there is some other way to live such that one becomes neither affectively dead nor mimetically violent, a way out of the circle of violence altogether. This possibility has to do with demanding a world in which bodily vulnerability is protected without therefore being eradicated and with insisting on the line that must be walked between the two."[5]

To find political virtue in vulnerability is no easy thing in our era nor was it in Spenser's. *The Faerie Queene* is full of gratuitous violence, violence often deliciously described and that serves to differentiate and demarcate. What is equally clear in recent political philosophy and in the ideological operations of early modern epic-romance is that the positive values to be associated with vulnerability exist in tension with the uneven, structural distribution of vulnerability. To some, a greater share of susceptibility to physical, emotional, and political suffering is consistently allocated. An ethics and aesthetics of vulnerability that serves as an antidote to violence would face a significant challenge in forms of social and structural violence that distribute vulnerability in predictably uneven ways. While an overattention to violence has obscured Spenser's patient attention to vulnerability, our understanding of the project of *The Faerie Queene* would be incomplete without a deeper analysis of social and structural violence.

The excised stanzas of the 1590 *Faerie Queene* index Spenser's realization of the need to widen the scope of his inquiry. In 1590 the Legend of Chastity ended with the reunion of Amoret and Scudamour who, in their loving embrace, form what has been, for many critics, a controversial unit: "No word they spake, nor earthly thing they felt, / But like two senceles stocks in long embracement dwelt" (3.7.45). Moreover, the narration continues, "Had ye them seene, ye would haue surely thought, / That they had beene that faire *Hermaphrodite*" (3.7.46).

For many, the figure of the hermaphrodite suggests "an emblem of completeness and fulfillment," as Donald Cheney sums up that figure's critical reception, and the harmonious union of male and female in a state of either the one flesh of Christian marriage or, as A. R. Cirillo argues, "a spiritual union . . . one in which the lovers are united so that they become one another, not physically but spiritually."[6] David Lee Miller sees the figure of the hermaphrodite as an extension of the 1590 *Faerie Queene*'s ideal of "integral wholeness" with the union of Amoret and Scudamour constituting a "sacramental embrace."[7] Although Lauren Silberman finds in the figure of the hermaphrodite a "denial of sexual difference," the union of Amoret and Scudamour exists as "an ideal of chaste love" that, because it is ideal is "therefore not something fully available to us in our sublunary existence."[8] In spite of this apparently perfect union, Spenser canceled these stanzas and extended the search for Amoret into the Legend of Friendship in the 1596 *Faerie Queene*.

While critics disagree about precisely why these stanzas were excised, some, including Jonathan Goldberg, diagnose this as a resistance to closure.[9] One might also see this as a resistance to the petrifying ideality of this closed circle of lovers. For Circillo, Silberman, and others, the phrase "no earthly thing they felt" cements the ideality of Amoret and Scudamour, yet it is hard not to linger on the simile that makes them "like two senceles stocks" and thus, unlike the union of Adonis and Venus, denudes these lovers of sensation and vitality. Ovid's *Metamorphoses* too imagines the lovers with respect to vegetative imagery, but these figures are endowed with life: "As when one grafts a twig on some tree, he sees the branches grow one, and with common life come to maturity, so were these two bodies knit in close embrace."[10] The irony of the ending stanzas of the 1590 *Faerie Queene* is that the ideal union of lovers has a prettifying and deadening effect on a poem that consistently finds in vegetative forms vulnerability and vitality. But the violent excision of those stanzas made possible the continuation of the poem as an inquiry into the nature of violence.

It would be impossible not to understand *The Faerie Queene* in reference to the violence distributed to particular subjects considering, if not exclusively, the Irish context for Spenser's life and Spenser's poem (which are by no means the same thing). What is the solution for a poet on the one hand, engaging in the imaginative project of recovering vulnerability as a political and aesthetic virtue even as the everyday value and virtue associated with suffering and vulnerability comes to be occluded while, on the other hand, participating in the infrastructure of the extraordinarily violent Tudor occupation of Ireland? The answer is the 1596 *Faerie Queene*, a poem that excavates the dark underside of vulnerability and the intersection of violence and political justice. What follows here is a brief attempt to suggest the future of the 1590 *Faerie Queene* while also suggesting the outlines for future research, which would take into account the dominant affect and ethic of the 1596 *Faerie Queene*: shame, an affect that some describe as "the painful feeling of exposed vulnerability."[11]

If at one point it could be argued that "Literary scholars," unlike practitioners of other disciplines, "have been rather slow in showing interest" in affect more generally and shame specifically, shame has garnered great interest of late, from literary critics of various kinds, scholars of early modernity, and theoreticians of sexuality.[12] The growth of a veritable shame industry (both in therapeutic discourse and in academic conversation) represents part of a larger attempt to account for negative affects and what Sianne Ngai refers to in a recent study as the "politically ambiguous work" of "ugly feelings."[13] What I will suggest here, briefly, is that in Spenser's age, as in our own, literature cannot be thought without recourse to the politically ambiguous operations of shame. Spenser is at once a theorist of shame and its relationship to literature, creativity, and the imagination in early modernity *and* an exemplary instance of the mutually imbricated nature of shame, literature, and literary studies in his relationship to Ireland.

Critical genealogies of the import of shame, concerned with the cultural and historical modalities of that affect, often begin with Ruth Benedict's formative study *The Chrysanthemum and the Sword*, which divided East and West into cultures of shame and guilt respectively, which is to say cultures of external and internal mechanisms of moral monitoring. Bernard Williams extended this insight historically, arguing for the appearance of a transition from shame to guilt in fifth-century Greece.[14] Shame has been no stranger to the study of early modernity, as the pioneering work of Norbert Elias, for whom shame constitutes a central node of the civilizing process, and a number of subsequent studies indicate.

Most notable in early modernity, however, is the relationship between shame and literature itself. In a major reevaluation of the literature of Spenser's age, Georgia Brown has argued that "Shame is not only produced by late Elizabethan culture, it actually produces late Elizabethan literary culture."[15] Shame, then, is not merely an object of representation; it is, rather, a field of affective force from which literature emerges: "In the 1590s a new kind of defense becomes popular, one which does not deny the traditional association of literature with the trivial and the transgressive, but capitalizes upon it to uncover the paradoxical value of marginality, error, ornamentality and excess. By exploiting shame, these texts set limits on literature, defining it as a thing apart, with its own rules, personnel and history, and challenge the idea that literature is primarily the vehicle for historical, political or religious truth."[16] Brown locates this strategy for "turning the negative potential in literature into something productive" in a variety of literary works (prose romance, Ovidian epyllion, and others) from the 1590s. These authors form a counterpoint to Brown's exemplary literary proponent of appropriate forms of shame: Edmund Spenser.

While Brown detects in both the 1590 and 1596 *Faerie Queene* "varied, even contradictory, roles played by shame in social, political and cultural self-definition," she attends quite closely to "the ethical, social and nationalistic ideals that are defined by Spenserian courtesy [and that] involve a particular sensitivity to shame, which controls the interactions between individuals, and generates order."[17] As Brown notes, "Shame plays an important role in mediating the transactions between individuals in Spenser's text. It defines an emergent and vulnerable space of privacy that is usually figured by a female body that needs to be shielded from the indulgences of voyeurism."[18] Clearly, Spenser knew how to wield shame to maintain a sense of propriety and order. In a study of Shakespeare's relationship to shame, Ewan Fernie contrasts Christopher Marlowe, noted for his shamelessness, with Spenser who "demonstrates a clear commitment to shame, which is exemplified by women but which men must learn to emulate."[19]

Spenser wielded rather effectively the forces of shame in the interests of maintaining a sense of order, but he also keenly observed shame as a form of *social vulnerability*. Aristotle famously defines shame as "a kind of pain or uneasiness in respect of misdeeds, past or present, or future, which seem to tend to bring dishonor."[20] *The Faerie Queene* is, indeed, full of social uneasiness, and it would be easy to construe the project of the poem as a response to anxieties of social rank alone. But Spenser's understanding of his literary identity was quite personally inflected with a sense of shame. In a Latin poem included in the published *Letters* he exchanged with Gabriel Harvey, Spenser admits his greatest fears as a poet.[21] An apt student of Horace, Spenser defines the successful poet as he who combines what is sweet and pleasing with what is morally useful. In this regard, he found himself wanting:

> Omne tulit punctum, qui miscuit vtile dulci.
> Dij mihi, dulce diu dederant: verùm utile nunquam:
> Vtile nunc etiam, ô vtinam quoque dulce dedissent.
> Dij mihi, (quippe Dijs aequiualia maxima paruis)
> Ni nimis inuideant mortalibus esse beatis,
> Dulce simul tribuisse queant, simul utile
> (202–207)[22]

> He wins the prize who mingles the sweet with the useful.
> The gods long ago gave me sweetness, but never anything useful:
> How I wish even now that they had given me some utility along with sweetness.
> May the gods (for surely to them the greatest are equivalent to the small),
> Unless they envy mortals who are too happy,
> See their way to giving me the sweet and the useful together.

The articulation of familiar Horatian ambitions for poetry occurs negatively with Spenser as a failed instance. Early in his career, fresh from the publication of *The Shepheardes Calendar*, Spenser's identity as a poet is inflected with shame and waste:

Namque sinu pudet in patrio, tenebrisque pudendis
Non nimis ingenio Iuuenem infoelice, virentes,
Officijs frustra deperdere vilibus Annos,
Frugibus et vaucas speratis cernere spicas.
(217–220)

For one feels ashamed, as a youth not without talents,
To be wasting the green years uselessly,
At home with unworthy duties in the shameful shade,
Picking empty ears out of the hoped-for crops.

Disappointment and disillusionment are part of the youthful poet's impatience with a world that did not yet recognize his talent and with a sense that his literary potential that had yet to manifest itself definitively. But what duties, precisely, was Spenser referring to? He was, at this point, in the service of Leicester but soon to be passing into the service of Lord Grey de Wilton, shifting from the centrality of an English homeland for the margins of the Tudor settlement in Ireland. "Ad Ornatissimum Virum," published a year before Spenser took up residence in Ireland, where he would mature as a poet and establish himself as a New English settler, reveals the poet's constitutive concerns to be an entangled web of concerns: the poet's vocation, the cultural import of poetry, the duties appropriate to literary ambition, the green landscape in which such ambitions might come to fruition, and the equally constitutive experience of intense social and poetic shame.

"Ad Ornatissimum Virum" was, of course, not the first occasion in Spenser's career that he would convey a sense that shame, waste, and failure were the primary experiences of poetry. The "January" eclogue of *The Shepheardes Calendar* envisions an exhausted Colin Clout, "wasted" by the extremities of weather and love and culminates not only in the bitter plaints of the poet but also in the breaking of his signature instrument, the "oaten pipe" that marks his trade. The very same work that established, in Richard Helgerson's influential formulation, Spenser's laureate ambition opens with a poet wallowing in such shame, rage, waste, futility, and exhaustion that the eclogue becomes a poem about the making of art that culminates with the breaking of art. For the Colin Clout of Spenser's later career, of *Colin Clout Comes Home Again*, the wintry landscape of the "January" antipastoral eclogue, Ireland was the green place, the place of lyric exile and a pastoral possibility dependent on the absence of its inhabitants. The Spenser of *A Vewe of the Present State of Ireland* was more content with the easily idealized Irish landscape than its actual inhabitants, be they Gaelic natives or Old English settlers.

Critics have found various ways of understanding the problematic relationship between Spenser's residence in Ireland (and his civic career there), his poetic ambitions, and his poetic representations of his exilic homeland. Finding the problem of Ireland in Spenser's poetry analogically bound to contemporary concerns with the New World, Stephen Greenblatt describes the relationship as a battle between civility and savagery. The fashioning of a self depends on the exercise of a force "in relation to something perceived as alien, strange, or hostile. This threatening Other . . . must be discovered or invented in order to be attacked and destroyed."[23]

In the wake of Greenblatt, many have complicated and clarified Spenser's relationship to Ireland—Patricia Coughlan, Andrew Hadfield, Willy Maley, Richard McCabe, Andrew Murphy, Thomas Herron and others. Whereas Greenblatt imagines Spenser's Ireland through strategies of violent differentiation that typify European attitudes to the New World and a host of colonial subjects to be,[24] later critics concentrate on the violent consequences of contiguity. Murphy and McCabe both invoke proximity (and, to the consternation of some, the influential theories of Homi Bhaba[25]) as they attempt to explain the relationship between Spenser and Ireland. Murphy argues: "Ireland and Britain are 'proximate' in the sense that they lie close to each other geographically, but that geographical proximity has lead to a complex relationship of closeness between the populations . . . these relations of geographic and cultural proximity rendered the Irish, for the English, as 'proximate' Others . . . They are, in other words, imperfect aliens."[26] McCabe, describing *The Faerie Queene* as "a manifesto for the imperial ideal 'fashioned' by one of its most articulate proponents," describes the poem's "practice of defining civil ideals by their 'savage' antitheses" as "notoriously hazardous" and prone to failure. "In such circumstances," McCabe continues, "intended contrasts collapse all easily into unintentional comparisons, betraying the common heritage of the 'civil' and the 'savage,' the embarrassing kinship of self and other."[27]

This "embarrassing kinship" McCabe, Murphy, and others aptly describe shares with Greenblatt a focus on the formation of an identity.

I would suggest here that shame might offer a powerful way of understanding the forms of proximity and attachment that characterize Spenser's relationship to the place he spent the bulk of his adult life (and his writing life). It may also help us unpack our own relationship to writers, like Spenser, the canonicity of whose works provoke a potent and ambiguous mix of wonder and shame. The critical tendencies of the last decades have installed without necessarily examining fully the way literary and cultural criticism deploys shame. Take, for instance, the retrospective summary, however gently stated and attenuated by qualification, of the hermeneutic impulse articulated by Greenblatt and Catherine Gallaher in the introduction to *Practicing New Historicism*. There, they suggest that "explication and paraphrase are not enough; we seek something more, something that the authors we study would not have had sufficient distance upon themselves and their own era to grasp."[28]

But the experience of shame is not merely constituted by negative (internal or external) evaluation and differentiation. It is not merely a form of rejection, distinction, or exclusion. The major proponents of a turn to shame in literary and cultural studies have been not only historians and theorists of affect but also queer theorists and historians of sexuality, thinkers who understand shame as attachment and many of whom find shame's negativity generative. For some, shame provides a way of understand how individual or group identities are constituted by or sometimes against social norms. In Michael Warner's *The Trouble with Normal*, forms of sexual shame reinforce the production of norms and hobble even contemporary queer political activism. Sally Munt typifies many approaches that find shame and shaming generative of individual and group identities: "Shame is peculiarly intrapsychic: it exceeds the bodily vessel of its containment – groups that are shamed contain individuals who internalise the stigma of shame into the tapestry of their lives, each reproduce discrete, shamed subjectivities, all with their own specific pathologies."[29] This is perhaps what Eve Kosofsky Sedgwick and Adam Frank argued years earlier as they reintroduced the work of Silvan Tompkins to literary critics in *Shame and her Sisters*: "That's the double movement shame makes: toward painful individuation, toward uncontrollable relationality."[30] But Munt also suggests that "shame has political potential as it can provoke a separation between the social convention demarcated within hegemonic ideals, enabling a reinscription of social intelligibility. The outcome of this can be radical, instigating social, political and cultural agency amongst the formerly disenfranchised."[31]

It remains to be seen what insights or politics can emerge from revaluing shamed identities or groups. Indeed, Kathryn Bond Stockton's interest in "valuable, generative, beautiful shame" leads her to explore how "debasement informs us of hidden connections, cultural logics, and histories of fantasies, pain, and attractions far more telling than the weak conceptions of oppression and subversion."[32] Heather Love notices that while shame, once "a poison that must be purged from the queer community—has proved to be particularly attractive as a basis for alternative models of politics," work on sexuality should "pursue a fuller engagement with negative affects and with the intransigent difficulties of making feeling the basis for politics."[33] Perhaps Stockton and Love avoid the ethical pitfall Ruth Leys identifies "in the current tendency to replace guilt with shame," which is an impulse to displace questions about our moral responsibility for what we *do* in favor of more ethically neutral or different questions about our personal attributes."[34]

The politics associated with shame need not rest on overcoming negativity or consolidating identity, about which the work of Stockton, Love, and Leys seem usefully skeptical. What if shame were not an index of vulnerability (as a form of incapacity) but a response to the limits of vulnerability as a form of ethics? Silvan Tomkins describes shame as a thwarted affiliation: "shame is activated by the incomplete reduction of interest or joy . . . In shame the individual wishes to resume his or her contact with the exciting state of affairs, to reconnect with the other."[35] Tompkins distinguishes shame from disgust, in which "the bad other is spit out, or vomited forth," responses "appropriate to a hierarchically ordered society. These are not appropriate in a more egalitarian, democratic society." Elsewhere Tomkins identifies shame as a response to the failure to make contact with another: "one is suddenly looked at by one who is strange, or . . . one wishes to look at or commune with another person but suddenly cannot because is strange, or one expected him to be familiar but he suddenly appears unfamiliar, or one started to smile but found one was smiling at a stranger (*Shame* 135)."[36] Gerhart Piers and Milton B. Singer similarly describe shame as thwarted affiliation, quoting Hegel to support this position: "Shame does not mean to be ashamed of loving, say on account of exposing or surrendering the body . . . but to be ashamed that love is not complete, that . . . there still be something inimical in oneself which keeps love from reaching completion and perfection."[37]

Shame names the social pain of thwarted attachment, be it love, sympathy, friendship, or identification, all of which are affects of affiliation. And just as the 1590 *Faerie Queene* is motivated by vulnerability so too is the 1596 *Faerie Queene* motivated by shame. That is to say, the legends of Holiness, Temperance, and Chastity elaborate an ethics of vulnerability rooted in the disarming and reformation of those notions of masculinity at the heart of virtue or virtuous work. The extended legends of Friendship, Justice, and Courtesy transform the 1590 *Faerie Queene* into a poem concerned with shame, rage, and waste that derive from the failure to sustain an ethics of vulnerability. Friendship may hold out the promise of social bonds consolidated through shared vulnerability but it also threatens with a dizzying expansion of networks of affiliation. Thus the Legend of Friendship sparks a kind of crisis answered by the legends of Justice and Courtesy, which examine violence and the politics of community.[38]

In tracing the transit from vulnerability to shame, we stand to learn as much about Spenser's poem and his era as about our own era, one in which literature, literary studies, and the wide sweep of the humanities seem particularly vulnerable not to mention subject to shame as well as outright scorn for their apparent lack of utility. To be open to those ambivalent attachments is to understand how profoundly important are those works of art that help us imagine and therefore understand our vulnerabilities, our shames, and our participation in a shared capacity for the aesthetic from which a sense of ethics also derives. The task of fashioning virtue, gentility, and discipline, Spenser understood, would not be served by an instrumental or crudely didactic poetics. Rather, cultivation of the self required immersion in the imagination, from which any true understanding of the real must emerge. A poet like Spenser helps us remember that the power of the aesthetic, its capacity to constitute a politics, rests, as Jacques Rancière has argued, not in the moral or political messages it communicates but in "a certain recasting of the distribution of the sensible, a reconfiguration of the given perceptual forms" and a cultivation of "other networks of the sensible."[39]

The cultivation and alteration of the "networks of the sensible" seems just what Spenser was after when he wrote to Raleigh about *The*

Faerie Queene: "To some I know this Methode will seeme displeasaunt, which had rather haue good discipline deliuered plainly in way of precepts, or sermoned at large, as they vse, then thus clowdily enwrapped in Allegorical deuises. But such, me seeme, should be satisfied with the vse of these days, seeing all things accounted by their showes, and nothing esteemed of, that is not delightfull and pleasing to commune sence."[40] It has always seemed that Spenser's communiqué to Raleigh smacks of elitism, but perhaps it is most fitting to close with another gesture he makes: a dedication to dwell in and imaginatively alter what "commune sence" might be.

Notes

INTRODUCTION

1. John Milton, *Complete Prose Works of John Milton* (New Haven, CT: Yale University Press, 1959), 516.

2. Ibid., 514–15.

3. This issue is treated fully in Milton, *Complete Prose Works*, 515n.

4. Isa. 35:8 (Authorized King James Version).

5. Ibid, 514–15.

6. Thomas Luxon, "Allegory and the Puritan Self," *English Literary History* 60 (1993): 918.

7. John Milton, *The Major Works*, ed. Stephen Orgel and Jonathan Goldberg (Oxford: Oxford University Press, 1991), 247n.

8. All citations in text and notes of *The Faerie Queene* (to book, canto, and stanza) are to Edmund Spenser, *The Faerie Queene*, ed. A. C. Hamilton, 2nd ed. (London: Longman, 2007).

9. An innumerable host of essays and books place Spenser and Milton in a common lineage or trajectory, but the two singularly strongest readings of that literary relationship remain John Guillory's *Poetic Authority: Spenser, Milton, and Literary History* (New York: Columbia University Press, 1983) and Maureen Quilligan's *Milton's Spenser: The Politics of Reading* (Ithaca, NY: Cornell University Press, 1983).

10. Gordon Teskey, "Literature," in *Cultural Reformations: Medieval and Renaissance in Literary History*, ed. Brian Cummings and James Simpson (Oxford: Oxford University Press, 2010), 381.

11. Virgil, *Aeneid* 1.1, in *Eclogues, Georgics, Aeneid 1–6*, trans. H. Rushton Fairclough, Loeb Classical Library 63 (Cambridge, MA: Harvard University Press, 1999). All citations of this work (to book and line number) are from this edition.

12. Titus Lucretius Carus, *On the Nature of Things*, trans. W. H. D. Rouse, Loeb Classical Library 118 (Cambridge, MA: Harvard University Press, 1975), 1.29–34.

13. Edmund Spenser, *A Vewe of the Present State of Ireland*, in *The Works of Edmund Spenser: A Variorum Edition*, ed. Edwin Greenlaw et al., 11 vols. (Baltimore, MD: Johns Hopkins University Press, 1932–57), 10:43.

14. Ibid., 10:16.

15. Richard Helgerson, *Forms of Nationhood: The Writing of Elizabethan England* (Chicago: University of Chicago Press, 1992), 22.

16. Ibid., 28.

17. Georgia Ronan Crampton, *The Condition of Creatures: Suffering and Action in Chaucer and Spenser* (New Haven, CT: Yale University Press, 1974), 178.

18. Ibid., 47, 48.

19. Edmund Spenser, "Letter of the Authors," *The Faerie Queene*, ed. A. C. Hamilton, 2nd ed. (New York: Longman, 2007), 714.

20. Maurice Evans, *Spenser's Anatomy of Heroism: A Commentary on "The Faerie Queene"* (Cambridge: Cambridge University Press, 1970), vii.

21. Robin Headlam Wells, *Shakespeare on Masculinity* (Cambridge: Cambridge University Press, 2008), 2.

22. Ibid., 6.

23. Diana Purkiss, *Literature, Gender, and Politics during the English Civil War* (Cambridge: Cambridge University Press, 2005), 1.

24. Bruce R. Smith, *Shakespeare and Masculinity* (Oxford: Oxford University Press, 2000), 4.

25. Lisa Cevlosky, "Early Modern Masculinities and *The Faerie Queene*," *English Literary Renaissance* 35 (2005): 210. For a more complete social history of early modern masculinity, see Alexandra Shepard, *Meanings of Masculinity in Early Modern England* (Oxford: Oxford University Press, 2003).

26. Purkiss, *Literature, Gender, and Politics*, 1.

27. Catherine Bates, *Masculinity, Gender and Identity in the English Renaissance* (Cambridge: Cambridge University Press, 2007), 1.

28. Lynn Enterline, *The Tears of Narcissus: Melancholia and Masculinity in Early Modern Writing* (Stanford, CA: Stanford University Press, 1995), 1. Although Marion Wells does not focus so directly on masculinity in her study of romance, *The Secret Wound: Love-Melancholy and Early Modern Romance* (Stanford, CA: Stanford University Press, 2007), she understands masculine affect through medical accounts of melancholia, while Jennifer Vaught's *Masculinity and Emotion in Early Modern English Literature* (Burlington, VT: Ashgate, 2008) also focuses on grief as she

attempts to backdate to the Renaissance the man of feeling typical of the cult of sentimentality.

29. Michel Foucault, *The Use of Pleasure*, vol. 2 of *The History of Sexuality* (New York: Vintage, 1985), 51–52.

30. Ibid., 83.

31. Max Weber, *The Protestant Ethic and the "Spirit" of Capitalism* (New York: Penguin, 2002), 7.

32. Patricia Cahill, *Unto the Breach: Martial Formations, Historical Trauma, and the Early Modern Stage* (Oxford: Oxford University Press, 2008), 2.

33. Sigmund Freud, *Beyond the Pleasure Principle*, trans. James Strachey (New York: Norton, 1961), 30.

34. Jacques Lacan, *Écrits: A Selection*, trans. Alan Sheridan (New York and London: W. W. Norton, 1977), 4.

35. Headlam Wells, *Shakespeare on Masculinity*, 8.

36. See Stephen Greenblatt, *Renaissance Self-Fashioning: From More to Shakespeare* (Chicago: University of Chicago Press, 1980); and Cynthia Marshall, *The Shattering of the Self: Violence, Subjectivity, and Early Modern Texts* (Baltimore, MD: Johns Hopkins University Press, 2002).

37. Harry Berger Jr., "Displacing Autophobia in Faerie Queene I: Ethics, Gender, and Oppositional Reading in the Spenserian Text," *English Literary Renaissance* 28, no. 2 (1998): 165. Berger reconsiders his position in this essay in "Sexual and Religious Politics in Book I of Spenser's *Faerie Queene*," *English Literary Renaissance* 34, no. 2 (May 2004): 201–42. See also Theresa Krier's amplification and complication of this argument in "Hosea and the Play of Identifications in the *Faerie Queene I*," *Religion and Literature* 32, no. 2 (Summer 2000): 105–22.

38. William Shakespeare, *Macbeth* 5.10.10–11, in *The Oxford Shakespeare*, ed. John Jowett, William Montgomery, Gary Taylor, and Stanley Wells, 2nd ed. (Oxford: Oxford University Press, 2005). All Shakespeare references (to act, scene, and line) are from this edition.

39. For recent use of Nietzsche's concept of *ressentiment* articulated in *On the Genealogy of Morals*, see Wendy Brown's *States of Injury: Power and Freedom in Late Modernity* (Princeton, N.J.: Princeton University Press, 1995).

40. Virgil, *Aeneid*, 1:250–53.

41. Ibid., 1:407–9.

42. Barbara J. Bono, *Literary Transvaluation: From Vergilian Epic to Shakespearean Tragicomedy* (Berkeley: University of California Press, 1984), 64–65.

43. Ibid., 3–4n.

44. Edgar Wind, *Pagan Mysteries in the Renaissance* (London: Faber and Faber, 1958), 81.

45. Wind, *Pagan Mysteries*, 84.

46. Pico della Mirandola, "On the General Nature of Beauty," quoted in Wind, *Pagan Mysteries*, 81.

47. Marsilio Ficino, *Commentary on Plato's Symposium on Love*, trans. Sears Jayne (Woodstock, CT: Spring Publications, 1985), 97.

48. Roy Strong, *Britannia Triumphans: Inigo Jones, Rubens, and Whitehall Palace* (London: Thames and Hudson, 1980), 7.

49. Lisa Rosenthal, *Gender, Politics, and Allegory in the Art of Rubens* (Cambridge: Cambridge University Press, 2005), 2.

50. Ibid., 19.

51. Mary Beth Rose, *Gender and Heroism in Early Modern English Literature* (Chicago: University of Chicago Press, 2002), xii.

52. Richard Stanyhurst, *Thee first foure bookes of Virgil his Aeneis* (Leiden, 1582), 1.1–4.

53. David Lee Miller, *The Poem's Two Bodies: The Poetics of the 1590 "Faerie Queene"* (Princeton, NJ: Princeton University Press, 1988), 4–5.

54. A. Bartlett Giamatti, *Play of Double Senses: Spenser's "Fairy Queene"* (Englewood Cliffs, NJ: Prentice Hall, 1975), 49.

55. Thomas M. Greene's landmark study *The Light in Troy: Imitation and Discovery in Renaissance Poetry* (New Haven, CT: Yale University Press, 1982) finds that practices central to Renaissance humanism, such as imitation, produced in authors a sense of vulnerability resulting from their belatedness with respect to the achievements of classical antiquity and their anxiety with respect to the historical contingency of their own writing, which they worried might not be understood by future readers and future cultures. More recently Jane Tylus's *Writing and Vulnerability in the Late Renaissance* (Stanford, CA: Stanford University Press, 1993) extends Greene's thesis, arguing that the bankruptcy of a Senecan ideal of invulnerability was made most apparent to writers by their social circumstances. Spenser, Shakespeare, Tasso, and their contemporaries "were dependent for recognition and livelihood on the various institutions of power they served. Their intensely individual responses to this dependency produced a complicated array of textual performances designed to protect themselves and their writing from the *vulnus* that late Renaissance authorities increasingly had the power to inflict" (3).

56. Colin Burrow, *Epic Romance: Homer to Milton* (Oxford: Clarendon Press, 1993), 3.

57. Leo Braudy, *From Chivalry to Terrorism: War and the Changing Nature of Masculinity* (New York: Random House, 2004), xiii.

58. Burrow, *Epic Romance*, 3–4.

59. Ibid., 4.

60. David Quint, *Epic and Empire: Politics and Generic Form from Virgil to Milton* (Princeton, NJ: Princeton University Press, 1993), 8–9.

61. Ibid., 9.

62. Ibid., 34.

63. Patricia Parker, *Inescapable Romance: Studies in the Poetics of a Mode* (Princeton, NJ: Princeton University Press, 1979), 4. On forms of deferral and *différance* in *The Faerie Queene*, see also Jonathan Goldberg's *Endlesse Worke: Spenser and the Structures of Discourse* (Baltimore, MD: Johns Hopkins University Press, 1981).

64. Quint, *Epic and Empire*, 45.

65. Geraldine Heng, "Cannibalism, the First Crusade, and the Genesis of Medieval Romance," *Differences* 10 (1998): 99.

66. Ibid., 126.

67. Ibid., 137.

68. Geraldine Heng, *Empire of Magic: Medieval Romance and the Politics of Cultural Fantasy* (New York: Columbia University Press, 2003), 2.

69. Ibid., 3.

70. Eamon Duffy, *The Stripping of the Altars: Traditional Religion in England, 1400–1580*, 2nd ed. (New Haven, CT: Yale University Press, 2005), xiv.

71. Christopher Haigh, *The English Reformation Revised* (Cambridge: Cambridge University Press, 1987), 2.

72. Ibid., 4.

73. J. J. Scarisbrick, *The Reformation and the English People* (Oxford: Basil Blackwell, 1984), 1.

74. Norman Jones, *The English Reformation: Religion and Cultural Adaptation* (Malden, MA: Blackwell, 2002).

75. Christopher Haigh, *English Reformations: Religion, Politics, and Society under the Tudors* (Oxford: Clarendon Press, 1993), 12.

76. David Aers and Nigel Smith, "English Reformations," *Journal of Medieval and Early Modern Studies* 40, no. 3 (2010): 426.

77. Ibid., 434.

78. Ibid., 435.

79. Duffy, xxxiii.

80. Linda Gregerson, *The Reformation of the Subject: Spenser, Milton, and the English Renaissance Epic* (Cambridge: Cambridge University Press, 1995), 4, 5.

81. Headlam Wells, *Shakespeare on Masculinity*, 8.

82. Richard McCabe, *Spenser's Monstrous Regiment: Elizabethan Ireland and the Poetics of Difference* (Oxford: Oxford University Press, 2005), 11.

83. Ephesians 4:22–24 (Authorized King James Version).

84. Ibid., 6:10–11.

85. Ibid., 4:31–21.

86. Plato, *The Republic*, 607a.

87. Philip Sidney, *A Defence of Poetry*, ed. J. A. Van Dorsten (Oxford: Oxford University Press, 1966), 25.

88. The wealth of scholarship on Renaissance Ovidianism prevents an expansive survey, but signature recent studies include Lynn Enterline, *The Rhetoric of the Body from Ovid to Shakespeare* (Cambridge: Cambridge University Press, 2000); Jonathan Bate, *Shakespeare and Ovid* (Oxford: Clarendon Press, 1993); Patrick Cheney, *Marlowe's Counterfeit Profession: Ovid, Spenser, Counter-Nationhood* (Toronto: University of Toronto Press, 1997); Syrithe Pugh, *Spenser and Ovid* (Aldershot, UK: Ashgate, 2005); M. L. Stapleton, *Spenser's Ovidian Poetics* (Newark: University of Delaware Press, 2009); and Cora Fox, *Ovid and the Politics of Emotion in Elizabethan England* (New York: Palgrave Macmillan, 2009).

89. William Keach, *Elizabethan Erotic Narratives: Irony and Pathos in the Ovidian Poetry of Shakespeare, Marlowe, and Their Contemporaries* (New Brunswick, NJ: Rutgers University Press, 1977).

90. A relatively small body of scholarship on Renaissance neo-Stoicism and English literature exists. For an account of Senecan tragedy and Renaissance drama, see Gordon Braden, *Renaissance Tragedy and the Senecan Tradition: Anger's Privilege* (New Haven, CT: Yale University Press, 1985). There are two general if not up to date accounts of Renaissance English literature and neo-Stocism: Gilles D. Monsarrat, *The Light from the Porch: Stoicism and English Renaissance Literature* (Paris: Didier-Erudition, 1984); and Audrey Chew, *Stoicism in Renaissance English Literature: An Introduction* (New York: Peter Lang, 1988). For an account of the thought of Justus Lipsius, see Jason Lewis Saunders, *Justus Lipsius: The Philosophy of Renaissance Stoicism* (New York: Liberal Arts Press, 1955); and Justus Lipsius, *On Constancy*, ed. John Sellars (Exeter, UK: Bristol Phoenix Press, 2006), which is a gently updated edition of Sir John Stradling's 1596 translation of *De Constantia* with a useful introduction. For Ben Jonson's relationship to Renaissance neo-Stoic philosophy and the works of Justus Lipsius, see Robert C. Evans, *Jonson, Lipsius, and the Politics of Renaissance Stoicism* (Wakefield, NH: Longfield Academic, 1992). For an account of the political ramifications of Stoic philosophy

in Renaissance Europe, see Gerhard Oestreich, *Neostoicism and the Early Modern State*, ed. Brigitta Oestreich and H. G. Koenigsberger and trans. David McLintock (Cambridge: Cambridge University Press, 1982). For an account of neo-Stoicism and the literature of seventeenth-century England, see Andrew Shifflett, *Stoicism, Politics, and Literature in the Age of Milton: War and Peace Reconciled* (Cambridge: Cambridge University Press, 1998).

91. Shifflet, *Stoicism, Politics, and Literature*, 18.

92. Michael C. Schoenfeldt's *Bodies and Selves in Early Modern England: Physiology and Inwardness in Spenser, Shakespeare, Herbert, and Milton* (Cambridge: Cambridge University Press, 1999) remains exemplary and most germane to Spenser studies, as does the edited collection *Reading the Early Modern Passions: Essays in the Cultural History of Emotions*, ed. Gail Kern Paster, Katherine Rowe, and Mary Floyd-Wilson (Philadelphia: University of Pennsylvania Press, 2004), including Douglas Trevor's essay "Sadness in *The Faerie Queene*," 204–52. For an account of the erotics of melancholy in Spenser and, more broadly, the epic tradition, see Marion Wells, *The Secret Wound.*

93. In addition to Schoenfeldt, see Bruce Smith, *The Key of Green: Passion and Perception in Renaissance Culture* (Chicago: University of Chicago Press, 2008) and *Phenomenal Shakespeare* (Malden, Mass.: Wiley-Blackwell, 2010), and Gail Kern Paster's *The Body Embarrassed: The Disciplines of Shame in Early Modern England* (Ithaca, NY: Cornell University Press, 1993) and *Humoring the Body: Emotions and the Shakespearean Stage* (Chicago: University of Chicago Press, 2004).

94. John Milton, *Paradise Lost*, ed. Alastair Fowler, 2nd ed. (London: Longman, 1998), 12.561. All citations of this work (to book and line) are to this edition.

1. READING BLEEDING TREES: THE POETICS OF OTHER PEOPLE'S PAIN

1. As Donald Cheney argues, "Fradubio's human reason is the first to fail him when he chooses Duessa." Moreover, he provides "an emblem of man trapped by the flesh" (*Spenser's Images of Nature: Wild Man and Shepherd in "The Faerie Queene"* [New Haven, CT: Yale University Press, 1966], 37).

2. Readings of the Legend of Holiness tend to contextualize the most obvious moral evaluation of Redcrosse's progress. See, for example, Kerby Neill, "The Degradation of the Red Cross Knight," *English Literary His-*

tory 19 (1952): 173–90; and John W. Shroeder, "Spenser's Erotic Drama: The Orgoglio Episode," *English Literary History* 29 (1962): 140–59. In most readings of the Fradubio episode, Fradubio is merely a moral signpost of the failing Knight of Holiness. As Maureen Quilligan puts it, "The Redcrosse Knight meets a character who is a projection of his own psyche" (*The Language of Allegory* [Ithaca, NY: Cornell University Press, 1978], 111). William Kennedy confirms this reading as he examines the dialectic of doubt and fear that explains the intersection of rhetorical, dramatic, and allegorical significance in the episode in "Rhetoric, Allegory, and Dramatic Modality in Spenser's Fradubio Episode," *English Literary Renaissance* 3 (1973): 351–68; and in his entry "Fradubio" in *The Spenser Encyclopedia*, ed. A. C. Hamilton (Toronto: University of Toronto Press, 1990), 317. Shirley Clay Scott ("From Polydorus to Fradubio: The History of a Topos," *Spenser Studies* 7 [1986]: 27–57) and Elizabeth Bellamy read the episode in light of a struggle with literary forebears in the epic tradition, while Bellamy also describes an "ongoing Renaissance battle between the romance and epic genres" that is "a key to understanding the incompletion of *The Faerie Queene* itself" ("The Broken Branch and the 'Liuing Well': Spenser's Fradubio and Romance Error in *The Faerie Queene*," *Renaissance Papers* [1985]: 2).

3. A tradition of distinguishing sensual beauty, of Duessa's variety, from Platonic beauty, of Una's variety, allows us to ignore the question of how beauty functions by asking us to focus on the source of beauty (the material or the spiritual). See Linwood E. Orange, "Sensual Beauty in Book I of *The Faerie Queene*," *Journal of English and Germanic Philology* 61 (1962): 555–61. On another recent attempt, by Richard Halpern, to "rescue" Una from the "critical consensus . . . that Una is a Very Good Girl," see his 2009 Hugh Maclean Memorial Lecture (*Spenser Review* 40, no. 3 [2010]: 1).

4. Michael Schoenfeldt, "Aesthetics and Anaesthetics: The Art of Pain Management in Early Modern England" in *The Sense of Suffering: Constructions of Physical Pain in Early Modern Culture*, ed. Jan Frans van Dijkhuizen and Karl A.E. Enenkel (Leiden: Brill, 2009), 19.

5. Jan Frans van Dijkhuizen, "Religious Meanings of Pain in Early Modern England," in *The Sense of Suffering: Constructions of Physical Pain in Early Modern Culture*, ed. Jan Frans van Dijkhuizen and Karl A. E. Enenkel (Leiden: Brill, 2009), 190.

6. Ibid., 189.

7. C. S. Lewis, *The Problem of Pain* (New York: HarperCollins, 2000), 122.

8. Ibid., 177.

9. Scarry, *Body in Pain*, 6.

10. Ibid., 167, 14.

11. Ibid., 3, 4.

12. Deborah K. Shuger, *The Renaissance Bible* (Berkeley: University of California Press, 1994), 89.

13. Ibid., 12.

14. Ernst B. Gilman, *Iconoclasm and Poetry in the English Reformation: Down Went Dagon* (Chicago: University of Chicago Press, 1986), 11.

15. Luxon, 918.

16. Patrick Collinson, *The Reformation: A History* (New York: Modern Library, 2004), 187.

17. John Phillips, *The Reformation of Images* (Berkeley: University of California Press, 1973), 102. As Mary Aston indicates, "The contentious rood images are assumed to be gone [by the 1560s]. . . . And now, in the central place of the proscribed crucifixion, stood the royal arms" (Aston, *England's Iconoclasts* [Oxford: Oxford University Press, 1988], 313).

18. Graham Hough, *The First Commentary on "The Faerie Queene"* (privately published, 1964), 1.

19. John N. King, *English Reformation Literature: The Tudor Origins of the Protestant Tradition* (Princeton, NJ: Princeton University Press, 1982), 445. See also Andrea Hume, *Edmund Spenser: Protestant Poet* (Cambridge: Cambridge University Press, 1984). King, quite influentially, defines Spenser's poetics by virtue of "unpretentious devices of native satire and allegory that were adopted by English Protestant authors," which some identify with Puritan doctrine (446).

20. Jeffrey Knapp, "Spenser the Priest," *Representations* 81 (Winter 2003): 62. See Richard Mallette, *Spenser and the Discourses of Reformation England* (Lincoln: University of Nebraska Press, 1997).

21. John N. King, "Spenser's Religion," in *The Cambridge Companion to Spenser*, ed. Andrew Hadfield (Cambridge: Cambridge University Press, 2001), 208. For an account of the reception history of Spenser's religion, see King's survey "Religion," in *A Critical Companion to Spenser Studies*, ed. Bart van Es (New York: Palgrave Macmillan, 2006), 58–75. See also King, *Spenser's Poetry and the Reformation Tradition* (Princeton, NJ: Princeton University Press, 1990).

22. Kenneth Gross, *Spenserian Poetics: Idolatry, Iconoclasm and Magic* (Ithaca, NY: Cornell University Press, 1985), 29.

23. Sean Kane, *Spenser's Moral Allegory* (Toronto: University of Toronto Press, 1989), 31.

24. Stephen Orgel, "Margins of Truth," in *The Renaissance Text*, ed. Andrew Murphy (Manchester, UK: Manchester University Press, 2000),

104. Orgel is not alone in associating a quasi-Catholic affiliation with the poetics of *The Faerie Queene*. Darryl Gless, in attempting to correlate Spenser's poetics and the wide array of Reformation doctrines, explores a series of theological struggles common to Protestants and post-Tridentine Catholics. See Gless, *Interpretation and Theology in Spenser* (Cambridge: Cambridge University Press, 1994). Harold Weatherby explains the apparently Catholic resonances in the poem with reference to the remnants of Augustinian theology, Greek and Latin patristic authors, and Greek Orthodox liturgy. See Harold Weatherby, *Mirrors of Celestial Grace* (Toronto: University of Toronto Press, 1994).

25. Deborah Shuger, "'Gums of Glutinous Heat' and the Stream of Consciousness: The Theology of Milton's *Maske*," *Representations* 60 (Autumn 1997): 16. "By silencing confession," Shuger argues, "the Reformation may have intensified, although it did not create, the felt disjunction between one's public identity and the unspeakably complex and strange inner creature known only to oneself. . . . In post-Reformation England . . . the intimate movements of thought, desire, and flesh disclose themselves *only* in poetry, which thus functions—I think for the first time—as the primary cultural language of inwardness."

26. Regina Schwartz, "Real Hunger: Milton's Version of the Eucharist," *Religion and Literature* 31, no. 3 (Autumn 1999): 1, 2. See also Schwartz, "From Ritual to Poetry: Herbert's Mystical Eucharist," in *Mystics: Presence and Aporia*, ed. Michael Kessler and Christian Shepherd (Chicago: University of Chicago Press, 2003), 138–60. Schwartz also examines the lingering presence of the Mass and sacrificial theories of Christ's death in "Tragedy and the Mass," *Literature and Theology* 19, no. 2 (June 2005): 139–58; and "*Othello* and the Horizon of Justice," in *Transcendence*, ed. Regina Schwartz (New York: Routledge, 2004), 81–104. These articles form the basis of Schwartz's recent, *Sacramental Poetics at the Dawn of Secularism: When God Left the World* (Stanford, CA: Stanford University Press, 2008).

27. Jan Frans van Dijkhuizen and Karl A. E. Enenkel, introduction to *The Sense of Suffering: Constructions of Physical Pain in Early Modern Culture*, ed. Jan Frans van Dijkhuizen and Karl A. E. Enenkel (Leiden: Brill, 2009), 11.

28. John Calvin, *Sermons on Job* (Edinburgh, UK: Banner of Truth Trust, 1993), 27.

29. Ibid., 20.

30. Ibid., 1.

31. Thomas More, who finds great value in the suffering of Christ and in Christians who bear up under the experience of suffering, saw Job

differently: "Now it is true [Tobias and Job] bore their calamities bravely and patiently, but neither of them, so far as I know, was exactly jumping with joy or clapping his hands out of happiness" (*The Sadness of Christ* [New York: Scepter Press, 1993], 41–42).

32. Orgel, "Margins of Truth," 103.

33. *Spenser Review* 36, no. 1 (Winter 2005): 18.

34. Ibid., 24.

35. It is notable, as well, that in marking time in this canto reference is made to the constellation Cassiopeia, thus suggesting the narrative of Andromeda, the damsel saved by Perseus, which provides a model for the legend of St. George. Thus, Una's vulnerability is stressed immediately following and immediately prior to extraordinary acts of violence committed on her behalf.

36. Friedrich Nietzsche, *Basic Writings of Nietzsche*, trans. Walter Kaufman (New York: Random House, 2000), 473.

37. Wendy Brown, *States of Injury* (Princeton, NJ: Princeton University Press, 1995), 52–76.

38. William Tyndale, *The Obedience of a Christian Man* (New York: Penguin, 2000), 11.

39. Ibid., 58.

40. Ibid., 133.

41. Ibid., 30.

42. Ibid., 27, 45.

43. Valentin Groebner, *Defaced: The Visual Culture of Violence in the Late Middle Ages*, trans. Pamela Selwyn (New York: Zone Books, 2004), 96–97.

44. William Flesch, "The Poetics of Speech Tags," in *Renaissance Literature and Its Formal Engagements*, ed. Mark David Rasmussen (New York: Palgrave, 2002), 159–84.

45. That this is maple rind reminds us of the opening catalogue of trees, of course, and the characteristic of the maple that is "seldom inward sound" (*FQ* 1.19).

46. Shuger, *Renaissance Bible*, 12.

47. Walter Benjamin, *Origins of German Tragic Drama* (London: New Left Books, 1977), 217.

48. Julia Reinhard Lupton, *Afterlives of the Saints* (Stanford, CA: Stanford University Press, 1996), 42.

49. Niklaus Largier, *In Praise of the Whip* (New York: Zone Books, 2007), 64.

50. Thomas A. Prendergast, "'Wanton Recollection': The Idolatrous Pleasures of *Beowulf*," *New Literary History* 30 (1999): 130.

51. René Girard, *Violence and the Sacred* (Baltimore: Johns Hopkins University Press, 1977), 14.

52. Eamon Duffy, *The Stripping of the Altars* (New Haven, CT: Yale University Press, 1992), 480.

53. Ibid., 593.

2. SPENSER'S DARK MATERIALS: REPRESENTATION IN THE SHADOW OF CHRIST

1. Giovanni Boccaccio, *Boccaccio on Poetry: being the preface and the fourteenth and fifteenth books of Boccaccio's Genealogia deorum gentilium in an English version*, ed. and trans. Charles G. Osgood (New York: Bobbs-Merril, 1956), 43.

2. Ibid., 46.

3. Michel Foucault, *The Order of Things: An Archaeology of the Human Sciences* (New York: Random House, 1970), 43.

4. Regina Schwartz, *Sacramental Poetics at the Dawn of Secularism: When God Left the World* (Stanford, CA: Stanford University Press, 2008), 12.

5. Michael O'Connell, *The Idolatrous Eye: Iconoclasm and Theater in Early-Modern England* (Oxford: Oxford University Press, 2000), 38.

6. Jacobus de Voragine, *The Golden Legend; or, Lives of the Saints*, trans. William Caxton, ed. F. S. Ellis (Philadelphia, PA: Temple University Press, 1900), 46.

7. Spenser confirms what Alastair Fowler has referred to as *The Faerie Queene's* participation in "a contemporary vogue for the figura etymologica" or "etymological conceit" in the naming of characters. Fowler, "Spenser's Names," in *Unfolded Tales: Essays on Renaissance Romance*, ed. George Logan and Gordon Teskey (Ithaca, NY: Cornell University Press, 1989), 43.

8. Ibid., 45.

9. Jean-François Lyotard, *The Inhuman: Reflections on Time*, trans. Geoffrey Bennington and Rachel Bowlby (Stanford, CA: Stanford University Press, 1991), 38.

10. Edmund Spenser, "Letter of the Authors," in *The Faerie Queene*, ed. A. C. Hamilton, 2nd ed. (London: Longman, 2007), 714.

11. Demetrius, *On Style*, ed. and trans. Doreen C. Innes, based on W. Rhys Roberts (Cambridge, MA: Loeb Classical Library), 2.101.

12. See Kaske, "The Eucharistic Cup: Romanist, Establishment, and Communitarian," *Reformation* 6 (2002): 125–32 and *Spenser's Biblical Poetics* (Ithaca, NY: Cornell University Press, 1999).

13. Anne Lake Prescott, "Complicating the Allegory: Spenser and Religion in Recent Scholarship," *Renaissance and Reformation* 15 (2001): 9.

14. O'Connell, *The Idolatrous Eye*, 58.

15. Gilman, 11.

16. John N. King, "Sacramental Parody in *The Faerie Queene*," *Reformation* 6 (2002), 111. See King's *Spenser's Poetry and the Reformation Tradition* (Princeton: Princeton University Press, 1990) and *English Reformation Literature: The Tudor Origins of the Protestant Tradition* (Princeton: Princeton University Press, 1982).

17. Prescott, 10.

18. Harold L. Weatherby, "Spenser and the Sacraments," *Reformation* 6 (2002): 122. Weatherby's article extends arguments he made in *Mirrors of Celestial Grace: Patristic Theology in Spenser's Allegory* (Toronto: University of Toronto Press, 1994).

19. Clinton Allen Brand, "Sacramental Initiation and Residual Catholicism in the Legend of Holiness," *Reformation* 6 (2002): 133.

20. Ibid., 144.

21. See Prescott, "Why Arguments over Communion Matter to Allegory: Or, Why are Catholics like Orgoglio?" *Reformation* 6 (2002): 163–79.

22. Kenneth Borris, "The Sacraments in *The Faerie Queene*," *Reformation* 6 (2002): 145.

23. Lee Palmer Wandel, *The Eucharist in the Reformation: Incarnation and Liturgy* (Cambridge: Cambridge University Press, 2006), 6.

24. Schwartz describes a sacramental poetics as one that "entails a radical understanding of signifying, one that points beyond the life and presence of the artists, to manifest a new world . . . a sacramental poetics is hence not afflicted by embarrassment at the poverty of signs, at the inept ways in which language falls short of conveying the sacred. In it, signs are empowered to be effective—if not to confer grace, then to change their hearer; if not to grant him eternity, then to manifest a world" (7).

25. Kenneth Gross, *Spenserian Poetics: Idolatry, Iconoclasm, and Magic* (Ithaca, NY: Cornell University Press, 1985), 18.

26. Ibid., 27.

27. W. J. T. Mitchell, *Iconology: Image, Text, Ideology* (Chicago: University of Chicago Press, 1987), 165.

28. Henri Bergson, *Creative Evolution*, trans. Arthur Mitchell (New York: Random House, 1944), 299.

29. Henri Bergson, *The Creative Mind: An Introduction to Metaphysics*, trans. Mabelle Andison (New York: Citadel Press, 1992), 64.

30. Daniel Tiffany, *Toy Medium: Materialism and Modern Lyric* (Berkeley: University of California Press, 2000), 33. For a further development of these concerns, see Tiffany's more recent article "Lyric Substance: On Riddles, Materialism, and Poetic Obscurity," *Critical Inquiry* 28, no. 1 (Autumn 2001): 72–98.

31. Augustine, *On Christian Teaching*, trans. R. P. H. Green (Oxford: Oxford University Press, 1997), 48.

32. Boccaccio, *Boccaccio on Poetry*, 44.

33. Augustine, *On Christian Teaching*, 16.

34. Tertullian, *De idolatria* (Leiden: Brill, 1987), 78.

35. Augustine, *On Christian Teaching*, 72.

36. Clifford Ando, "Signs, Idols and the Incarnation in Augustinian Metaphysics," *Representations* 73 (Winter 2001): 26.

37. Ibid., 37.

38. Augustine, *On Christian Teaching*, 64.

39. Of the many accounts of this Christian adequation of pagan *materia*, see particularly Leonard Barkan, *The Gods Made Flesh: Metamorphosis and the Pursuit of Paganism* (New Haven, CT: Yale University Press, 1986).

40. Jean Calvin, *Institutiones Christianae Religionis* (London, 1583).

41. Jean Calvin, *Institutes of the Christian Religion*, trans. Henry Beveridge (Grand Rapids, MI: Eerdmans, 1989), 1.11.8.

42. Sean Kane, "Idolatry," in *The Spenser Encyclopedia*, ed. A. C. Hamilton (Toronto: University of Toronto Press, 1990), 387. Kane uses the following edition: *Institutes of the Christian Religion*, trans. Ford Lewis Battles, ed. John T. McNeill (Philadelphia, PA: Westminster Press, 1960).

43. Thomas Luxon, "Allegory and the Puritan Self," *English Literary History* 60 (1993): 924.

44. O'Connell, *The Idolatrous Eye*, 37.

45. Desiderlius Erasmus, *The Paraclesis*, in *Humanism and the Northern Renaissance* (Toronto: Canadian Scholars' Press, 2000), 136.

46. Luxon, "Allegory and *England's Iconoclasts* the Puritan Self," 902.

47. Aston, *England's Iconoclasts*, 13.

48. Marie-José Mondzain, *Image, Icon, Economy: The Byzantine Origins of the Contemporary Imaginary* (Stanford, CA: Stanford University Press, 2005), 5–6.

49. Aston, *England's Iconoclasts*, 5.

50. St. John of Damascus, *On the Divine Images* (Crestwood, NY: St. Vladimir's Seminary Press, 1980), 23.

51. St. Theodore the Studite, *On the Holy Icons*, trans. Catherine P. Roth (Crestwood, NY: St. Vladimir's Seminary Press, 2001), 109.

52. Mondzain includes translations of two of the primary iconoclastic voices of the Byzantine controversy. In the extracts from the *Antrirhetics* by Nikephorous, Patriarch of Constantinople, and from the writings of Horos of Hiera, an easily conflated series of critiques of icons and idols emerges—the usurping of God's power to create, the overvaluation of material things, and the insubstantial nature of icons relative to divinity. Nikephorous refers to the idol as "the formation of nonexistent and insubstantial things," though it is also, later, described as being "the obsession of those addicted to their passions and to material things" *(Image, Icon, Economy*, 237). For iconoclasts, then, the idol and the icon were guilty of the same fault, while for the Byzantine iconophile, the idol was purely the work of deranged imagination.

53. Gaston Bachelard, *Water and Dreams: An Essay on the Imagination of Matter* (Dallas: Dallas Institute Publications, 1983), 1.

54. O'Connell, *The Idolatrous Eye*, 5.

55. Jeffrey Cohen, *Of Giants: Sex, Monsters and the Middle Ages* (Minneapolis and London: University of Minnesota Press, 1999), 11.

56. Martin Heidegger, *The Question concerning Technology and Other Essays*, trans. William Lovitt (New York: Harper & Row, 1977), 126.

57. Ibid., 168.

58. Heidegger, "The Origin of the Work of Art," in *Poetry, Language, Thought*, trans. Albert Hofstader (New York: Harper and Row, 1971), 46.

59. In Golding's translation: "Yit like a woman labring was the tree, and bowing downe / Gave often sighes, and shed foorth teares as though she there should drowne // The tree did crayne, and the barke deviding made away, / And yielded out the child alive, which cryde and wayld streyght away" (10.583–84; 587–88). *Ovid's Metamorphoses*, ed. John Frederick Nims (Philadelphia, PA: Paul Dry Books, 2000).

60. Lawrence F. Rhu, "Romancing the Word: Pre-texts and Contexts for the Errour Episode," *Spenser Studies* 11 (1994): 101.

61. It has been argued that early modernity witnesses the translation of monsters into machines amid the rise of scientific knowledge and the resulting secularization. For an account of this process in early modern Italy, see Zakiya Hanafi, *The Monster in the Machine: Magic, Medicine, and the Marvelous in the Time of the Scientific Revolution* (Durham, NC: Duke University Press, 2000).

62. Elizabeth Spiller, "Poetic Parthenogenesis and Spenser's Idea of Creation in *The Faerie Queene*," *Studies in English Literature, 1500–1900* 40 (Winter 2000): 70.

63. See Terry Eagleton, *The Ideology of the Aesthetic* (London: Black-

well, 1990), 13; Susan Buck-Morrs, "Aesthetics and Anaesthetics: Walter Benjamin's Artwork Essay Reconsidered," *October* 62 (1992): 3–41.

64. Richard Broxton Onians, *The Origins of European Thought about the Body, the Mind, the Soul, the World, Time, and Fate* (Cambridge: Cambridge University Press, 1951), 74–75.

65. Ludovico Ariosto, *Orlando Furioso*, trans. Barbara Reynolds (London: Penguin, 1975), 9.75.1–2.

66. Ibid., 9.91.

67. See Spenser, *Faerie Queene*, 2.11.11. It is interesting to note that Spenser seems to have a particular affinity for this word. His are the first recorded usages in a number of those recorded in the *Oxford English Dictionary*.

68. Åke Bergvall, "The Theology of the Sign: St. Augustine and Spenser's Legend of Holiness," *Studies in English Literature, 1500–1900* 33 (1995): 28. See also Wendy Olmsted, "Deconstruction and Spenser's Allegory," *Spenser Studies* 11 (1994). The highly influential accounts of the poststructural Spenser are Parker; and Jonathan Goldberg, *Endlesse Worke: Spenser and the Structures of Discourse* (Baltimore: Johns Hopkins University Press, 1981).

69. Harry Berger Jr., "Archimago: Between Text and Countertext," *Studies in English Literature, 1500–1900* 43, no.1 (Winter 2003): 20.

70. Jean Calvin, *Four Godlye Sermons against the Pollution of Idolatries* (London: n.p., 1561).

71. Prescott, "Allegory," 166.

72. Calvin, Biir.

3. ON NOT DEFENDING POETRY: SPENSER, SUFFERING, AND THE ENERGY OF AFFECT

1. Although difficult poetry was not a recognized category, George Chapman does praise difficulty and obscurity as potentially valuable poetic qualities. In the dedicatory epistle to *Ovids Banquet of Sence* (1595), Chapman laments, "But that poesy should be as perviall," or easily seen through, "as oratory, and plainness her special ornament, were the plain way to barbarism" (George Chapman, *Ovids Banquet of Sence* [London, 1595], A2r). See Brian Vickers, ed., *English Renaissance Literary Criticism* (Oxford: Clarendon, 1999), 392–94.

2. Philip Sidney, *A Defence of Poetry*, ed. J. A. Van Dorsten (Oxford: Oxford University Press, 1966), 23.

3. Ibid., 32–33.

4. The exemplary figure of eloquent defense in the exordium of Sidney's treatise is the Italian riding master John Pietro Pugliano, who was of "the noblest of soldiers . . . the masters of war and ornaments of peace, speedy goers and strong abiders, triumphers in both camps and courts" (Sidney, *Defence of Poetry*, 17). As he speaks of poetry, Sidney assumes the language of triumph and mantle of heroic romance. Robert Matz describes heroic masculinity, the ideal of "warrior service" born of "feudal nostalgia" (*Defending Literature in Early Modern England* [Cambridge: Cambridge University Press, 2000], 22), as central to how Sidney imagined himself as a poet, courtier, and critic: "Poetry's warrior content must repress what is most basic to the form of that poetry, its existence as a piece of writing, the product of a writer's activity" (73).

5. As Chapman indicates, it is not visuality that poses a problem for poetry but the desire for iconic clarity: "It serves not a skillful painter's turn to draw the figure of a face only to make it known who it represents, but he must limn, give luster, shadow and heightening; which though ignorants will esteem spiced and too curious, yet such as have the judicial perspective will see it hath motion, spirit and life" (Chapman, *Ovids Banquet of Sence*, A2r).

6. Paul Alpers finds a "rhetorical mode" in *The Faerie Queene*, but one that is to be distinguished from Sidney's desire to discover in poetry clear rhetorical images of moral truth. On the contrary, Alpers argues, Spenser's "poetic motive in any given stanza is to elicit a response—to evoke, modify, or complicate feelings and attitudes" (*The Poetry of the Faerie Queene* [Columbia: University of Missouri Press, 1982], 5).

7. One may wonder about the *English Poet*, a "lost" work ascribed to Spenser by E. K., who, in the argument of the October eclogue, promises its future publication. See James Oruch, "Lost Works," in *The Spenser Encyclopedia*, ed. A. C. Hamilton (Toronto: University of Toronto Press, 1990).

8. M. H. Abrams, "Belief and the Suspension of Belief," in *Literature and Belief*, ed. Abrams (New York: Columbia University Press, 1958), 2.

9. Margaret W. Ferguson, *Trials of Desire: Renaissance Defenses of Poetry* (New Haven, CT: Yale University Press, 1983), 2.

10. Abrams, "Belief and the Suspension of Belief," 1.

11. Ibid., 2–3.

12. Matz, *Defending Literature*, 128.

13. Dana Gioia, "Can Poetry Matter?" in *Can Poetry Matter?: Essays on Poetry and American Culture* (Saint Paul: Graywolf, 2002), 18.

14. Ibid., 17.

15. See Jean H. Hagstrum, *The Sister Arts* (Chicago: University of Chicago Press, 1958); Wendy Steiner, *The Colors of Rhetoric* (Chicago: University of Chicago Press, 1982).

16. Horace, *Satires, Epistles, [and] Ars Poetica*, trans. H. R. Fairclough, Loeb Classical Library (Cambridge, MA: Harvard University Press, 1926), lines 180–82.

17. Attention to the pictorial or visual quality of Spenser's poetry dates to the early reception of the poem and continues in importance in the reception of *The Faerie Queene*. Studies by John Bender (*Spenser and Literary Pictorialism* [Princeton, NJ: Princeton University Press, 1972]), Rudolf Gottfried ("The Pictorial Element in Spenser's Poetry," *ELH* 19, no. 3 (1952): 203–13; and Camille Paglia (*Sexual Personae: Art and Decadence from Nefertiti to Emily Dickinson* [New York: Vintage, 1991]) identify visuality, even violent, iconic visuality (especially Paglia), as a central virtue of *The Faerie Queene*. Theresa M. Krier's *Gazing on Secret Sights: Spenser, Classical Imitation, and the Decorums of Vision* (Ithaca, NY: Cornell University Press, 1990) brought much needed attention to the erotic dynamics of sight. More recently, Jane Grogan's *Exeplary Spenser: Visual and Poetic Pedagogy in The Faerie Queene* (Burlington, VT: Ashgate Publishing, 2009) interrogates the heuristic value of visuality in *The Faerie Queene*, thus emphasizing the importance of pedagogy in Spenser, a subject at the heart of Jeff Dolven's impressive *Scenes of Instruction in Renaissance Romance* (Chicago: University of Chicago Press, 2007).

18. John Hughes, "An Essay on Allegorical Poetry," in *Penguin Critical Anthologies: Edmund Spenser*, ed. Paul Alpers (London: Penguin, 1969), 80.

19. For the philosophical valences of *enargeia* and *energeia*, see F. E. Peters, *Greek Philosophical Terms: A Historical Lexicon* (New York: New York University Press, 1967).

20. Aristotle, *The "Art" of Rhetoric*, trans. J. H. Freese (Cambridge, MA: Harvard University Press, 1926), 3.11.1–2.

21. Martin Jay has argued that not only does the privileging of vision in Greek thought contribute to an "ocularcentricism" increasingly characteristic of Western modernity, it also results in the denigration of other forms of sensory experience and of language itself (*Downcast Eyes* [Berkeley: University of California Press, 1994], 33).

22. Longinus, *On the Sublime*, trans. W. H. Fyfe (Cambridge, MA: Harvard University Press, 1995), 25–26.

23. Quintilian never uses the term *energeia*; he does discuss *enargeia* and *phatasiai* ("visions . . . by which the images of absent things are presented to the mind") in the course of explaining rhetorical appeals not

to *ēthos* (temperate, reasonable morality) but to *pathos* (fierce emotional experience) (*The Orator's Education: Books 6–8*, trans. Donald Russell [Cambridge, MA: Harvard University Press, 2001], 6.2.26).

24. Ibid., 6.2.29–30.

25. George Puttenham, *The Arte of English Poesie* (Kent, OH: Kent State University Press, 1970), 155.

26. Ibid., 61.

27. Sidney, *Defence of Poetry*, 19.

28. Ibid., 33.

29. Quintilian, *Orator's Education*, 6.2.13.

30. Stephen Greenblatt, "The Touch of the Real," in *Practicing New Historicism*, ed. Catherine Gallagher and Greenblatt (Chicago: University of Chicago Press, 2000), 29.

31. Stephen Greenblatt, *Shakespearean Negotiations* (Oxford: Clarendon, 1988), 2–20.

32. "Poetry" is not "the path to a transhistorical truth" but "the key to particular historically embedded social and psychological formations" (Greenblatt, "Touch of the Real," 7).

33. Gallagher and Greenblatt, *Practicing New Historicism*, 9.

34. Greenblatt, "Touch of the Real," 30. As Matz notes, "contemporary analyses" of early modern poetry often "unconsciously repeat sixteenth-century anxieties about the place of literature, especially in relationship to the 'political'" (*Defending Literature in Early Modern England*, 3).

35. Gallagher and Greenblatt, *Practicing New Historicism*, 15.

36. Spenser, *The Faerie Queene*, 716.

37. See Gross; Sean Kane, *Spenser's Moral Allegory* (Toronto: University of Toronto Press, 1989).

38. Augustine, *Confessions*, trans. Henry Chadwick (Oxford: Oxford University Press, 1990), 10.8.12.

39. Bergson, 14, 23.

40. John Milton, *Areopagitica. Prose Writings* (London: Dent, 1958), 158.

41. Stephen Greenblatt, *Renaissance Self-Fashioning* (Chicago: University of Chicago Press, 1980), 170.

42. Max Weber, *The Protestant Ethic and the "Spirit" of Capitalism* (New York: Penguin, 2002), 7.

43. Ibid., 74.

44. Karl Marx, *Capital: A Critique of Political Economy*, ed. Frederick Engels (New York: International, 1967), 667–70.

45. Weber, *Protestant Ethic*, 89.

46. I treat allegory in greater detail in Chapter 6, where I engage not only with Spenser's Legend of Chastity but also with accounts of allegory as the capture of wayward matter by violent form in Gordon Teskey, *Allegory and Violence* (Ithaca, NY: Cornell University Press, 1996) and as demonic personification in Angus Fletcher, *Allegory: Theory of a Symbolic Mode* (Ithaca, NY: Cornell University Press, 1964).

47. Sigmund Freud, "The Economic Problem of Masochism," in *On Metapsychology: The Theory of Psychoanalysis*, Penguin Freud Library 2 (London: Penguin, 1991), 413.

48. Max Horkheimer and Theodor Adorno, *Dialectic of Enlightenment*, trans. Edmund Jephcott (Stanford, CA: Stanford University Press, 2002), 116.

49. On Mammon's gold and the New World, see David Read, *Temperate Conquests: Spenser and the Spanish New World* (Detroit, MI: Wayne State University Press, 2000).

50. Torquato Tasso, *Jerusalem Delivered*, trans. Edward Fairfax (Oxford: Clarendon, 1981), 7.78–83.

4. BOY TOYS AND LIQUID JOYS: PLEASURE AND POWER IN THE BOWER OF BLISS

1. James Carscallen, "The Goodly Frame of Temperance: The Metaphor of Cosmos in *The Faerie Queene*, Book II," *University of Toronto Quarterly* 37 (1968): 136.

2. Joshua Scodel, *Excess and Mean in Early Modern Literature* (Princeton, NJ: Princeton University Press, 2002), 84.

3. Aristotle, *The Nichomachean Ethics*, trans. David Ross (Oxford: Oxford University Press, 1998), 2.3.1104b4.

4. Plato, *The Republic*, trans. Paul Shorey (Cambridge, MA: Harvard University Press, 1935), 395c–d.

5. Ibid., 606d (emphasis added).

6. Stephen Gosson, *The Schoole of Abuse* (London, 1587), A4r.

7. Philip Sidney, *A Defence of Poetry*, ed. Jan Van Dorsten (Oxford and London: Oxford University Press, 1966), 51.

8. Walter J. Ong, *Rhetoric, Romance, and Technology: Studies in the Interaction of Expression and Culture* (Ithaca, NY: Cornell University Press, 1971), 130.

9. Roger Ascham, *English Works: Toxophilus, Report of the Affaires and State of Germany, The Scholemaster*, ed. William Aldis Wright (Cambridge: Cambridge University Press, 1904), 231.

10. Patricia Parker, *Literary Fat Ladies: Rhetoric, Gender, and Property* (London: Methuen, 1987), 56. See also W. W. Barker, "Rhetorical Romance: The 'Frivolous Toys' of Robert Greene," in *Unfolded Tales: Essays on Renaissance Romance*, ed. George M. Logan and Gordon Teskey (Ithaca, NY: Cornell University Press, 1989).

11. John Harington, *Orlando Furioso in English Heroical Verse* (London, 1591), 4v.

12. "Vaine toyes" was a signature phrase appearing in a variety of early modern authors, including William Painter's *Palace of Pleasure* (1567), John Lyly's *Euphues* (1578), Philip Stubbes's *The Anatomie of Abuses* (1583), Robert Greene's *Morando* (1584), and Spenser's *The Faerie Queene* (1590).

13. George Puttenham, *The Arte of English Poesie*, ed. Baxter Hathaway (Kent, OH: Kent State University Press, 1970), 90, 91.

14. Sidney's *"The Defence of Poesy" and Selected Renaissance Literary Criticism*, ed. Gavin Alexander (New York: Penguin, 2004), 284, 239, 259, 284.

15. *Oxford English Dictionary*, 2nd ed., s.v. "boy toy." That, since then, the phrase has come to be used more frequently to describe the young playthings of wealthier *men* suggests a certain liquidity of terminology that reflects developments in the intertwining realms of sexuality and economy, a development marked by Madonna's appropriation of the term, which appears on her belt buckle on the cover of her 1984 album *Like a Virgin* and which was notable enough to earn her a mention in the *OED*.

16. Catherine Belsey, "Cleopatra's Seduction," in *Alternative Shakespeares*, vol. 2, ed. Terrence Hawkes (London: Routledge, 1996), 60.

17. Sidney, *Defence of Poetry*, 18.

18. Ibid., 40.

19. Michel Foucault, *The Use of Pleasure*, vol. 2 of *The History of Sexuality*, trans. Robert Hurley (New York: Random House, 1985), 51–52.

20. Ibid., 249.

21. Ibid., 65.

22. On the classical and Christian distinctions between "continence" and "temperance" that may have influenced Spenser, see Harold Weatherby, "Spenser's Legend of Enkrateia," *Studies in Philology* 93, no. 2 (Spring 1996): 207–17.

23. Harry Berger, Jr., *The Allegorical Temper: Vision and Reality in Book II of Spenser's "Faerie Queene"* (New Haven, CT: Yale University Press, 1957), 67.

24. Foucault, *Use of Pleasure*, 97.

25. Alphonso Lingis, *Libido: The French Existential Theories* (Bloomington: Indiana University Press, 1984), vii.

26. Paul Alpers, "Bower of Bliss," in *The Spenser Encyclopedia*, ed. A. C. Hamilton (Toronto: University of Toronto Press, 1989), 105. Alpers argues that the Bower of Bliss is not only "peculiarly representative of Spenser's poetry" but that it appears in what "is much the longest canto in *The Faerie Queene* . . . and it has always been felt to have an importance commensurate with its length" (105).

27. W. B. Yeats, *Essays and Introductions* (New York: Macmillan, 1961), 370.

28. Arlene Okerlund, "Spenser's Wanton Maidens: Reader Psychology and the Bower of Bliss," *PMLA* 88, no. 1 (January 1973): 62. Okerlund cites an anonymous letter to the February 27, 1930, *Times Literary Supplement* that argues, "Spenser's heart was not in his morality. When, as in this episode, it came to a struggle between his morality and his sense of beauty, his sense of beauty, very properly, triumphed."

29. C. S. Lewis, *The Allegory of Love: A Study in Medieval Tradition* (Oxford: Oxford University Press, 1938), 332–33.

30. N. S. Brooke, "C. S. Lewis and Spenser: Nature, Art and the Bower of Bliss," in *Essential Articles for the Study of Edmund Spenser*, ed. A. C. Hamilton (Hamden, CT: Archon Books, 1972), 27.

31. Roland Barthes, *The Pleasure of the Text*, trans. Richard Miller (New York: FSG, 1975), 22.

32. Jonathan Goldberg, "Spenser's Familiar Letters," in *Sodometries: Renaissance Texts, Modern Sexualities* (Stanford, CA: Stanford University Press, 1992), 22.

33. William Keach's study of early modern Ovidian erotic narratives concludes by arguing for the ironic and expansive nature of the epyllion as a "challenge Spenser's vision of the 'glorious fire' of love ideally realized in the creative chastity of marriage" (*Elizabethan Erotic Verse* [New Brunswick, NJ: Rutgers University Press, 1972], 232). Keach quite clearly articulates a commonly held position regarding *The Faerie Queene*, which is that Spenserian pleasure and sexuality of necessity participate almost exclusively in the formation or deformation of idealized heterosexual coupling. See, among others, particularly Thomas Roche, *The Kindly Flame: A Study of the Third and Fourth Books of Spenser's "Faerie Queene"* (Princeton, NJ: Princeton University Press, 1964); and Lauren Silberman, *Transforming Desire: Erotic Knowledge in Books Three and Four of the "Faerie Queene"* (Berkeley: University of California Press, 1995).

34. See Goldberg, "Spenser's Familiar Letters"; and Bruce R. Smith, "The Passionate Shepherd," in *Homosexual Desire in Shakespeare's England: A Cultural Poetics* (Chicago: University of Chicago Press, 1991).

35. See Richard Rambuss, *Spenser's Secret Career* (Cambridge: Cambridge University Press, 1993), 56–61, and "Spenser's Life and Career," in *Cambridge Companion to Spenser*, ed. Andrew Hadfield (Cambridge: Cambridge University Press, 2001), 13–16.

36. Only a scattering of articles on the presence of female homoerotic or "lesbian" encounters in *The Faerie Queene* exists. See Camille Paglia, "The Apollonian Androgyne and *The Faerie Queene*," *English Literary Renaissance* 9 (1979): 42–63; Valerie Traub, *The Renaissance of Lesbianism in Early Modern England* (Cambridge: Cambridge University Press, 2002), 147–50; Kathryn Schwartz, "Dressed to Kill: Looking for Love in *The Faerie Queene*," in *Tough Love: Amazon Encounters in the English Renaissance* (Durham, NC: Duke University Press, 2000), 137–74; and Tracey Sedinger, "Women's Friendship and the Refusal of Lesbian Desire in *The Faerie Queene*," *Criticism* 42, no. 1 (Winter 2000): 91–113.

37. See David M. Halpern, *How to Do the History of Homosexuality* (Chicago: University of Chicago Press, 2002), 24–48. For a response to Halpern, see Carla Freccero, *Queer/Early/Modern* (Durham, NC: Duke University Press, 2006), 31–50.

38. David Macey, *The Lives of Michel Foucault* (New York: Vintage, 1993), 358.

39. Quoted in Macey, *Lives of Michel Foucault*, 364, 365.

40. Traub, *Renaissance of Lesbianism*, 6.

41. Ibid., 15.

42. Anthony Esolen, "Spenser's 'Alma Venus': Energy and Economics in the Bower of Bliss," *English Literary Renaissance* 23 (Spring 1993): 86.

43. Greenblatt, *Renaissance*, 173. Greenblatt famously diagnoses in the Bower of Bliss a profound hostility to pleasure, which confirms the complicity of Spenserian poetics in the violence of early modern politics associated with Protestant iconoclasm, New World colonialism, and political oppression in Ireland.

44. Greenblatt, *Renaissance Self-Fashioning*, 173, 192. For critiques of Greenblatt, see David Lee Miller, "*The Faerie Queene* (1590)," in *A Critical Companion to Spenser Studies*, ed. Bart van Es (Houndsmill, UK: Palgrave Macmillan, 2006), 139–65; and Richard McCabe, *Spenser's Monstrous Regiment: Elizabethan Ireland and the Poetics of Difference* (Oxford: Oxford University Press, 2002).

45. McCabe, *Spenser's Monstrous Regiment*, 122. While McCabe takes up the relationship between Temperance and Ireland, others explore the relationship between Temperance and the New World. See Read.

46. Ibid., 126.

47. Roland Greene, "Spenser's Worldmaking: A Primer," in *Worldmaking Spenser: Explorations in the Early Modern Age*, ed. Patrick Cheney and Lauren Silberman (Lexington: University of Kentucky Press, 2000), 21.

48. Isobel Armstrong, *The Radical Aesthetic* (Oxford: Blackwell, 2000), 1–2.

49. See Joseph Campana, "On Not Defending Poetry: Spenser, Suffering, and the Energy of Affect," *PMLA* 120, no. 1 (January 2005): 33–48.

50. Michel Foucault, *An Introduction*, vol. 1 of *The History of Sexuality* (New York: Random House, 1978), 136.

51. Ibid., 144, 139.

52. Spenser, *The Faerie Queene*, 717.

53. Michael Schoenfeldt, *Bodies and Selves in Early Modern England: Physiology and Inwardness in Spenser, Shakespeare, Herbert, and Milton* (Cambridge: Cambridge University Press, 1999), 73.

54. Fredric Jameson, "Pleasure: A Political Issue," in *Formations of Pleasure*, ed. Fredric Jameson (London: Routledge, 1983), 9.

55. Karl Marx, *Economic and Philosophical Manuscripts of 1844* (New York: International Publishers, 1964), 111.

56. See Greenblatt, *Renaissance Self-Fashioning*, 176.

57. In a well-known analogy from Plato's *Phaedrus*, the soul is like a charioteer (reason) directing two horses, one white (passion) and one black (appetite). This tripartite soul appears as well in book 4 of Plato's *Republic*, which describes the three drivers immediately following a lengthy discussion of the virtue of temperance.

58. Parker, *Literary Fat Ladies*, 55.

59. Ibid., 64.

60. "Spenser depicts the elevation of nature to deity as unnatural and idolatrous and the Lucretian Venus as ungenerative unless Christianized—that is, remasculinized and absorbed into the theological and social hierarchies implicit in Alma's castle" (Esolen, "Spenser's 'Alma Venus,'" 285).

61. Tasso, 16.19.1–2.

62. Early in Shakespeare's *Venus and Adonis*, Venus exercises physical mastery over Adonis, humiliating him in the process: "Being so enrag'd, desire doth lend her force / Courageously to pluck him from his horse"

(29–30). All references are to *The Riverside Shakespeare*, ed. G. Blakemore Evans (New York: Houghton Mifflin, 1997).

63. Jameson, "Pleasure," 9.

64. Traub, *Renaissance of Lesbianism*, 148.

65. On the power traditionally associated with masculine pleasure and spectatorship, see Nancy Vickers, "Diana Described: Scattered Woman and Scattered Rhyme," *Critical Inquiry* 8 (Winter 1981): 265–79; and the influential article by Laura Mulvey, "Visual Pleasure and Narrative Cinema," *Screen* 16 (Autumn 1975): 6–18.

66. Lingis, *Libido*, 52.

67. Howard Hendrix, "'Those Wandring Eyes of His': Watching Guyon Watch the Naked Damsels Wrestling," *Assays* 7 (1992): 71.

68. Guillaume de Lorris and Jean de Meun, *The Romance of the Rose*, trans. Charles Dahlberg (Princeton, NJ: Princeton University Press, 1995), 41.

69. Ibid.

70. Marx, *Economic and Philosophical Manuscripts*, 111.

71. Marshall McLuhan, *Understanding Media: The Extensions of Man* (New York: Signet, 1964), 43.

72. Jameson, "Pleasure," 13–14.

5. VULNERABLE SUBJECTS: AMORET'S AGONY, BRITOMART'S BATTLE FOR CHASTITY

1. Judith H. Anderson, "Narrative Reflections: Re-envisaging the Poet in *The Canterbury Tales* and *The Faerie Queene*," in *Refiguring Chaucer in the Renaissance*, ed. Theresa Krier (Miami: University Press of Florida, 1998), 93.

2. Andrew Escobedo, "Daemon Lovers: Will, Personification, and Character." *Spenser Studies* 22 (2007): 217.

3. Jonathan Goldberg, *The Seeds of Things: Theorizing Sexuality and Materiality in Renaissance Representations* (New York: Fordham University Press, 2009), 63.

4. Cynthia Marshall, *The Shattering of the Self: Violence, Subjectivity, and Early Modern Texts* (Baltimore: Johns Hopkins University Press, 2002), 90.

5. Goldberg, 67.

6. Michel Foucault, "Sexuality and Solitude," in *Religion and Culture*, ed. Jeremy R. Carrette (Manchester: Manchester University Press, 1999), 183.

7. Ibid., 186.

8. Ibid., 193.

9. Ibid., 196.

10. Foucault, *Ethics: Subjectivity and Truth*, ed. Paul Rabinow (New York: New Press, 1997), 177.

11. Jeffrey Nealon, *Foucault Beyond Foucault: Power and its Intensifications since 1984* (Stanford: Stanford University Press, 2007), 8.

12. Susan Sontag, "The Artist as Exemplary Sufferer," in *Against Interpretation and Other Essays* (New York: Picador, 1961), 47–48.

13. As Janet Groth summarizes in her introduction to the volume, "the stories of Dickens' childhood trauma in the blacking factory, of Kipling's abandonment by his parents, of Edith Wharton's unhappy marriage, Casanova's illegitimacy, Joyce's near blindness, and Hemingway's ambivalence toward women and his compensating machismo." Janet Groth, introduction to Edmund Wilson, *The Wound and the Bow* (Athens: University Press of Ohio, 1997), xi.

14. Scarry, *Body in Pain*, 11.

15. Greenblatt, *Renaissance Self-Fashioning*, 120.

16. Louis Montrose, "*A Midsummer Night's Dream* and the Shaping Fantasies of Elizabethan Culture: Gender, Power, Form," in *Rewriting the Renaissance: The Discourses of Sexual Difference in Early Modern England*, ed. Margaret Ferguson, Maureen Quilligan, and Nancy Vickers (Chicago: University of Chicago Press, 1986); Philippa Berry, *Of Chastity and Power: Elizabethan Literature and the Unmarried Queen* (London: Routledge, 1989).

17. Roland Greene, *Post-Petrarchism: Origins and Innovations in the Western Lyric Sequence* (Princeton, NJ: Princeton University Press, 1991), 5–6.

18. Christopher Warley, *Sonnet Sequences and Social Distinction in Renaissance England* (Cambridge: Cambridge University Press, 2005), 4.

19. Judith Butler, *The Psychic Life of Power: Theories in Subjection* (Stanford, CA: Stanford University Press, 1997), 3.

20. Mark Breitenberg, *Anxious Masculinity in Early Modern Europe* (Cambridge: Cambridge University Press, 1996), 99.

21. Sally Minogue, "A Woman's Touch: Astrophil, Stella, and 'Queen Vertue's Court,'" *English Literary History* 63, no. 3 (1996): 555.

22. Laura Mulvey, "Visual Pleasure and Narrative Cinema," *Screen* 16, no. 3 (Autumn 1975): 27, 29. D. N. Rodowick discusses the extent to which Mulvey forbids male masochism in her vision. See "The Difficulty of Difference," *Wide Angle* 5, no. 1 (1982): 4–15. Mulvey, interestingly, refers to the fragmentation of the male gaze—its denial of a

certain "Renaissance space" conveying interiority and subjectivity to women.

23. Nancy J. Vickers, "Diana Described: Scattered Women and Scattered Rhyme," in *Writing and Sexual Difference*, ed. Elizabeth Abel (Brighton, Sussex, UK: Harvester, 1982), 103.

24. Vickers, "Diana Described," 107.

25. Petrarch, *Canzoniere*, ed. Mark Musa (Bloomington: Indiana University Press, 1996), 23.83. All translations are my own, unless otherwise noted.

26. Breitenberg, *Anxious Masculinity*, 136.

27. Ibid., 56.

28. Carol Siegel, *Male Masochism: Modern Revisions of the Story of Love* (Bloomington: Indiana University Press, 1995), 47.

29. Barbara Estrin, *Laura: Uncovering Gender and Genre in Wyatt, Donne, and Marvell* (Durham, NC, and London: Duke University Press, 1994), 27.

30. Dorothy Stephens, *The Limits of Eroticism in Post-Petrarchan Narrative* (Cambridge: Cambridge University Press, 1998); Gordon Braden, "Gaspara Stampa and the Gender of Petrarchism," *Texas Studies in Language and Literature* 38, no. 2 (1996): 115–39; Catherine Bates, "Astrophil and the Manic Wit of the Abject Male," *Studies in English Literature, 1500–1900* 41, no. 1 (2001): 1–24; Diana Henderson, *Passion Made Public: Elizabethan Lyric, Gender, and Performance* (Urbana: University of Illinois Press, 1995); Lynn Enterline, *The Rhetoric of the Body from Ovid to Shakespeare* (Cambridge: Cambridge University Press, 2000).

31. Gilles Deleuze, *Masochism* (New York: Zone Books, 1989), 37.

32. Theodor Reik, *Of Love and Lust* (New York: FSG, 1957), 178.

33. Ibid., 204.

34. Reik speaks eloquently to the fallacious account of masochism as capitulation: "The description of the masochistic character as weak, dependent, easily influenced, helpless, continues to amaze us. All these features serve the purpose of concealing the utmost determination and stubbornness. What the masochist has to say to the existent ruling forces sounds like slavish submissiveness. It is however a scornful 'No' to the world of appearances that became dominant. He submits—in order to never yield" (280).

35. Adela Pinch, "Female Chatter: Meter, Masochism, and the Lyrical Ballads," *English Literary History* 55, no. 4 (1988): 848. See also Eve Kosofsky Sedgwick, "A Poem Is Being Written," *Representations* 17 (1987): 110–43.

36. Foucault, *Ethics*, 165.

37. Deleuze, *Masochism*, 31.

38. See Spenser, *Amoretti*, sonnets 10–14 and 57, among others. Hereafter quotations from *Amoretti* will be cited in the text by sonnet number(s) and line number(s) from *The Yale Edition of the Shorter Poems of Edmund Spenser*, ed. William Oram, et. al. (New Haven: Yale University Press, 1989).

39. See Anne Lake Prescott, "The Thirsty Deer and the Lord of Life: Some Contexts for *Amoretti* 67–70," *Spenser Studies* 6 (1985): 33–76.

40. Roche sees her torments as visualizations of the "physical torments of sexual love" in *The Kindly Flame*, 76.

41. Helen Cheney Gilde, "'The Sweet Lodge of Love and Deare Delight': The Problem of Amoret," *Philological Quarterly* 50 (1971): 63–74.

42. See Lewis, *Allegory of Love*, 297–360.

43. Maureen Quilligan, *Milton's Spenser: The Politics of Reading* (Ithaca, NY: Cornell University Press, 1983), 45.

44. Roche, *Kindly Flame*, 76.

45. Sheila Cavanagh, *Wanton Eyes and Chaste Desire: Female Sexuality in* The Faerie Queene (Bloomington: Indiana University Press, 1994), 2.

46. James Broaddus, "Renaissance Psychology and Britomart's Adventures in *Faerie Queene III*," *English Literary Renaissance* 17 (1987): 199. One of the more fascinating if inscrutable readings indicates that Busyrane is, perhaps, the temptation for Amoret (and Britomart?) of perverse lesbian love. See J. E. Hankins, *Source and Meaning in Spenser's Allegory* (Oxford: Oxford University Press, 1973).

47. Lauren Silberman, "Singing Unsung Heroines: Androgynous Discourse in Book 3 of The Faerie Queene," in *Rewriting the Renaissance: The Discourses of Sexual Difference in Early Modern Europe*, ed. Margaret Ferguson et al. (Chicago: University of Chicago Press, 1986).

48. Katherine Eggert, "Spenser's Ravishment: Rape and Rapture in the *Faerie Queene*," *Representations* 70 (2000): 1–26.

49. Susan Frye, "Of Chastity and Violence: Elizabeth I and Edmund Spenser in the House of Busirane," *Signs* 20 (1994): 49–78. Frye's impassioned if overwrought appeal for a reading of Amoret's captivity as rape evidences a telling breakdown in its interpretation of Britomart. Not only does she claim that Britomart is vulnerable, because chaste, but she claims that this is clear in two attempted rape scenes—in the House of Busyrane and in Castle Joyeous. By the latter claim she positions the diffident Malecasta as a rapist and reads female same-sex desire as a kind of perverse violation.

50. Chih-hisin Lin, "Amoret's Sacred Suffering: The Protestant

Modification of Courtly Love in Spenser's *The Faerie Queene*," *Studies in Philology* 106, no. 3 (2009): 354–77.

51. Kaja Silverman, *Male Subjectivity at the Margins* (London: Routledge, 1992), 187.

52. Deleuze, *Masochism*, 151–52.

53. While Guyon and Redcrosse's equipment seems more talismanic than enchanted, Arthur wields enchanted weapons and arms, as does Artegall.

54. Kathryn Schwartz, *Tough Love: Amazonian Encounters in the English Renaissance* (Durham, NC: Duke University Press, 2000), 152.

55. See Schwartz, *Tough Love* and Traub, *Renaissance of Lesbianism*.

56. Theodora Jankowski, *Pure Resistance: Queer Virginity in Early Modern English Drama* (Philadelphia: University of Pennsylvania Press, 2000), 6.

57. Phillipa Berry, *Of Chastity and Power: Elizabethan Literature and the Unmarried Queen* (London: Routledge, 1989), 18.

58. Hankins, 30–1. See Lewis for the classic account and Elizabeth Heale's *The Faerie Queene: A Reader's Guide* (Cambridge: Cambridge University Press, 1987) for that view as canonical. Heale even replaces the image of desire in the scene, claiming that Britomart's wound represents her vulnerability to Arthegall's image. Not only will I question, in Chapter 6, the status of that image, I would also suggest that we not simply erase Malecasta.

59. Thomas Roche, *The Kindly Flame: A Study of the Third and Fourth Books of Spenser's* Faerie Queene (Princeton: Princeton University Press, 1964), 70.

60. See Camille Paglia, "The Apollonian Androgyne and *The Faerie Queene*," *English Literary Renaissance* 9 (Winter 1979): 42–63; and James Norhnberg, *The Analogy of The Faerie Queen* (Princeton, NJ: Princeton University Press, 1980). Gary Grund, "The Queen's Two Bodies," *Cahiers Elisabethans* 20 (1981): 19.

61. Susanne Woods, "Spenser and the Problems of Women's Rule," *Huntington Library Quarterly* 48.2 (1985): 151.

62. Foucault, *Ethics*, 195.

63. See Schwartz, *Tough Love*, 138–74; Gross, *Spenserian Poetics*, 145–57; Elizabeth J. Bellamy, *Translations of Power: Narcissism and the Unconscious in Epic History* (Ithaca, NY: Cornell University Press, 1992), 195–211; Gregerson, *Reformation of the Subject*, 9–47.

64. Jacques Lacan, *Écrits: A Selection*, trans. Alan Sheridan (New York and London: W. W. Norton, 1977), 2.

65. Ibid., 4.

66. Ibid., 6, 2.

67. Ibid., 2.

68. Ibid., 4.

69. Ibid., 1.

70. Ibid., 3.

71. Bellamy, *Translations of Power*, 201.

72. Mikkel Borch-Jacobsen, *The Freudian Subject*, trans. Catherine Porter (London: Macmillan, 1989), 28.

73. Susanne Lindgren Wofford, "Gendering Allegory: Spenser's Bold Reader and the Emergence of Character in *The Faerie Queene* III," *Criticism* 30 (1988): 3. See also Wofford, "Britomart's Petrarchan Lament: Allegory and Narrative in *The Faerie Queene III*, iv," *Comparative Literature* 39, no. 1 (1988): 28–57.

74. See *FQ* 3.10.1–10.

75. Sedgwick, "Poem Is Being Written," 134.

76. Berry, *Of Chastity and Power*, 2.

77. Bellamy, *Translations of Power*, 203.

78. Alan Stewart, "The Early Modern Closet Discovered," *Representations* 50 (1995): 77.

79. Ibid., 83. Stewart's analysis of architecture and furnishing supports a reading of the closet as a space between the lord and his secretary.

80. See Rambuss on Spenser's role as secretary in *Spenser's Secret Career*.

81. Broaddus, "Renaissance Psychology," 186.

82. Graham Hough, *A Preface to "The Faerie Queene"* (New York: Norton, 1962), 167–80.

83. See Joel Fineman, *The Subjectivity Effect in Western Literature: Essays Toward the Release of Shakespeare's Will* (Cambridge, MA: MIT Press, 1991).

84. Hough, *A Preface*, 111–12.

85. Ibid., 109–10.

86. Edgar Wind, *Pagan Mysteries in the Renaissance* (Harmondsworth: Penguin, 1967), 91–92.

87. Judith H. Anderson, "Britomart's Armor in Spenser's *Faerie Queene*: Reopening Cultural Matters of Gender and Figuration," *English Literary Renaissance* 39, no. 1 (2009): 79.

88. Foucault, *Ethics*, 136.

89. Ibid., 136–37.

90. I have written more extensively on this subject in "Letters (1580)," forthcoming in *The Oxford Handbook of Edmund Spenser* (Oxford: Ox-

ford University Press, 2010), 178–97. On the eroticism of letters, friendship, and the Spenser-Harvey correspondence see Jonathan Goldberg's seminal treatment in "Spenser's Familiar Letters," in *Sodometries: Renaissance Texts, Modern Sexualities* (Stanford, CA: Stanford University Press, 1992), 63–81. On the eroticism of male friendship and epistolarity see Jeffrey Masten, "Toward a Queer Address: The Taste of Letters and Early Modern Male Friendship," *GLQ* 10.3 (2004): 367–84.

6. DAMAGED GODS: ADONIS AND THE PAIN OF ALLEGORY

1. C. S. Lewis, *Allegory of Love: A Study in Medieval Tradition* (Oxford: Oxford University Press, 1958), 45.

2. Ibid., 46.

3. Ibid., 298.

4. Ibid., 113.

5. Angus Fletcher, *Allegory: Theory of a Symbolic Mode* (Ithaca, NY: Cornell University Press, 1967), 1, 3.

6. See Maureen Quilligan, *The Language of Allegory: Defining the Genre* (Ithaca, NY: Cornell University Press, 1979).

7. Lewis, *Allegory of Love*, 68.

8. Fletcher, *Allegory*, 23.

9. Gordon Teskey, *Allegory and Violence* (Ithaca, NY: Cornell University Press, 1996), 25.

10. Ibid., 19.

11. This chapter joins a series of recent alternative accounts to Fletcher's and Teskey's powerful understandings of allegorical personification as daemonic personification or as violent capture. For an extension of notions of allegorical personification into the terrain of justice, see Jeff Dolven, "Spenser's Sense of Poetic Justice," *Raritan* 21, no. 1 (2001): 127–40. For an account that traces the influence of characterological distinctions on notions of personification to Milton's Satan, see Andrew Escobedo, "Allegorical Agency and the Sins of Angels," *English Literary History* 75 (2008): 787–818. For an account of the relationship between personification, will, and character in Spenser see Escobedo, "Daemon Lovers: Will, Personification, and Character," *Spenser Studies* 22 (2007): 203–25. For a psychoanalytic account of thinking and allegory in Spenser see Theresa Krier, "Psychic Deadness in Allegory: Spenser's House of Mammon and Attacks on Linking," in *Imagining Death in Spenser and Milton*, ed. Elizabeth Jane Bellamy, Patrick Cheney, and Michael Schoen-

feldt (New York: Palgrave Macmillan, 2003): 46–64. For Krier's Irigirayan revision of Angus Fletcher's notion of daemonic personification, see "Daemonic Allegory: The Elements in Late Spenser, Late Shakespeare, and Irigaray," *Spenser Studies* 18 (2003): 315–42.

12. Judith Butler, *Bodies That Matter: On the Discursive Limits of "Sex"* (London: Routledge, 1993), 29–30.

13. Ibid., 53.

14. Teskey, *Allegory and Violence*, 16.

15. *The "Cosmographia" of Bernardus Silvestris*, trans. Winthrop Wetherbee (New York: Columbia University Press, 1973), 66.

16. Winthrop Wetherbee, *Platonism and Poetry in the Twelfth Century: The Literary Influence of the School of Chartes* (Princeton, NJ: Princeton University Press, 1972), 158.

17. Brian Stock, *Myth and Science in the Twelfth Century: A Study of Bernard Sylvester* (Princeton, NJ: Princeton University Press, 1972), 117.

18. Ibid., 122.

19. Silvestris, *Cosmographia*, 12.

20. Stock, *Myth and Science*, 133.

21. Alan of Lille, *Plaint of Nature*, trans. James J. Sheridan (Toronto: Pontifical Institute of Medieval Studies, 1980), 67.

22. Ibid., 68–69.

23. Ibid., 146.

24. Alexandre Leupin, *Barbarolexis: Medieval Writing and Sexuality*, trans. Kate Cooper (Cambridge, MA: Harvard University Press, 1989), 62.

25. Marsilio Ficino, *Commentary on Plato's Symposium on Love*, trans. Sears Jayne (Dallas: Spring Publications, 1985), 53.

26. Ovid, *Metamorphoses*, trans. Frank Justus Miller (Cambridge, MA: Harvard University Press, 1977), 10.515–20.

27. Ibid., 10.311–12.

28. Ibid., 10.524.

29. Ibid., 10.706.

30. Ibid., 10.730–31.

31. Deleuze, *Masochism*, 99.

32. Teskey, *Allegory and Violence*, 76.

33. *Ovid's Metamorphoses: The Arthur Golding Translation of 1567*, ed. John Frederick Nims (Philadelphia, PA: Paul Dry Books, 2000), 10.577–79.

34. Ibid., 10.580–82.

35. Ibid., 10.583–85.

36. Ibid., 10.585–88.

CONCLUSION

1. Titus Lucretius Carus, *On the Nature of Things*, trans. W. H. D. Rouse, Loeb Classical Library 118 (Cambridge, MA: Harvard University Press, 1975), 1.1

2. Ibid., 1.2–5.

3. Ibid., 1.19–20.

4. Judith Butler, *Precarious Life: The Powers of Mourning and Violence* (London: Verso, 2004), 28.

5. Ibid., 42. Or, as Butler later argues, "Suffering can yield an experience of humility, of vulnerability, of impressionability and dependence, and these can become resources, if we do not 'resolve' them too quickly; they can move us beyond and against the vocation of the paranoid victim who regenerates infinitely the justifications for war," (*Precarious Life*, 150). For a critique of Butler's nonviolent ethics rooted in vulnerability, see a special issue of *differences*, including Catherine Mills, "Normative Violence, Vulnerability, and Responsibility," *Differences* 18, no. 2 (2007): 133–56; as well as responses to Mills, from Fiona Jenkins, "Toward a Non-Violent Ethics: A Response to Catherine Mills," *Differences* 18, no. 2 (2007): 157–79; and Butler, "Reply from Judith Butler to Mills and Jenkins," *Differences* 18, no. 2 (2007): 180–95.

6. Donald Cheney, "Spenser's Hermaphrodite and the 1590 *Faerie Queene*," *PMLA* 87, no. 2 (1972): 193; A. R. Cirillo, "The Fair Hermaphrodite: Love-Union in the Poetry of Donne and Spenser," *Studies in English Literature, 1500–1900* 9, no. 1 (1969): 85.

7. David Lee Miller, "Spenser's Poetics: The Poem's Two Bodies," *PMLA* 101, no. 2 (1986): 171. Miller extends this argument in *The Poem's Two Bodies: The Poetics of the 1590 "Faerie Queene"* (Princeton, NJ: Princeton University Press, 1988), which sees in the poem a "quest for the body's wholeness and informs every realm of social and cultural experience" (4–5).

8. Lauren Silberman, *Transforming Desire: Erotic Knowledge in Books III and IV of* The Faerie Queene (Berkeley: University of California Press, 1995), 70.

9. Jonathan Goldberg, *Endlesse Work: Spenser and the Structures of Discourse* (Baltimore: Johns Hopkins University Press, 1981), 1–4.

10. Ovid, *Metamorphoses: Books I–VIII*, trans. Frank Justus Miller, 3rd ed. (Cambridge: Harvard University Press, 1977), 4:375–7.

11. Joseph Adamson and Hilary Clark, "Introduction: Shame, Affect, and Writing," in *Scenes of Shame: Psychoanalysis, Shame, and Writing*, eds.

Joseph Adamson and Hilary Clark (Albany: State University of New York Press, 1998), 28.

12. Ibid., 1.

13. Sianne Ngai, *Ugly Feelings* (Cambridge, MA: Harvard University Press, 2005), 1.

14. Bernard Williams, *Shame and Necessity*. Sather Classical Lectures, vol. 57. (Berkeley: University of California Press, 1993).

15. Georgia Brown, *Redefining Elizabethan Literature* (Cambridge: Cambridge University Press, 2004), 5.

16. Ibid., 6.

17. Ibid., 6–7.

18. Ibid., 8.

19. Ewan Fernie, *Shame in Shakespeare* (London: Routledge, 2002), 65.

20. Aristotle, *The Art of Rhetoric*, trans. John Henry Freese, The Loeb Classical Library (Cambridge, MA: Harvard University Press, 1982 [1926]), II.vi.

21. On Spenser's letters and his relationship to Gabriel Harvey see Joseph Campana, "*Letters* (1580)," *Oxford Handbook of Edmund Spenser* (Oxford: Oxford University Press, 2010), 178–97.

22. *The Works of Edmund Spenser: The Prose Works*, vol. 10, eds. Edwin Greenlaw et al. (Baltimore: Johns Hopkins University Press, 1949). The translation that appears in my conclusion is an unpublished translation by John Quitslund.

23. Stephen Greenblatt, *Renaissance Self-Fashioning from More to Shakespeare* (Chicago: University of Chicago Press, 1980), 9.

24. Murphy argues that the consequence of this strategy of strict differentiation is the collapse of all "colonial subjects" in an undifferentiated "Other." See Andrew Murphy, *But the Irish Sea Betwixt Us: Ireland, Colonialism, and Renaissance Literature* (Lexington: University Press of Kentucky, 1999).

25. See particularly the introduction to Thomas Herron, *Spenser's Irish Work: Poetry, Plantation, and Cultural Reformation* (Burlington, VT: Ashgate, 2007).

26. Murphy, *But the Irish Sea Betwixt Us*, 6–7.

27. Richard McCabe, *Spenser's Monstrous Regiment: Elizabethan Ireland and the Poetics of Difference* (Oxford: Oxford University Press, 2005), 26.

28. Catherine Gallagher and Stephen Greenblatt, *Practicing New Historicism* (Chicago: University of Chicago Press, 2001), 8.

29. Sally Munt, *Queer Attachments* (London: Ashgate, 2008), 3.

30. *Shame and Its Sisters: A Sylvan Tompkins Reader*, eds. Eve Kosofsky Sedgwick and Adam Frank (Durham, NC: Duke University Press, 1995), 37.

31. Munt, *Queer Attachments*, 4.

32. Kathryn Bond Stockton, *Beautiful Bottom, Beautiful Shame: Where "Black" Meets "Queer"* (Durham, NC: Duke University Press, 2006), 24, 26.

33. Heather Love, *Feeling Backwards: Loss and the Politics of Queer History* (Cambridge, MA: Harvard University Press, 2009), 13–14.

34. Ruth Leys, *From Guilt to Shame: Auschwitz and After* (Princeton, NJ: Princeton University Press, 2009), 131.

35. Silvan Tomkins, *The Many Faces of Shame*, ed. Donald L. Nathanson (New York: Guilford Press, 1987), 144.

36. Quoted in Eve Kosofsky Sedgwick, *Touching Feeling: Affect, Pedagogy, Performativity* (Durham, NC: Duke University Press, 2002), 35.

37. Gerhart Piers and Milton B. Singer, *Shame and Guilt: A Psychoanalytic and a Cultural Study* (New York: Norton, 1971), 28.

38. Scholarship approaching the structure of *The Faerie Queene* and the relationship between the 1590 and 1596 poems is too extensive to survey in a brief conclusion. However, for one of the most invigorating approaches to the progress of the 1596 *Faerie Queene* and particularly the unfolding of the Legend of Courtesy from the Legend of Justice see Gordon Teskey, "And Therefore as a Stranger Give it Welcome: Courtesy and Thinking," *Spenser Studies* 18 (2003): 343–59.

39. Jacques Rancière, *The Politics of Aesthetics*, trans. Gabriel Rockhill (London: Continuum, 2004), 63, 64.

40. Edmund Spenser, "Letter of the Authors," *The Faerie Queene*, ed. A. C. Hamilton, 2nd ed. (New York: Longman, 2007), 715–6.

Index